Niels Streekmann

Clustering-Based Support for Software Architecture Restructuring

VIEWEG+TEUBNER RESEARCH

Software Engineering Research

Herausgeber/Editor:

Prof. Dr. Wilhelm Hasselbring

Im Software Engineering wird traditionell ein Fokus auf den Prozess der Konstruktion von Softwaresystemen gelegt. Der Betrieb von Systemen, die kontinuierlich Dienste mit einer geforderten Qualität bieten müssen, stellt eine ebenso große Herausforderung dar. Ziel der Reihe Software Engineering Research ist es, innovative Techniken und Methoden für die Entwicklung und den Betrieb von nachhaltigen Softwaresystemen vorzustellen.

Traditionally, software engineering focuses on the process of constructing and evolving software systems. The operation of systems that are expected to continuously provide services with required quality properties is another great challenge. It is the goal of the Series Software Engineering Research to present innovative techniques and methods for engineering and operating sustainable software systems.

Niels Streekmann

Clustering-Based Support for Software Architecture Restructuring

With a foreword by Prof. Dr. Wilhelm Hasselbring

VIEWEG+TEUBNER RESEARCH

Bibliographic information published by the Deutsche Nationalbibliothek
The Deutsche Nationalbibliothek lists this publication in the Deutsche Nationalbibliografie;
detailed bibliographic data are available in the Internet at http://dnb.d-nb.de.

Dissertation University of Kiel, 2011

1st Edition 2012

All rights reserved
© Vieweg+Teubner Verlag | Springer Fachmedien Wiesbaden GmbH 2012

Editorial Office: Ute Wrasmann | Anita Wilke

Vieweg+Teubner Verlag is a brand of Springer Fachmedien.
Springer Fachmedien is part of Springer Science+Business Media.
www.viewegteubner.de

Cover design: KünkelLopka Medienentwicklung, Heidelberg
Printed on acid-free paper

ISBN 978-3-8348-1953-6

Foreword

Successful software systems are long-living systems. During their lifetime the underlying development platforms, programming languages and software architectures eventually become obsolete. When this happens, these software systems are often called *legacy systems:* those engineers responsible for maintaining the systems are usually not the engineers who built the systems. An emerging question is how the resulting requirements for modernization may be achieved. As a first step, it is useful to reconstruct the existing software architecture via reverse engineering techniques. If we aim at a real modernization, just a transformation of legacy code into the syntax of a new programming language will not lead to a maintainable system. Therefore, as a second step, the target architecture for the modernized software system needs to be defined. Then, a migration strategy from the legacy systems architecture toward the chosen target architecture is needed.

Niels Streekmann introduces in this research work a new approach to restructuring software architectures, meant to support engineers with modernizing existing legacy systems. From the above-mentioned modernization tasks, the work presented in this book focuses on finding an appropriate migration strategy on the architectural level. To support this task, a semi-automatic method is introduced which groups elements of the reconstructed legacy architecture via clustering algorithms. These clustered groups of source code elements are then mapped to components of the target architecture.

Besides the presented conceptual research work, this book reports on an extensive experimental evaluation of the restructuring approach. In particular, the reconstruction of the architectural elements of a large industrial system is presented. Thus, this book will be a valuable resource for both researchers and practitioners interested in restructuring (legacy) software systems.

Wilhelm Hasselbring

Acknowledgements

During the past five years many people influenced this thesis by providing helpful comments, criticism and reviews to my ideas and publications. I would like to express my deepest gratitude to all of them, even though they may not be mentioned explicitly in the following.

First of all I would like to thank Willi Hasselbring for supervising my thesis and giving me useful hints and suggestions from the selection of the topic to the final completion. I also thank the second examiner of this thesis Andreas Winter for his extensive remarks on reengineering and graph clustering.

My former employer, the OFFIS - Institute for Information Technology, had a vital part in the creation of this thesis by giving me the time to develop and try out my ideas in the context of interesting research projects and to write down this thesis. I thank all my former colleagues and especially all current and former members of the Software Engineering for Business Information Systems Group for the pleasant and productive working atmosphere. I very much appreciated working with you.

Furthermore, I would like to thank all participants of the PhD student seminars (*Doktorandenrunden*) of the software engineering groups of the universities in Oldenburg and Kiel and the former OFFIS division Business Information Management. These seminars have been a source for many helpful remarks and inspiring discussions. I also thank all participants of the talks I gave at other universities, workshops, and conferences and the reviewers of my submitted papers for their expert feedback. Moreover, I would like to thank all people who helped me during the evaluation of my approach by providing assistance, experiment subjects, tools and advice.

However, my biggest thanks go to my family. My parents Ulla and Rolf Streekmann, who made all this possible with their long lasting financial and above all personal support, and my girlfriend Silvia, who endured the temporal constraints in the past five years and who was always there for me with much understanding.

Niels Streekmann

Abstract

The modernisation of existing software systems is an important topic in software engineering research and practice. A part of the modernisation of software systems is the restructuring of their architecture. This has to be done in numerous contexts, including the evolution to service-oriented architectures, the re-establishment of the maintainability of a system or the smooth migration of a system to a new development environment. Architecture restructurings are coarse-grained changes to the internal structure of the system that are performed in temporally limited projects. The planning of the transfer of a existing implementation to the target architecture of a system is currently a mostly manual task. While the analysis of the existing system is supported by e.g. architecture reconstruction approaches, the actual restructuring process is not supported by current approaches.

The MARE approach, which is introduced in this thesis, was developed to provide support for the stepwise restructuring of the implementation towards a target architecture. MARE supports architecture restructurings by semi-automatically creating a complete mapping of elements of the existing implementation to components of the target architecture. The creation of the mapping bases on explicit knowledge about the target architecture and its decomposition criteria. MARE employs graph clustering to implement the creation of the complete mapping.

The MARE Method describes an iterative process model for the overall architecture restructuring process. It emphasises the target architecture as the basis for the architecture restructuring. The iterations of the process model allow for a stepwise restructuring of the system and the integration of human influence on the result of MARE.

The clustering algorithm employed by MARE to create the complete mapping bases on agglomerative hierarchical clustering. It is adjusted to incorporate knowledge about the target architecture. The decomposition criteria are considered by the definition of weights for the different types of dependencies that relate the elements of the existing implementation.

The MARE approach was evaluated in three case studies. These examined the application of MARE in small and middle-sized open source projects as well as for an industrial system with 3.5 million lines of code. The main goal of the evaluation is to show the quality and stability of the clustering algorithm. It furthermore shows the influence factors for the creation of the complete mapping.

Contents

III Evaluation   145

IV Conclusion   211

List of Figures

List of Tables

1 Introduction

This chapter presents the motivation for the support of software architecture re-structuring (Section 1.1) that is researched in this thesis and introduces the proposed solution approach (Section 1.2). The consequent scientific contributions of the thesis are summarised in Section 1.3. Finally, Section 1.4 gives an overview of the remainder of the thesis.

1.1 Motivation

Architecture restructurings become necessary in a number of software evolution projects. The reasons for architecture restructuring are manifold and include changing requirements regarding different quality attributes as e.g. maintainability and performance as well as extensive changes to functional requirements. Further reasons include the accommodation to new technical platforms, frameworks, or development paradigms. These are often linked with the improvement of quality attributes or with organisational necessities as e.g. the ceasing of vendor support of used hard- and software.

Architecture restructuring is defined as a coarse-grained change in the component structure of a system or the change of its architectural style in the context of this thesis. Such restructurings are planned on the architectural level, but also have to be transferred to the implementation of the system to make it fit to the new target architecture. In object-oriented systems this e.g. necessitates the reassignment of classes to packages.

Section 6.2 describes typical application scenarios for architecture restructuring. The evolution to service-oriented architectures is a frequently performed paradigm shift that often also requires the restructuring of single applications to target architectures that support service-orientation. Since existing systems are often not designed based on services, an overall restructuring of the systems or the extraction of implementation of single services become necessary in order to fulfil current requirements. Both restructuring tasks require a mapping of source elements to the services they implement.

The second application scenario targets the improvement of the quality of a system by re-establishing its maintainability. The goal of the restructuring in this case is the decomposition of the system into maintainable modules. These can differ from the grown structure of the system and hence necessitate the relocation of fine-grained modules as e.g. functions or classes into more coarse grained modules.

Another scenario in which restructuring becomes necessary, is the migration of a system to a new development environment. To execute such a migration in a feasible way, it is often done in small steps. Hence, it is necessary to partition the system into suitable migration increments. These constitute the target components of the architecture restructuring. The goal of a restructuring project is to separate these increments in the implementation in order to transform them independently into the new development environment. This also makes it necessary to map source elements to target components.

Since restructuring projects often are of an individual nature, there are many more contexts besides these three examples. One of these individual contexts is the restructuring of the openArchitectureWare framework in the course of its integration into the Eclipse Modeling Project as described in the case study in Section 10.2. Hence, the proposed solution approach has to be generic regarding the target architecture and its decomposition criteria as wells as the programming paradigms and languages of the existing systems.

The aforementioned application scenarios represent different contexts for architecture restructurings. A common task of all scenarios is the mapping of source elements to target components in order to transfer the structure given by the target architecture to the implementation of the system. Hence, this has to be supported by the solution approach.

The support for the planning of architecture restructurings, both on the architectural level as well as for the transfer to the implementation, is limited. Garlan et al. (2009) introduce support for the former. They provide methods for modelling and analysing different restructuring alternatives on the architectural level to enable more sound decisions on coarse-grained evolution paths.

Current support for the transfer of a new architecture to the implementation of a system mainly focuses on the analysis of the existing implementation and on the reconstruction of the implemented architecture. This field is well-researched (cf. Koschke (2005)), but does not involve the target architecture. Thus, such approaches improve the foundation for architectural decisions, but do not support the restructuring directly.

Such support can be found for fine-grained restructurings as e.g. the merging and separation of classes to improve the modularisation of a system. However, this support is missing for more coarse-grained restructurings, e.g. on the level of packages and components. This lack of support is the main motivation for the introduction of MARE, as described in the following section.

1.2 Solution Approach

To support the transformation of an existing implementation of a software system so that it conforms to a target architecture in the course of an architecture restructuring project, this thesis introduces the MARE approach. The goal of MARE is to propose a complete mapping of the structural implementation artefacts (called source elements in the remainder of the thesis) of the existing system to the components of the target architecture (called target components in the remainder of the thesis; a definition is given in Section 6.5 on page 81). Thus, it actively supports the restructuring process. Thereby, MARE is a generic method that is applicable for systems following different programming paradigms and for different types of target architectures.

The creation of the complete mapping bases on the decomposition criteria of the target architecture. In this way, human methods and criteria are adopted by MARE. This is done to produce results that are similar to an according human mapping. Thus, the complete mapping created by MARE is comprehensible for the user and the user has the possibility to provide feedback and change the configuration of MARE in order to improve the result.

MARE provides an iterative process model for the whole architecture restructuring process with a focus on the creation of the complete mapping. Further preliminary and follow-up activities like the creation of the target architecture and the actual restructuring of the implementation are considered in the process model and discussed in this thesis, but are not part of the contribution.

MARE is a semi-automated approach. The creation of the complete mapping bases on a configuration provided by the user. This configuration consists of the target architecture and a model of the source system as well as a partial initial mapping and weights for certain dependencies types that connect source elements in the source system model. This mapping and the dependency type weights represent the decomposition criteria of the target architecture in the models employed by MARE. Another human task is the validation of the complete mapping. Since restructuring projects are highly individual and there are no extensive experiences with the configuration of MARE yet, it is intended to adjust the configuration in an iterative process.

MARE employs graph clustering to create the complete mapping. The goal of the MARE clustering algorithm is to create cohesive clusters that are as close as possible to a mapping a human expert would create. Therefore, existing hierarchical clustering techniques are extended by the consideration of the target architecture in the clustering algorithm. Furthermore, the dependency weights are the main factor for the composition of clusters.

1.3 Scientific Contribution

The contribution of this thesis has three major parts.

- The MARE Method to support architecture restructuring which incorporates the target architecture as an essential constituent of the restructuring approach

- The MARE Clustering algorithm that provides a complete mapping of source elements to target components

- The evaluation of the use of MARE in three case studies

Thus, the thesis makes contributions to the scientific knowledge in the methodical support of architecture restructuring projects and the evaluation of these methods. The contributions are outlined in the following subsections.

1.3.1 MARE Method

The MARE approach contributes to the scientific knowledge by providing support for the task of architecture restructuring. Its objective is to reduce the human effort for creating a complete mapping of source elements to target components. MARE supports the user by semi-automating this task.

The MARE Method provides an iterative process model that guides the entire restructuring process. The focus of the method is on the central role of the target architecture for the restructuring process and the possibility to formalise the its decomposition criteria for the semi-automation of this otherwise manual task.

MARE proposes the representation of the decomposition criteria by weights of the types of dependencies between source elements that exist in the implementation. An important task for the user is the selection of the types of dependencies and source elements for the representation of the source system as well as the weights of the dependency types, which are decisive for the quality of the clustering. For the selection of the dependency types and their weights, it is important to consider which properties the target components should have and which dependencies are allowed between them.

1.3.2 MARE Clustering Algorithm

There are several use cases for clustering in software reengineering, mainly in program understanding and architecture reconstruction. This thesis shows that clustering can also be applied for architecture restructuring. It is shown how hierarchical clustering can be adjusted in order to better suit the requirements of architecture restructuring. Furthermore, the impact of inputs to the clustering algorithm, namely dependency type weights and information about the target architecture, is discussed.

A clustering algorithm is defined that incorporates this information to create cohesive clusters of source elements. These clusters are directly mapped to target components and thus do not require further human interpretation.

1.3.3 Evaluation of MARE

This thesis provides an extensive evaluation of MARE. The evaluation comprises three case studies. In these, the approach is evaluated with software systems between 1400 and 3.5 million lines of code, which are written in Java and C/C++. The systems are from an open source as well as from an industrial context.

The contribution of the evaluation is to show the applicability of MARE for these different types of systems. Thereby, it mainly targets the quality and the stability of the MARE clustering algorithm. The evaluation results also show the influence of different types of source elements as well as the dependency type weights. Thus, it allows the conclusion of early strategies for the configuration of the semi-automatic approach that has to be provided by the user.

1.4 Overview

This thesis consists of four parts. The first part introduces the underlying foundations of the MARE approach. Chapter 2 introduces the necessary basics of software architecture. Based on this, Chapter 3 discusses the state of the art of software evolution and modernisation. The foundations and applications of graph clustering are described in Chapter 4, while Chapter 5 completes the foundations presenting the concepts of model-driven software development.

The second part presents the MARE approach, which is the core of this thesis. Chapter 6 states the goals of MARE and the underlying research questions. It also defines central terms and deepens the motivating application scenarios. The underlying process of MARE as well as its particular activities are presented in Chapter 7. The essential clustering algorithm that creates the resulting complete mapping is introduced in Chapter 8.

The evaluation of the MARE approach is the topic of the third part. The methods that were used to structure the evaluation are described in Chapter 9. The actual case studies and their results are presented in Chapter 10. Chapter 11 discusses related work of MARE .

   The fourth part concludes this thesis with a summary of the results (Chapter 12), a discussion of future work (Chapter 13), and final conclusions (Chapter 14).

Part I

Foundations

2 Software Architecture

Software architecture is a subdiscipline of software engineering that deals with high-level views on software systems. Its goal is to make the development and evolution of complex systems manageable. The following sections introduce aspects of software architecture that are needed for the understanding of this thesis. Its fundamental basics (Section 2.1) are described as well as the distinction to the detailed design of a software system (Section 2.2). In addition architectural styles (Section 2.3), which form the basis of the target architecture considered in MARE and the relevant architecture metrics (Section 2.4) in the context of MAREare examined. Furthermore, the phenomenon of architecture erosion (Section 2.5), which is one reason for architecture restructurings, is introduced.

2.1 Software Architecture Basics

Software architectures are essential to develop and maintain large-scale software systems. Garlan (2000) introduces six main goals of software architecture:

- **Understanding** Architecture improves the understanding by a high-level abstract view on a system.

- **Reuse** Architecture supports the reuse of components and frameworks.

- **Construction** Architecture defines the abstract structure and major interfaces and constraints, that guide the construction of a system.

- **Evolution** Architecture makes expected evolution explicit and separates functionality and connection mechanisms of components, so that they can evolve separately.

- **Analysis** Architectures allow for several analyses of the system under study.

- **Management** Architecture can guide the development process and support the understanding of aspects of the process.

Various definitions for software architecture exist. The most agreed on definitions are given by the IEEE Recommended Practice for Architectural Description of Software-Intensive Systems-Description and the Carnegie Mellon Software Engineering Institute (SEI)[1]:

Definition: Software Architecture (IEEE Architecture Working Group (2000))
The fundamental organization of a system embodied in its components, their relationships to each other, and to the environment, and the principles guiding its design and evolution.

Definition: Software Architecture (Bass et al. (2003)) *The software architecture of a program or computing system is the structure or structures of the system, which comprise software elements, the externally visible properties of those elements, and the relationships among them.*

The definition of Bass et al. (2003) emphasises the structure of the system and its externally visible properties, which are both important aspects of architecture restructuring (cf. Section 3.5). The IEEE definition is broader and adds a focus on the process of architecting, which is not in the scope of MARE. Thus, the latter definition will be the reference for the remainder of this thesis.

The documentation of software architecture is manifested in *views* that concentrate on different concerns of the architecture. The IEEE Architecture Working Group (2000) defines a view as follows:

Definition: View (IEEE Architecture Working Group (2000)) *A representation of a whole system from the perspective of a related set of concerns.*

There are several publications that define sets of views for the description of a software system. The 4+1 view model of software architecture by Kruchten (1995) describes five views and their dependencies. The central view is called *scenarios* and describes the functionality of a software system as use cases. Based on this view four further views show different aspects of the system, namely the *logical view*, the *process view*, the *physical view* and the *development view*.

Hofmeister et al. (2000) describes four architecture views. The *conceptual architecture view* describes the components of a system on a level that is close to the application domain. The *module architecture view* describes the decomposition of the software into implementation units. These units are mapped to hardware and software platforms in the *execution architecture view*. The *code architecture*

---

[1]http://www.sei.cmu.edu/architecture/start/definitions.cfm

view describes the organisation of the system in terms of source code units, release management, and testing.

Matevska-Meyer et al. (2004) describe views for component-based software systems (cf.Szyperski et al. (2002)), which are also used by Reussner and Hasselbring (2008). They distinguish a structural, a dynamic and a resource mapping view. The structural view describes the components and connectors that make up the system. The dynamic view models the runtime behaviour of the system. The resource mapping view contains the mapping of components to deployment units or organisational entities.

· Based on the views introduced before, Clements et al. (2003, p. 18) define three abstract viewtypes: the *module viewtype*, the *component-and-connector viewtype* and the *allocation viewtype*. The viewtypes focus on structural aspects of a software system and are therefore well-suited as a basis for the considerations taken in this thesis on architecture restructuring. Furthermore, the module viewtype and the component-and-connector viewtype can be directly mapped to the different application scenarios of the MARE method (cf. Section7.3.3). Thus, the following subsections describe these viewtypes and the modelling of according views in more detail.

The allocation viewtype subsumes views that map the elements of the other two viewtypes to non-software structures. This corresponds to the resource mapping view of Matevska-Meyer et al. (2004) and the physical view of Kruchten (1995). The allocation view is not employed in MARE since restructuring in the meaning of change of the deployment unit allocation of components or change of the allocation of modules to development teams is not in the scope of MARE.

2.1.1 Module Viewtype

The module viewtype is concerned with the structure of implementation units and their relationships. The units are called *modules* and are defined as follows:

Definition: Module (Clements et al. (2003, p. 43)) *A module is an implementation unit of software that provides a coherent unit of functionality.*

A module encapsulates design decisions and has clearly defined interfaces. Parnas (1972) provides early work about the criteria on how to design modules and define the information encapsulated in a module. Further information on this topic is provided in Section 2.3.2. Modules are units of the design time and thus also the units of maintenance (cf. Clements et al. (2003, p. 22)). For this thesis the term module is further restricted to implementation units that are subject of a systems architecture.

2.1.2 Component-and-Connector Viewtype

The component-and-connector viewtype is concerned with runtime units and their relationships. These runtime units are called components. The relationships between components are modelled by connectors. Connectors can e.g. be remote procedure calls or database accesses. Components are runtime entities and units of deployment. Thereby, there is not mandatorily a unique mapping of components and modules. Components can contain code from several modules and modules can be used in several components. Nevertheless, atomic components are often referred to as modules (cf. Szyperski et al. (2002, p. 420) or Siedersleben (2004, p. 43).

Component-based architectures describe software systems in terms of components. In the thesis the component definition of Szyperski et al. (2002) is used.

Definition: Software Component (Szyperski et al. (2002)) *A software component is a unit of composition with contractually specified interfaces and explicit context dependencies only. A software component can be deployed independently and is subject to composition by third parties.*

Siedersleben (2004, p. 42) defines six features of components:

1. A component provides one or more interfaces, that are contractually guaranteed and include a semantic description.

2. A component requires interfaces of other components.

3. A component hides its implementation.

4. A component is a unit of reuse.

5. Components can contain other components.

6. A component is an essential unit of design, implementation and planning.

Feature 1 to 5 are based on Szyperski et al. (2002), D'Souza and Wills (1999), and the Object Management Group (OMG) (2007). The last feature is derived from these features and describes the central role of a component from the viewpoint of Siedersleben (2004).

In the context of architecture restructuring the runtime aspect of the component-and-connector viewtype is of secondary interest. In the terms of Matevska-Meyer et al. (2004) only the structural view of this viewpoint is considered in the remainder of this thesis. The main difference to the structural view of the module viewtype is, that the module viewtype represents the implementation, while the component-and-connector viewtype represents an abstract functional decomposition of the system, which is the way many users think of software systems in early design phases. Another difference is, that the module decomposition is strictly hierarchical. A component on the other hand can be contained in more than one other component, which leads to further challenges in the configuration of a restructuring method and the interpretation of the results.

2.1.3 Allocation Viewtype

To complete the overview of the viewtypes described by Clements et al. (2003), this section describes the allocation viewtype. The views of the allocation viewtype define the mapping of the software artefacts introduced in the other viewtypes to their environment. Clements et al. (2003) present three different mappings for this purpose:

- The mapping of components and connectors to the hardware, they are executed on (*Deployment*).

- The mapping of modules to the file system in order to manage the development.

- The mapping of modules to developers or development teams in order to support project management.

2.1.4 Viewtype Modelling

Clements et al. (2003) describe typical modelling notations for the different architecture viewpoints. Besides other modelling languages, the UML (Rumbaugh et al. (2005)) is described as a commonly used formal notation for software architectures. More detailed, UML class diagrams are introduced to create models of the module viewtype, while UML component diagrams are used for the component-and-connector viewtype. For the latter also architecture description languages (ADL)[2] are frequently used.

In the remainder of this thesis UML component diagrams are used to represent structural models of component-and-connector views as well as module views. This simplification is made due to the fact that MARE is designed to be able to work on structural models of both viewtypes without a difference in the method itself. The specifics and delimitations of this decision are discussed in Section 7.3.3.

2.2 Detailed Design

As stated by Clements et al. (2003, p. 5ff.) the difference between architecture and detailed design is not strict and depends on context and purpose. Based on this differentiation, the term detailed design is introduced here. A definition is provided, that aims at the context of architecture restructuring and has the purpose to differentiate the inputs and results of the MARE approach.

In addition to the differentiation of detailed design and architecture by Clements et al. (2003) a differentiation between modules in architectural and detailed design descriptions is introduced for the remainder of this thesis. To avoid misunderstandings, fine-grained modules that are subject to the detailed design, but not to the architecture of a system, are called *structural elements*.

2.2.1 Definition

According to Abran et al. (2004) the detailed design of a software system describes the specific behaviour of the components of a software system. In this thesis the detailed design describes the specific structure of components in the component-and-connector viewtype or of modules in the module viewtype, respectively.

Definition: Detailed Design *Detailed design is the representation of the structural elements of a software system and their dependencies.*

According to the context, the elements of detailed design can be manifold. In the context of architecture restructuring the level of detail depends on the level on which entities of the source system shall not be divided in order to perform the restructuring. For the different case studies presented in Chapter 10 the elements of detailed design are e.g. classes or files.

---

[2]For a comparison of ADLs cf. e.g. Giesecke (2008, p. 57ff.)

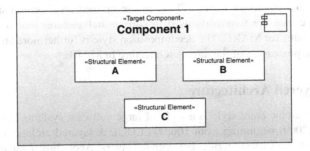

Figure 2.1: Mapping Example

2.2.2 Modelling

As described in 2.1.4, coarse-grained architectural elements like modules, subsystems or runtime components are modelled using UML component diagrams. The mapping of structural elements, which are considered to be the entities of detailed design, to these coarse-grained elements is depicted by components containing classes, which represent the fine-grained modules. Figure 2.1 gives an example of the component *Component 1* containing the structural elements *A*, *B* and *C*.

2.3 Architectural Styles

Only the coarse-grained architectural styles, which contribute to the understanding of the thesis are introduced in this section. These coarse-grained styles are the basis for the target architecture and thus influence the architecture restructuring process. Further detail on architectural styles is presented by Clements et al. (2003) and Giesecke (2008). Early work on architectural styles was published by Abowd et al. (1993) and Perry and Wolf (1992). Clements et al. (2003) define architectural style as follows:

Definition: Architectural Style (Clements et al. (2003)) *An architectural style is a specialisation of element and relation types, together with a set of constraints on how they can be used.*

In the following *Layered Architecture* and *Decomposition* are introduced as styles of the module view as well as *Service-Oriented Architecture* as a style of the component-and-connector view. These coarse-grained architectural styles were chosen since they are frequently used in current architectures that serve as target architectures for MARE. The decomposition style is furthermore an important basis for the processing of the target architecture in MARE.

2.3.1 Layered Architecture

The layered architecture style is a style of large software systems (according to Lilienthal (2009) beginning from 100,000 LOC). A layered architecture defines layers of modules with strict rules between the layers. According to Clements et al. (2003) each layer represents a virtual machine, where a virtual machine is defined as follows: *A virtual machine is an abstract computing device; typically, it is a program, that acts as an interface between other software and actual hardware (or another virtual machine).* Such a layer should provide an interface offering cohesive services. Layers have a strict ordering, such that a higher layer is only allowed to use the next lower layer, but no higher layers. Many layered architectures in practice are non-strict layered architectures, i.e. layers are allowed to use the next lower layer or layers below it.

2.3.2 Decomposition

Clements et al. (2003) describe decomposition as an architectural style of the module viewpoint. The style represents the partitioning of a system in modules and their submodules. The decomposition style serves several purposes: the allocation of responsibilities, the communication of a broad picture of the architecture, and the predefinition of the modifiability of the system. Typically two dimensions of decomposition are relevant in practice: technological and functional decomposition (cf. Heckel et al. (2008)).

The technological decomposition of a system represents a mapping of source elements to the chosen technological implementation and their relations to technological frameworks and libraries. The functional decomposition of a system represents a mapping of source elements to the functional requirements of the system. In service-oriented architectures, services provide functional interfaces to the system, that conform to business functions. Services are typically implemented by components; these encapsulate the implementation of a services from a particular domain.

Siedersleben (2004) views decomposition on the level of single systems. He introduces software categories and states that atomic components should belong to exactly one category. Composite components may contain components of several categories. The categories defined for information systems are A for application-specific software and T for technology specific software. The idea behind this distinction is that A- and T-software have different change cycles and hence the separation of these categories improves maintainability. Arsanjani et al. (2008) also distinguish *Functional Components* and *Technical components* in the context of service-oriented architectures.

Typically the technological decomposition in form of a layered architecture (cf. Section 2.3.1) is the dominant decomposition in the development of single software systems or system families. For system landscapes paradigms as SOA (cf. Section 2.3.3) a functional decomposition for the definition of domains and services is proposed.

For single systems, the technological decomposition eases the separation of concerns in the development and is assumed to improve the maintainability of the system and support the reusability of its implementation. Parnas (1972) proposes a decomposition based on design decisions and their foreseen frequency of change in favour of a decomposition based on functional requirements. The functional decomposition on the other side allows a more direct mapping of requirements to the implementation and eases the communication with users and domain experts. E.g., Stahl et al. (2007) propose to concentrate on technological aspects (architecture-centric model-driven software development) for the introduction of model-driven software development, since it supports the maintainability of a system and the development efficiency. But they also propose to put domain-specific abstractions on top of mature technology-centric methods to improve the communication with other stakeholders (cf. Stahl et al. (2007, p. 336)). Similar methods are developed in the context of Domain-Specific Modelling (cf. Tolvanen and Rossi (2003)).

Evans (2004) introduces Domain-Driven Design (DDD). The core of DDD are methods to build a domain model and to map this model to the implementation of the system. As such DDD provides methods for the functional decomposition of the domain. It also describes how to fit this into the technological decomposition of a corresponding software system.

Clements et al. (2003) describe the following three purposes of the decomposition:

- The achievement of quality attributes as e.g. modifiability and performance

- The decision whether modules from other systems or commercial modules are (re-)used

- The implementation of a product line

The decomposition criteria for a concrete architecture base on the decisions that are associated with this purposes and have to be customised for the given context. In MARE, the concrete decomposition criteria are the basis for the mapping of source elements to target components.

2.3.3 Service-Oriented Architectures

Service-oriented architecture (SOA) is an architecture paradigm for distributed systems, that is especially promoted in the domain of business information systems. It can also be seen as an architectural style (Baresi et al. (2006)). There is no common definition of SOA. Nevertheless, the literature (e.g. Erl (2005), Krafzig et al. (2004), and Josuttis (2007)) exposes common features of a SOA as e.g. separation of concerns, loose coupling, interoperability, and heterogeneity. Methods for the introduction of a SOA are provided by *Quasar Enterprise* (Engels et al. (2008)) and the *Service-Oriented Modeling and Architecture (SOMA)* method (Arsanjani et al. (2008)). Channabasavaiah et al. (2004) examine the industrial motivation for the introduction of a SOA, while Gimnich (2007) concentrates on abstract technological tasks for the introduction.

The definition of the term service as the central concept of a SOA is also controversial in literature and practice. The OASIS Reference Model for Service Oriented Architecture abstractly defines a service as follows.

Definition: Service (Organization for the Advancement of Structured Information Standards (OASIS) (2006)) *The performance of work (a function) by one for another.*

The term is concretised by the following properties (Organization for the Advancement of Structured Information Standards (OASIS) (2006)):

- A service is a mechanism to enable access to one or more capabilities.

- A service is provided by an entity (the service provider).

- A service is accessed by means of a service interface.

- A service is opaque in that its implementation is typically hidden from the service consumer.

In SOA the functional decomposition of a domain becomes the guiding aspect of development (Engels et al. (2008)). Functional decomposition is the basis for the definition of services and applications that provide these services. From the viewpoint of component-based systems, a service can also be seen as a deployed component. The concentration on the functional decomposition does not contradict the best practice of technological decomposition and layered architectures for single software systems, since the focus of SOA is on application landscapes or large software systems.

Services can be combined to business processes in order to fulfil more coarse-grained functionalities. This combination of services in an enterprise is called *orchestration*. In contrast to orchestration, *choreography* of services describes the service-oriented collaboration of different enterprises. An example for the application of orchestration in the context of grid computing was introduced by the BIS-Grid project as described by Hasselbring (2010).

2.4 Architecture Metrics

To measure the quality of an architecture, appropriate metrics are needed. Since this thesis focuses on the structural aspects of architectures coupling and cohesion were chosen as main quality metrics. They are commonly referred to as major design principles of software architectures. Existing metrics for coupling and cohesion are described in the following subsections. There are further metrics for special paradigms, as e.g. the depth of the class hierarchy for object-oriented systems, which are not considered here. For further details see Harrison et al. (1997) which give an overview of object-oriented metrics. Bengtsson (1998) adapts chosen object-oriented metrics to the architecture level to support the prediction of maintainability.

2.4.1 Coupling

The IEEE (1990) defines coupling as follows:

Definition: Coupling (IEEE (1990)) *The manner and degree of interdependence between software modules.*

Stevens et al. (1974) describe the reduction of coupling as the minimisation of connections between modules. They further state, that coupling is lower for connections to the interface of a module than for connections to internal elements of a module, which are assumed to change more frequently. Martin (1994) accordingly terms dependencies to stable targets as good dependencies. A simple example are external accesses to attributes in contrast to external accesses to methods that use these attributes in object-oriented systems. The latter use the stable interface of a class, while the former access internals of a class that should be hidden.

In the context of architecture restructuring in this thesis it is not intended to measure the quality of the target architecture in terms of the coupling induced by the intended interface uses. It is rather necessary to measure the quality of the complete mapping which can introduce dependencies that do not conform to the target architecture. These types of coupling, which conform to dependencies to unstable target in terms of Martin (1994), should be minimised, since they influence the restructuring of the implementation.

2.4.2 Cohesion

Stevens et al. (1974) describe cohesion as the binding of elements inside a module. They introduce cohesion as a counterpart to coupling and as a concept to maximise relationships among elements in the same module and minimise relationships between elements in different modules. The IEEE (1990) defines cohesion as *the manner and degree to which the tasks performed by a single software module are related to one another.*

There are also several definitions of concrete metrics for cohesion based on different notions of the term module. Emerson (1984) defines a cohesion metric on the procedure or function level. The definition is based on paths through a function and defined using flow graphs. Emerson (1984) formulates conditions for the application of the metric, which require a single entry point for each module and special properties for executable statements. Thus, the metric is not usable in the context of modules and components as defined in this thesis.

Chidamber and Kemerer (1994) define the cohesion of classes in object-oriented system in terms of lack of cohesion between methods in a class. Their LCOM (Lack of Cohesion in Methods) metric counts the pairs of methods, that do not use the same instance variables. Hitz and Montazeri (1995) show cases in which LCOM provides unintuitive results. They redefine LCOM in graph-theoretic terms as the number of connected components in a graph. The basis of the definition is a graph with methods as vertices and method calls and accesses to equal instance variables as edges.

Hitz and Montazeri (1995) provide further cases in which all methods use the same instance variables, but that nevertheless intuitively show different cohesion. Figure 2.2 depicts an example, that shows two graphs for which LCOM = 1. To

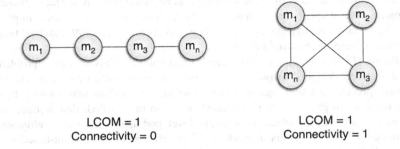

LCOM = 1
Connectivity = 0

LCOM = 1
Connectivity = 1

Figure 2.2: LCOM Connectivity Example

distinguish these cases Hitz and Montazeri (1995) define a metric that maps the connectivity of the graph to the interval [0, 1]. The metric is defined as follows:

$$Connectivity = 2 * \frac{|E| - (n-1)}{(n-1)*(n-2)} \tag{2.1}$$

with n being the number of nodes (methods) and E being the set of edges (relationships between methods) in the graph. LCOM was chosen as an exemplary metric for cohesion, since it is one of the most widespread in literature. Furthermore, LCOM and Connectivity are used as a basis for the measurement of the cohesion of coarse-grained modules in the context of MARE.

2.5 Architectural Erosion

Perry and Wolf (1992) introduced the notions of *architectural erosion* and *architectural drift*. Both address the phenomenon that changes to software systems become harder to realise the longer the system is maintained. The two terms are distinguished by their cause and effect. Architectural erosion is defined as the result of architecture violations, which lead to an increase of problems in the system. Architectural drift on the other hand is described as the result of the insensitivity of the developers about the architecture, which leads to inadaptability of the system. Another term used for the description of the phenomenon is *architectural decay* (e.g. Riebisch and Bode (2009)).

Medvidovic and Jakobac (2006) use the term architectural erosion for the discrepancy between the documented and the implemented architecture. Frequently named reasons for these discrepancies are cost and time pressure for maintenance projects or inadequate documentation of the architecture and the rules it implies for the development of a system. According to Perry and Wolf (1992) architectural drift also causes architectural erosion.

Parnas (1994) talks about *software aging* and states that it is not only a problem of defectively designed software, but can occur in every software system. He describes preventive actions against software aging, but also lists reasons why these are not used in practice. In this context, it has to be clarified, that architecture erosion is not only a problem of software developed using outdated development paradigms, but also occurs in modern object-oriented or component-based systems. Following Parnas, many design principles that can help to prevent erosion are long known, but they are often ignored in practice. But even if these principles are applied, architecture erosion still remains a problem, since its avoidance is based on the predictability of future changes. These assumptions of Parnas are confirmed by van Gurp and Bosch (2002), who evaluated design erosion of an exemplary system.

Architectural erosion is one of the reasons that complicate the understanding and the maintenance of software systems and raise the costs of changes. That led to several research approaches in the field of software evolution and modernisation which are described in the next chapter. These approaches try to reduce the effect and the impact of architecture erosion and re-establish the intended architecture. The complication of maintainability by architectural erosion is also one of the reasons for architecture restructuring projects, if the implemented architecture shows large differences to the intended architecture or a new architecture is developed that better suits the current architectural requirements.

3 Software Evolution and Modernisation

This chapter presents in overview on the basics and current approaches in the area of software evolution and modernisation that are important in the context of MARE. Section 3.1 introduces the broad field of reengineering of which architecture restructuring is a subdiscipline. Section 3.2 gives a broad overview on migration which is a field of application for MARE. Reverse engineering, as described in Section 3.3 is used in MARE to gain knowledge about the existing system that is needed for the creation of the complete mapping. Section 3.4 introduces architecture reconstruction, which is a field of application of related approaches to MARE, which use similar methods. Sections 3.5 describes restructuring and architecture restructuring. It presents the current state of the art and related approaches of MARE with similar goals.

Software systems evolve over time. The evolution has several reasons and different scales during the software life cycle. The evolutionary process of software after its delivery is called *software maintenance*. The ISO/IEC (2006) defines software maintenance as follows:

Definition: Software Maintenance (ISO/IEC (2006)) *Software maintenance is the process of modifying a software system or component after delivery to correct faults, improve performances or other attributes, or adapt to a changed environment.*

Furthermore, they define four categories of maintenance:

- **Corrective maintenance** Reactive modification of a software product performed after delivery to correct discovered problems.

- **Adaptive maintenance** Modification of a software product performed after delivery to keep a software product usable in a changed or changing environment.

- **Perfective maintenance** Modification of a software product after delivery to improve performance or maintainability.

- **Preventive maintenance** Modification of a software product after delivery to detect and correct latent faults in the software product before they become effective faults.

A further categorisation is given by terming adaptive and perfective maintenance enhancements and preventive and corrective maintenance corrections, while preventive and perfective maintenance are proactive and corrective and adaptive maintenance are reactive. Table 3.1 gives an overview of these categories.

Table 3.1: Maintenance Categories (Source: Abran et al. (2004)

	Correction	Enhancement
Proactive	Preventive	Perfective
Reactive	Corrective	Adaptive

According to Ulrich (2004) software modernisation '*begins where existing practices fall short*'. He also states that '*modernization examines, exposes and facilitates the refactoring, redesign and redeployment of core application architectures with the intent of meeting critical business requirements in a way that lowers risks, costs and delivery timeframes*'. I.e. modernisation becomes necessary when requirements can not be implemented on the basis of the existing system anymore with reasonable effort. Modernisation is then used to transform the system into a state that enables the envisioned changes.

Thus, software modernisation can be seen as a large software evolution step. Typically software migration belongs to this category. Migration in the common understanding denotes the transformation of a software system from one environment to another without changing its functionality. Examples are the migrations to new operating systems or programming languages or migrations to new development paradigms as e.g. object-orientation or service-oriented architectures.

Abran et al. (2004) lists program comprehension, reengineering and reverse engineering as techniques for maintenance. The remainder of this chapter will describe these topics in more detail, beginning with reengineering, migration, and reverse engineering as basic terms in Sections 3.1 to 3.3. Further topics are architecture reconstruction in Section 3.4 as well as restructuring and architecture restructuring (Section 3.5) as fundamental reengineering methods, that are the basis for the topic of this thesis.

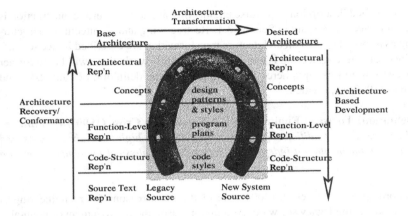

Figure 3.1: The Horseshoe Model (Source: Kazman et al. (1998))

3.1 Reengineering

Reengineering is a task that performs fundamental changes to an existing software system, mostly with the purpose to improve the quality of the system. The most common definition of reengineering is given by Chikofsky and Cross (1990):

Definition: Reengineering (Chikofsky and Cross (1990)) *Reengineering, also known as both renovation and reclamation, is the examination and the alteration of a subject system to reconstitute it in a new form and the subsequent implementation of the new form.*

Following this definition reengineering can be subdivided into three parts: *Reverse Engineering, Restructuring* and *Forward Engineering*. This conforms to the horseshoe model presented by Kazman et al. (1998). It is a metaphor for the integration of code-level and architectural reengineering. The model as shown in Figure 3.1 represents the reverse engineering of the current system on the left-hand side and the forward engineering of the new system on the right-hand side. The restructuring step is done by an architecture transformation from the recovered source system architecture to the target system architecture. According to Kazman et al. (1998) the architecture transformation is the context of further transformations on the lower levels of abstraction. The horseshoe model is used in this thesis as a basis for the architecture restructuring process in the MARE Method.

A detailed description on reverse engineering and architecture reconstruction is given in Section 3.3 and in Section 3.4. Restructuring and architecture restructuring as a special case of an architecture transformation are described in Section 3.5. Since forward engineering is not in the focus of this work, there will be no further discussion on this topic here. For completeness the definition of Chikofsky and Cross (1990) is provided.

Definition: Forward Engineering (Chikofsky and Cross (1990)) *Forward engineering is the traditional process of moving from high-level abstractions and logical, implementation-independent designs to the physical implementation of a system.*

According to Abran et al. (2004) one of the main reasons for reengineering is to replace aging legacy software. As a minor reason the improvement of maintainability of the system is mentioned.

3.2 Migration

The term migration is commonly used for the transformation of a system from one environment to another without changing its functionality. Gimnich and Winter (2005) distinguish four kinds of migration:

- **Hardware Migration** is the migration of a system between two hardware environments, e.g. from a mainframe to a server environment.

- **Runtime Environment Migration** is e.g. the migration from one operating system to another.

- **Development Environment Migration**, e.g. the migration from COBOL to Java.

- **Architecture Migration** is the change of the system structure. In the context of this thesis it is referred to as architecture restructuring. Practical aspects of the topic are also discussed by Krieghoff et al. (2008).

According to Brodie and Stonebraker (1995) there are two principal migration strategies: *Cold Turkey* and *Chicken Little*. The Cold Turkey strategy, also known as *Big Bang*, replaces the existing system in one step by a newly developed software system with the same functionality. The Chicken Little strategy, also known as *Smooth Migration*, on the other hand proposes an incremental replacement or transformation of the system. Based on these basic strategies several migration processes were introduced in the literature (e.g. Ackermann et al. (2005), Gimnich and Winter (2005) and Boos et al. (2006)).

Hasselbring et al. (2004) introduce a pattern for the smooth migration of information systems from a monolithic system to a multi-tier architecture. This pattern, called DUBLO (DUal Business Logic), promotes the dual definition of business logic in the new and the old environment. Both environments are connected via standardised interfaces. Thus, new logic, implemented in the new environment, can use functionality and data of the old implementation. The next step is to perform a stepwise transformation of the logic implementing these interfaces to the new environment in order to improve the maintainability of the system and in the end completely replace the old system. Teschke et al. (2004) describe methods for the identification of web service interfaces in the context of DUBLO. The further definition of migration steps and the decision process for the decision which parts of the implementation are to be migrated in a certain step are not discussed for DUBLO. Section 6.2.3 describes how MARE can be used to plan these steps on the basis of the identified web services.

In recent years several approaches were developed, that introduced the automation of migration scenarios using model-driven technologies (e.g. Hunold et al. (2008), Kühnemann and Rünger (2006) and Fleurey et al. (2007)). Most of these approaches concentrate on the migration of the development environment. They create complete models of the implementation of the software systems and transform these models to models based on programming language. Problems like the migration from one programming paradigm to another, the migration from procedural to object-oriented programming in the course of a migration from COBOL to Java, are however not addressed. Also, the restructuring of the architecture, that becomes necessary, when the environments require different architectural styles, is usually not subject of the discussion.

3.3 Reverse Engineering

Reverse engineering is an important method of software evolution and the initial phase of reengineering (Mens and Demeyer (2008)). This phase is used to gain information about a system under study by creating abstract views of the source code. A common definition of reverse engineering is given by Chikofsky and Cross (1990):

Definition: Reverse Engineering (Chikofsky and Cross (1990)) *Reverse engineering is the process of analyzing a subject system to identify the system's components and their interrelationships and create representations of a system in another form or at a higher level of abstraction.*

An important property of reverse engineering is, that it is passive (Abran et al. (2004)). I.e. it does not change the implementation of a system under study, but is only used to gain information about the system. A typical approach to reverse engineering is to extract all relevant facts from the source code of a system and store them in a repository (Ebert et al. (2008)). From this basis further analyses can be conducted to create more abstract views of the source code and improve the understanding of the system. Jahnke (2008) emphasises that reverse engineering is goal-driven. It is typically used from some point of the maintenance process, when the knowledge of the system is insufficient to adequately change the system and be able to predict the consequences of the change.

Müller et al. (2000) present a roadmap on reverse engineering that highlights present and future topics of reverse engineering. Furthermore, they give an overview on tools and reverse engineering processes. They also highlight, that reverse engineering and program understanding should be applied continuously to keep track of the properties of the implementation. The continuous update of information about the system ensures the quality of the implementation and can make expensive reverse engineering projects obsolete. Corresponding methods are e.g. provided by tools like Bauhaus,[1] Sotograph,[2] or CAST.[3]

The extraction of knowledge from the source code can be implemented using two principally different methods, namely static analysis and dynamic analysis. Both will be described in the following subsections. Another method to gain knowledge about a system is the analysis of further sources besides the programming language source code. Possible sources for this analysis are described in Section 3.3.3.

As can be seen in the left part of Figure 3.1, reverse engineering can lead to specific representations of a software system on different abstraction levels. For this thesis the architectural level is of special interest. Therefore approaches for the reverse engineering to an architectural abstraction level is covered in more detail in Section 3.4.

---

[1] http://www.axivion.com/
[2] http://www.software-tomography.ch/
[3] http://www.castsoftware.com/

3.3.1 Static Analysis

Static source code analysis is the most investigated method in literature to gain knowledge about a software system. It results in a model that contains the entities of the software system and their relationships. A limitation of static analysis is that it is only able to reconstruct which relations are possible in the system, but not which are really used in the running system.

3.3.2 Dynamic Analysis

Dynamic analysis tackles the limitation of static analysis not to be able to reconstruct dynamic properties of the running system. In order to gain such knowledge, the source code is instrumented or interpreted for special use cases. The instrumentation focuses on certain properties to be found and logs the data in *traces* or *call graphs*. These represent the control flow through a system and enable the analysis, which source code has really been executed. A current approach for nonintrusive instrumentation and subsequent monitoring of the system is the Kieker framework presented by van Hoorn et al. (2009).

Xie and Notkin (2002) present a case study about Java call graph extractors. They focus on the differences of call graph extraction for reverse engineering and other usages, such as compiler optimisation or performance analysis. They also state that *dynamic call graphs require some complementary static information and an effective representation to aid program understanding*. Thus, dynamic analysis is mostly combined with static analysis to gain a complete picture of the system under study.

3.3.3 Analysis of other Artefacts

For many software systems there are more artefacts than the mere source code that can be analysed to gain information about the system. These artefacts are e.g. source code comments and all kinds of further documentation from textually captured requirements to architectural documents and diagrams using UML or other formal or informal notations. Also information about the implementation history like repository logs that enable the reconstruction when a certain part of the code was developed or by whom it was developed can be of interest for reverse engineering.

3.4 Architecture Reconstruction

Architecture reconstruction, also known as architecture recovery, is a part of the reverse engineering process (cf. Bauer and Trifu (2004)). Van Deursen et al. (2004) describe it as *the process of obtaining a documented architecture for an existing system*. As such it is aimed at the high-level understanding of existing software systems for which documentation and especially architectural documents are rare.

Architecture reconstruction is a necessary precondition for manual architecture restructuring processes and also reveals design flaws in existing systems and can therefore be used to improve the quality of existing software systems. According to this, Medvidovic and Jakobac (2006) denominate architectural erosion (cf. Section 2.5) as the main motivation for architecture reconstruction methods. Van Deursen et al. (2004) state the realisation of migrations, auditing, application integration, or impact analysis as main drivers for architecture reconstruction.

Ducasse and Pollet (2009) present a taxonomy of architecture reconstruction. Figure 3.2 shows the categories of the taxonomy. The categories are subsumed in five groups: the goal of the reconstruction, the main process type, the inputs used as information source, the used techniques and the target output of the approach. In the paper they classified 34 different approaches using the taxonomy.

The following sections describe methods for architecture reconstruction based on different input data. Approaches are distinguished by the fact whether they employ architectural information or not. Since MARE makes strong use of architectural information for the restructuring, approaches that also include this input are methodologically close to MARE although they follow a different goal. Thus, this category of the aforementioned taxonomy is the most relevant in the context of MARE.

While most approaches only use the source code and its implicit architectural information to support the reconstruction of explicit architectural information of a system under study, there are also some approaches that employ hypothetical architectural information from the user. For these approaches reference architectures can e.g. be used as an initial starting point. Furthermore, these techniques can be used to reveal architectural flaws in the implementation. Subsequent to these approaches architecture conformance checking is briefly introduced. Conformance checking (cf. Section 3.4.3) is not directly concerned with architecture reconstruction, but can also be used to discover architectural flaws and as a starting point for manual architecture restructuring.

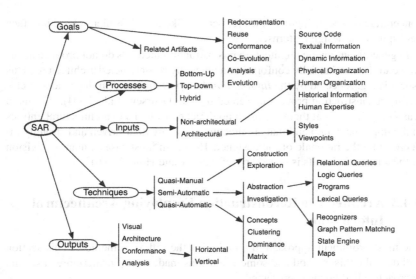

Figure 3.2: Architecture Reconstruction Taxonomy (Source: Ducasse and Pollet (2009))

3.4.1 Architecture Reconstruction Based on Source Code

Most architecture reconstruction approaches, that are documented in the literature focus on the reconstruction of architectural information from the source code as the only source of knowledge about the system. The reason for this is, that reconstruction in practice is mainly applied to legacy systems, for which the source code is the only source available. Typically architecture reconstruction approaches further concentrate on the reconstruction of structural information, i.e. the decomposition of the system into modules. The main criteria for the reconstruction of these modules are cohesion and coupling. Thus, the approaches assume that the system was build with at least an architectural blueprint in mind. Another implicit assumption is, that architectural erosion has not progressed too far, because this sophisticates the result of the reconstruction.

Koschke (2005) presents an extensive overview on the current state of architecture reconstruction methods. He also provides an overview which architecture viewtype (as described in Section 2.1) is reconstructed by these approaches. It is shown, that the major part of reconstruction methods create views in the module viewtype, while just a few approaches create views in the component-and-connector or the allocation viewtype. It can further be seen that most approaches concentrate on special parts of the architecture like e.g. class hierarchies, interface descriptions or design patterns.

In general, automatic architecture reconstruction methods do not produce an architectural view that fully conforms to a manually reconstructed architecture. This aspect is e.g. reflected by the *Information Interpretation* step in the general architecture reconstruction process presented by Van Deursen et al. (2004). The main reason for this is, that there are often no direct equivalents to architectural entities in the implementation and that architecture views are goal-driven and strongly influenced by the rationale of the designer. Hence, in most cases a manual revision of the automatic results is necessary (cf. Fahmy and Holt (2000)).

3.4.2 Architecture Reconstruction Employing Architectural Information

The most prominent approach in this field is the reflexion method. This section will describe this method and some extensions made to it. Furthermore, a second approach called Focus is presented.

3.4.2.1 Reflexion Method

The reflexion method was originally developed by Murphy et al. (1995) in order to provide support for architecture reconstruction based on the comparison of architectural models and the actual source code of a system. The reflexion method takes an architectural model and a mapping of its elements to the source code as user-defined inputs. The architectural model represents the hypothesised module view of the system under study and reflects the expectations of the user. The elements of the *hypothesised architecture* are mapped to implementation entities of the system under study.

From these inputs a reflexion model is computed. The reflexion model represents a comparison between the expected architectural model and the current implementation. It indicates convergent and divergent dependencies between the elements described in the architectural model in comparison to the source code as well as expected dependencies that do not exist in the source code. Figure 3.3 illustrates this procedure.

The process of the reflexion method is iterative. In each iteration further source code entities are added to the mapping and existing mappings can be changed. After that a new reflexion model is computed and presented to the user. The goal is to find a decomposition with minimal coupling and maximum cohesion.

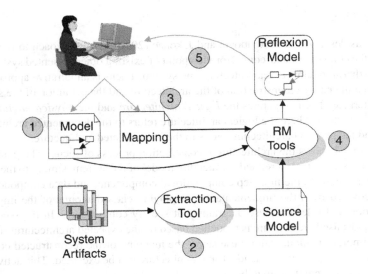

Figure 3.3: The Reflexion Method (Source: Murphy et al. (2001))

Koschke and Simon (2003) extend the reflexion method by the possibility to define hierarchical hypothesised module views, which is necessary to apply the method to complex systems. The main discussion of the paper is how lifted references between elements in the hypothesised architecture have to be handled.

In the original reflexion method the mapping of implementation entities to elements of the hypothesised architecture has to be done manually. Christl et al. (2005) extend the reflexion method by a semi-automatic mapping using clustering techniques. The mapping process is iterative and starts with the manual mapping as an initial seed of implementation entities. The clustering algorithm then automatically adds all implementation entities to this mapping that unambiguously belong to one of the seeds. Further entities are proposed for each seed, indicating the probability of their belonging to the different seeds. After an agreement of the user further entities can be iteratively mapped. In Christl et al. (2007) the attraction functions used to execute the clustering are described in more detail and the quality of the automatic mapping is evaluated in four case studies.

3.4.2.2 Focus

Focus, as described in Medvidovic and Jakobac (2006), is an approach to reconstruct the component-and-connector viewpoint of existing object-oriented systems and furthermore aims at rearchitecting the system. Focus is an iterative approach in which the partly reconstruction of the architecture and the evolution of the system alternate. Focus separates the *logical architecture* and the *physical architecture* of a system, where the logical architecture refers to the documented architecture and the physical architecture refers to the implemented architecture.

Figure 3.4 shows the architecture reconstruction process of focus. The goal of the process is to create a refined architecture model of the system, similar to the reflexion method. In the first step computational components and data components are recovered from the implementation employing class diagrams of the implementation and rules on these diagrams that specify components. In the second step an idealised architecture is modelled based on the expected architectural style of the implementation. After these steps, the mapping of the reconstructed components to components of the idealised architecture can be executed. This activity has to be done mainly manually.

The forth step is the identification of key use cases. The use cases as well as the idealised architecture focus on the current evolution goal and therefore only cover parts of the implementation. In the next step the interactions of the identified component are analysed in order to be able to integrate all of them into the idealised architecture. The last step is the generation of the refined idealised architecture. During this step inconsistencies between the components reconstructed in the physical architecture and the components defined in the idealised logical architecture are revealed. Inconsistencies include inconsistent dependencies as in the reflexion method. Furthermore, arising from the different mapping approach, the appearance and the granularity of components in the two architecture models can also be inconsistent.

The architecture reconstruction phase in Focus is followed by an evolution phase. In this evolution phase changes are made to the system on the basis of the refined idealised architecture. The changes made in the implementation are fed back to the architecture description. After the evolution phase another iteration can be started, setting the focus to another part of the system.

3.4.3 Architecture Conformance Checking

Architecture conformance checking is the process of finding source code dependencies that do not conform to the intended architecture of a system. Typically

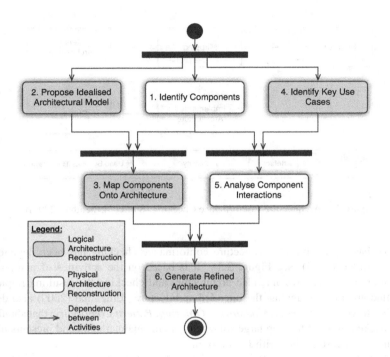

Figure 3.4: Architectural Reconstruction in Focus (Source: Medvidovic and Jakobac (2006))

architecture conformance checking bases on a mapping of the source code to intended architectural entities of the module view. One approach to architecture conformance checking is to use the reflexion method (see Section 3.4.2.1) with a concrete intended architecture instead of a hypothesised architecture to check the implementation against that architecture.

Knodel and Popescu (2007) compare the reflexion method with two other rule-based approaches to architecture conformance checking, that base on the names and interfaces of components. They present 13 dimensions for the comparison of static conformance checking methods. These dimensions include e.g. the kinds of architectural violations, that can be revealed and the probability of false positives. Further dimensions, that are also of interest for the topic of this thesis are multiple view support, restructuring scenarios, and architectural decision support.

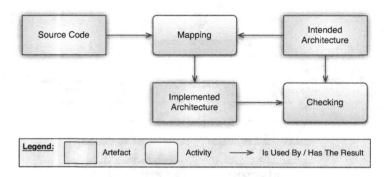

Figure 3.5: Architecture Conformance Checking (Source: Lilienthal (2009))

The basic principle of architecture conformance checking has been depicted
by Lilienthal (2009) (see Figure 3.5). It is based on the activities of mapping
the source code and the intended architecture and checking the resulting implemented architecture against the intended architecture. Lilienthal (2009) also describes three basic aspects (*Modularity, Ordering, Pattern Conformity*) that should
be checked in order to keep large software systems maintainable and presents the
results of 24 case studies with Java systems.

Bischofberger et al. (2004) present the tool *Sotograph*, that automates architecture conformance checking and allows for a continuous conformance and trend
analysis covering subsequent versions of a system. Sotograph is limited to layered
architectures. The layers are subdivided in subsystems which are mapped to Java
packages or directories containing C files. The tool checks for typical violations
in layered architectures as e.g. *Illegal Upward Relationships, Interface Violations,
Several Layer Downward Relationships*, and *Illegal Relationships within a Layer.*

Another way to establish the mapping between source code and the intended
architecture is source code annotation. Krahn and Rumpe (2006) propose to maintain an intermediate architecture description in terms of architectural annotations
to the source code during the development process. They highlight the advantages,
that the developers are always aware of the architecture and an up-to-date architecture description can always be easily derived from the annotations. Furthermore,
the intermediate description can be checked automatically against an intended architecture model to ensure the conformance between the intended architecture and
the source code. The consistency of the annotations to the source code on the other
side have to be checked manually.

3.5 Restructuring

According to the horseshoe model, restructuring is the second phase of reengineering. The goal of restructuring is to transform the structure of an existing software system to improve its internal quality. A widespread definition is given by Chikofsky and Cross (1990):

Definition: Restructuring (Chikofsky et al., 1990) *Restructuring is the transformation from one representation form to another at the same relative abstraction level, while preserving the subject system's external behaviour (functionality and semantics).*

As depicted in the horseshoe model in Figure 3.1, restructuring can be performed on different levels of abstraction from the source code to the architecture. In research the most examined form of restructuring is program restructuring. The level of abstraction in that case is low since it mainly deals with the restructuring on the level of functions and methods. Restructuring on the level of architectural elements such as components is called architecture restructuring in this thesis.

Traditionally common reasons for restructuring are the increase of understandability and the reduction of maintenance cost (Xu et al. (2004)). Parnas (1994) terms restructuring *major surgery* and emphasises the role of restructuring to consolidate similar modules in a system family to a common code base, also to support the goals mentioned before. In the case of restructuring on the architecture level further reasons like e.g. flexibility and integrability into new environments are further important factors.

Figure 3.6 shows a concept hierarchy for restructuring concepts. Hence, restructuring is a subconcept of evolution and can be partitioned into program restructuring, refactoring, architecture refactoring and architecture restructuring. The remainder of this section will describe these subconcepts in more detail. Section 3.5.1 and Section 3.5.2 examine restructuring on a fine-grained module-level, which is a lower level than the focus of MARE, but shares methodological similarities. Section 3.5.3 describes approaches the restructuring on the architecture level in small steps, while Section 3.5.4 examines approaches that are related to MARE, since they also consider the coarse-grained restructuring of architectures. Section 3.5.5 concludes the chapter describing approaches for the migration to SOA, which is a special case of architecture restructuring and one of the application scenarios for MARE.

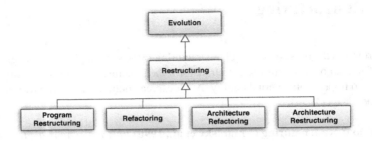

Figure 3.6: Restructuring Concept Hierarchy

3.5.1 Program Restructuring

Program restructuring denotes the restructuring of the implementation of a system on the statement or function level. It is the most established subconcept of restructuring. Its main concern is the restructuring of structural elements to improve their cohesion. Program restructuring is typically applied to imperative programming languages. Mens et al. (2003) give an overview of research on refactoring and program restructuring.

Frequently used methods for program restructuring are clustering (e.g. Wiggerts (1997) and Lung and Zaman (2004)) and formal concept analysis (Tonella (2001)), which are used to rearrange the existing structure.

3.5.2 Refactoring

Refactoring is the object-oriented equivalent to program restructuring (Mens et al. (2003)). The term has originally been introduced by Opdyke (1992) and gained prominence through the book of Fowler (1999). In this book Fowler defines refactoring as follows:

Definition: Refactoring (Fowler (1999)) *A change made to the internal structure of software to make it easier to understand and cheaper to modify without changing its observable behaviour.*

The definition is similar to the definition of restructuring by Chikofsky and Cross (1990), while highlighting the goals stated by Xu et al. (2004). In the book, a number of refactorings on object-oriented system are described. They mainly deal with the introduction of abstraction, simplification and the organisation of code and data. Refactorings are typically small changes to the code, that are executed regularly to keep a constant code quality. Serban and Czibula (2008) present an approach for the automatic recognition of refactorings using clustering analysis.

Mancl (2001) describes a refactoring case study and the migration from a legacy system to an object-oriented code base using design patterns. The conclusions of the case study are, that code discovery is an important but also very time-consuming step and that code modification should take place in small steps.

3.5.3 Architecture Refactoring

In contrast to coarse-grained architecture restructuring, which is the topic of Section 3.5.4, architecture refactoring in this thesis denotes architecture evolution approaches, that have a small-step and continuous character. The term refactoring has been chosen here, since the described approaches base on small evolutionary steps that are similar to refactorings, but applied on the architectural level.

Architecture refactorings are defined as *the first step in changing system implementation to match specific quality-improvement goals* by Ivkovic and Kontogiannis (2006). They also highlight the impact of architecture models on detailed design models and the implementation, which have to be changed, when the architecture evolves. For this technical aspect there is a parallel to methods of architecture conformance checking. For incremental changes these methods can reveal necessary changes to the implementation, when the refactored architecture is modelled as intended architecture of the system.

To keep the source code and the architecture description synchronised, Krahn and Rumpe (2006) propose an approach that adds architectural annotations to the source code. Using these annotations an architect is directly able to see which parts of the source code are affected by an architecture refactoring. Furthermore, the actual goal of the approach is to use the annotations to automate the synchronisation of the source code, when the architecture description is changed by refactorings. While the approach automates conformance checks between the architecture description and the source code annotations, the annotations themselves have to be created and checked by hand.

Krahn and Rumpe (2006) also propose exemplary architectural refactorings. They include the addition and removal of ports and connectors and the split of components. Ivkovic and Kontogiannis (2006) describe a framework to define and apply architecture refactorings on the basis of architecture models defined in the UML. However, they do not provide explicit architecture refactorings, but give a few specific examples for the application of the framework.

Fahmy and Holt (2000) view architectural changes as graph transformations and describe amongst others transformations for the modification of an architecture. These transformations mainly deal with fitting the concrete architecture implemented in the system and the architectural description.

Pashov (2004) presents an approach that joins feature-based requirements engineering and architecture refactorings. He proposes a software evolution process that introduces architecture refactorings for each change in the requirements features. Thus, it is ensured that the requirements, the architecture description and the source code are always synchronised.

Lung (1998) presents an approach, that uses clustering analysis for architecture recovery, but also uses the clustering results to propose refactorings of the system to improve the quality in terms of coupling and cohesion. A similar goal is stated by Bauer and Trifu (2004). They also propose to impose a new structure to a system based on a detailed architectural analysis of object-oriented systems.

As with refactorings on the source code level, *architectural bad smells* can be identified, which are indicators for the application of certain architecture refactorings. Garcia et al. (2009) introduce the term architectural bad smells and give four practical examples. Krahn and Rumpe (2006) also describe examples for architectural bad smells. Furthermore, architecture anti-patterns are e.g. described by Brown et al. (1998) In contrast to MARE the aforementioned approaches focus on small changes to an existing architecture, while MARE focuses on the coarse-grained change of the system's structure. Furthermore, many of the approaches only consider the architectural level and do not discuss the adjustment of the source code according to the architectural changes.

3.5.4 Architecture Restructuring

Where traditional restructuring approaches focus on restructuring smaller pieces of the source code, architecture restructuring focuses only on the overall structural organisation of the source code. Gimnich and Winter (2005) also refer to *architecture migration*. In this thesis the term architecture restructuring is used to avoid confusion with other migration approaches. Architecture restructuring itself is performed on the architectural level only. The result of the restructuring is a model or documentation of a system. After the restructuring on the architectural level the detailed design and the implementation also have to be restructured to conform to the new architecture. I.e. elements of the implementation have to be removed or restructured and dependencies between elements, which are not allowed in the target architecture, have to be resolved. The MARE approach introduced in this thesis is an approach that supports the adjustment of the detailed design to the restructured target architecture and thus prepares the restructuring of the implementation.

Aoyama (2001) introduces the distinction of continuous and discontinuous software evolution. In the context of this thesis one can refer to architecture refactoring as continuous evolution while architecture restructuring corresponds to discontinuous evolution. Discontinuous software evolution is associated by Aoyama (2001) with to main aspects: architectural change and feature change. While feature change can be a reason for architecture restructuring, this aspect is not considered here.

Typical architecture restructuring projects can be seen as enhancement according to Table 3.1. As stated by Tonella (2001) restructuring can also be seen as preventive maintenance, since it prevents faults that result from incomprehensible source code.

Although architecture erosion and poor software design are often stated as reasons for architecture restructuring tasks, this is not always the case. As mentioned by Garlan et al. (2009), another reason for architecture restructuring is the regular evolution of software systems. Mostly this evolution can be conducted in small steps, but in some cases, as e.g. changes to the environment, a system is used in, also larger restructurings become necessary. Another possible reason is the migration to a new execution environment, which can also involve architecture restructuring. An example for such a migration is the migration from COBOL to Java, where both execution environments base on completely different architectural foundations.

Garlan et al. (2009) focus on the planning of architecture restructuring projects on the architectural level. They introduce the notions of evolution paths and evolution patterns as building blocks for architecture evolution. An evolution path defines a series of intermediate architectures, starting from the current architecture of the system and ending with the intended target architecture. The intermediate architectures define the steps of the restructuring project. Evolution styles define a family of domain-specific architecture evolution paths and and common properties and constraints of these paths. However, the approach does not define concrete evolutionary steps. The evolution styles rather describe possible paths for the restructuring of an architecture based on the used architectural styles in the source and the target architecture. Furthermore, a mapping to changes of the implementation is missing.

Architecture restructuring is less researched than the restructuring of the source code. However, a number of methods and principles are similar on both abstraction levels. Furthermore, source code restructuring can be a necessary preceding step for architecture restructuring. Heckel et al. (2008) introduce the term *archi-*

tectural transformations. An architectural transformation combines architectural restructuring based on source code annotations with the automatic transformation to a new source representation.

Pashov et al. (2004) focus on the restructuring of systems, that contain disproportionally large components. They propose an approach based on feature models to identify these components. Feature analysis can also help to design smaller components in a new target architecture. However, it is not considered how the source code can be adjusted to the target architecture, i.e. how the implementation of the large components can be split up.

3.5.5 Migration to SOA

A current research topic is the migration to service-oriented architectures. In the terms introduced so far, SOA migration is an architecture restructuring towards an architecture that allows for the integration of the existing system into a service-oriented environment. A common strategy is to introduce wrappers for an existing system that realise a service interface (van den Heuvel (2007)). This approach has the advantage, that the existing system does not have to be changed and its internals do not have to be deeply understood to (re-)use it in a modern environment. A disadvantage of this approach is, that in the case of legacy systems it is still difficult to maintain the system and it is very difficult or almost impossible to only use parts of the functionality. The reason for this is, that many so-called legacy systems expose strong architectural erosion, that complicates the decoupling or extraction of single functionalities or services. In these cases an architecture restructuring of the existing system becomes necessary. This section presents current SOA migration approaches, which are a special case of architecture restructuring (cf. Section 6.2.1).

Heckel et al. (2008) present the following six technical SOA properties and state their importance for the reengineering of existing software system in order to (re-)use them in a service-oriented environment.

- Well-defined interfaces
- Loose coupling
- Logical and physical separation of business logic from presentation logic
- Highly-reusable services
- Coarse-grained granularity
- Multi-party and business process orientation

The first two properties concern the service interface and are also important properties when it comes to wrapping existing systems. The latter four properties can in most cases only be fulfilled by an architecture restructuring of these systems. Hence, MARE is an approach that can be employed to obtain these properties.

The approach by Heckel et al. (2008) has the goal to restructure a legacy system in order to be reusable in a service-oriented architecture. This goal is fulfilled by several technological and functional decomposition steps, each following the horseshoe model. They propose to start with a technological decomposition step in order to separate the user interface from the business logic to enable the definition of web service interfaces for the business logic. The further functional decomposition is mainly concerned with the granularity of services.

The technological decomposition of Heckel et al. (2008) bases on code annotation as introduced by Correia et al. (2007). Statements or larger units of code, such as methods and classes, are iteratively and semi-automatically annotated with the categories they belong to (categories are e.g. UI, business logic or data). The code is then reverse engineered to a graph model. Based on the code annotations, the model is automatically restructured using graph transformations. In the end, the source code is restructured by mapping the transformation rules to refactorings or by directly generating the source code.

The functional decomposition of the source code to services, described by Matos (2008) and Matos and Heckel (2008), employs the same methods used for the technological decomposition. It is separated in two tasks, namely *operation identification* and *grouping operations into services*. Thereby the functional categories are assumed not to be known beforehand, but to be defined during the annotation phase. The identification of service operations starts from entry points such as API's used by the UI or external systems. The grouping of the operations to services is done semi-automatically, supported by metrics such as *overlapping between operations, actors involved, information about data accessed*, and *similarity measure*.

Ziemann et al. (2006) describe an approach to SOA migration based on enterprise models. These models are used to define services in legacy systems on an appropriate level of detail and to integrate these services in processes. Winter and Ziemann (2006) extend the approach by adding a more technical reengineering view to support the SOA migration. They also present an adjusted horseshoe model for SOA migration and propose the model-based transformation of the existing system to a service-oriented environment. Winter and Ziemann (2007) provide more details on this topic and especially outline the role of metamodelling for the identification and transformation of services.

In the context of the SOAMIG project, Horn et al. (2009) present the application of model-driven development methods and graph technologies for SOA migration. They show how graph queries and transformations can be used to identify services and transform them to a SOA environment. Fuhr et al. (2010) present an extension of the SOMA method (Arsanjani et al. (2008)). They show which steps of SOMA have to be extended to allow for model-driven migration methods. The method is illustrated by an exemplary extraction of a service from an open-source application.

Sneed (2007) defines four steps for the extraction of services from existing systems. The paper concentrates on the implementation with web services, but the concepts are also applicable for other technological environments.

1. **Discovering potential services** in the existing systems. A potential service is functionality with an economic value in contrast to purely technical code.

2. **Evaluating potential services**. It has to be decided whether it is worthwhile to extract the code, i.e. whether the technically effort of reusing the code is appropriate.

3. **Extracting the source code**. Dependencies to other parts of the system have to be resolved.

4. **Adapting the source code** to the new environment. The code e.g. has to be adapted with a WSDL (Web Services Description Language) interface.

An overview on the different types of SOA migration approaches is provided by Razavian and Lago (2010). They conducted a review of current research approaches and define eight distinct categories called SOA migration families. These are again summarised into two sets: the *migration for modernisation*, which subsumes approaches that focus on the restructuring of the existing system, and the *migration for reuse in service-based development*, which focusses on the adaptation of the existing code.

The MARE approach can be used to support the restructuring of an existing system and the extraction of source code in terms of Sneed (2007). Thus, it complements the approaches described in this section. A more detailed discussion of the relation of MARE to these approaches is given in Section 11.1.

4 Graph Clustering

Graph clustering is used in MARE to create the complete mapping. This chapter gives an overview of the relevant foundations and applications of graph clustering. Section 4.1 describes the basic principles of graphs, while Section 4.2 introduces the graph clusterings. Hierarchical clustering, which is used as basis for the clustering in MARE as well as further common graph clustering algorithms are presented in Section 4.3. Section 4.4 ends the chapter with an overview of applications of graph clustering.

4.1 Graphs

A *graph* is typically defined as a pair of sets $G = (V, E)$, where V is a set of *vertices* (or *nodes*) and E is a set of *edges* (see e.g. Schaeffer (2007)). The pair $(v_1, v_2) \in E$ denotes an edge between the vertices $v_1 \in V$ and $v_2 \in V$. Edges can either be directed or undirected, so that (v_1, v_2) is either ordered or unordered. Furthermore they can be annotated with weights using a weight function $\omega : E \to \mathbb{R}$ leading to a *weighted graph*. A graph that contains more than one edge between two vertices is called *multigraph*. An edge that connects more than two nodes is called *hyperedge*.

A *path* in a graph is defined as a sequence of edges that connect two vertices. A graph is called *connected*, if a path exist between each pair of vertices in the graph. Else the graph is called *disconnected*.

Graphs and also edges can be typed according to the represented problem domain. In software reengineering nodes types can e.g. be classes, functions or files. Typed edges are e.g. used in the TGraph approach by Ebert et al. (2008). Edge types in software reengineering are e.g. containment or call relations.

4.2 Graph Clusterings

According to Schaeffer (2007), the goal of graph clustering is to *divide the data set into clusters such that the elements assigned to a particular cluster are similar or connected in some predefined sense.* Maqbool and Babri (2007) give a similar definition by stating that *Clustering is the process of forming groups of items or entities such that entities within a group are similar to one another and different from those in other groups.* Thus, a cluster is defined as a set $C = \{v_1, v_2, ..., v_x\}$.

Typically, clusters are formed based on a *similarity function* or *distance function*. Examples for traditional graph clustering functions are given in Schaeffer (2007). The similarity of two vertices is computed according to their internal properties. For software entities these properties are e.g. the name of the entity, its size or its developer. The similarity of two vertices can also be computed on the basis of the edges connecting the vertices, which can also be seen as external properties of the vertices. It is typically defined using the number of edges between two nodes, the weight of the edges between two nodes or the length of the path between two vertices. For graphs with a notion of space, the distance can be also defined using the length of edges.

For the remainder of this thesis the term *similarity function* is used. The reason for this is that distance implies a notion of space and vertices with a *low* distance are expected to be clustered. In software clustering, two nodes belong to the same cluster because of a functional relation for which the notion of similarity is more appropriate. Typically, vertices with high similarity are clustered together. Similarity functions can be defined on vertices or on clusters, where most algorithms operate on clusters only. The nodes are then assigned to initial clusters before the actual clustering. These initial clusters can contain one or more nodes, depending on the clustering algorithm. Thus, it can be said that a similarity function *Sim* returns a similarity value $sv_{C_1C_2}$, that states the similarity of the two input clusters $C1$ and $C2$.

$$sv_{C_1C_2} = Sim(C_1, C_2) \tag{4.1}$$

The similarity of two clusters bases on the similarity of their contained nodes. The computation of the similarity is described exemplarily for hierarchical clustering algorithms in Section 4.3.1.

Schaeffer (2007) describes a set of desirable graph theoretical properties of a cluster, which are also a notion of cohesion of a cluster. The properties are summarized in the following list:

- A cluster should be connected.

- Preferably each pair of vertices should be connected by several paths.

- The paths should be internal to the cluster. I.e. each pair of vertices should be connected by at least one path that only visits vertices that are part of the cluster.

- The vertices in a cluster should have more connections to other vertices in the cluster than to vertices outside the cluster. This also accords to the software architecture principle of low coupling.

4.3 Clustering Algorithms

There is a multitude of different clustering algorithms for different purposes. In practice, especially in software clustering, hierarchical clustering is most common and is also used in the MARE clustering approach. Therefore, this section will describe hierarchical clustering in greater detail. As examples for the vast number of other clustering algorithms, this section also shortly describes two algorithms with a broad distribution and different properties in comparison with hierarchical clustering, namely *Partitional Clustering* and *Search Based Clustering*.

4.3.1 Hierarchical Clustering

Hierarchical clustering is a clustering technique that bases on a hierarchical decomposition of nodes. Hierarchical clustering algorithms can be subdivided into agglomerative and divisive algorithms. Divisive algorithms start with the definition of the whole graph as one cluster. In each step of the algorithm this cluster is hierarchically divided into smaller clusters until each vertex is represented by one cluster. Agglomerative algorithms on the other side start by defining one cluster for each vertex in the graph. In each step of the algorithm the two clusters with the highest similarity are merged to form a new cluster. The result of hierarchical clusterings can be depicted in a *dendrogram*. Figure 4.1 shows an exemplary dendrogram for agglomerative hierarchical clustering.

Agglomerative hierarchical clustering will be in focus in the remainder of this section, since it is more commonly used in software reengineering and the basis for the MARE clustering algorithm presented in Section 8.2.

4.3.1.1 Stopping Condition

Agglomerative hierarchical clustering algorithms stop, if only one cluster is left. For many applications the order of the clustering and the resulting hierarchy are an adequate result of the clustering. Others, that are interested in a certain intermediate result search for an adequate cut through the dendrogram that defines a resulting hierarchy. Alternatively specific stopping conditions can be employed. Quante (2008) and Schaeffer (2007) mention two possible stopping conditions:

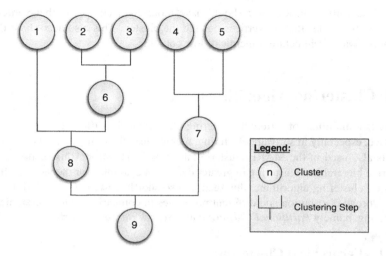

Figure 4.1: Dendrogram Example

dropping below a certain similarity threshold and reaching a predefined number of clusters.

4.3.1.2 Vertex Similarity

The similarity of two vertices is defined by a similarity function. This bases on the attributes of the vertices or the edges between the vertices. Depending on the context, two vertices that have similar attributes or a strong connectivity are assigned a high similarity value.

Many clustering approaches also introduce different kinds of weighting schemes in order to apply a more detailed definition of similarity. Andritsos and Tzerpos (2005) evaluate weighting schemes from different domains for their applicability for software clustering. Rayside et al. (2000) introduces a weighting scheme, that defines weights for different relations in object-oriented software systems. Koschke (2000) furthermore uses weights for different groups of properties, differentiating direct and indirect connections as well as informal information about software artefacts.

4.3.1.3 Cluster Similarity

The computation of the similarity between a newly formed cluster and the existing clusters in each step of a hierarchical clustering is often not newly computed based on the similarity of the single nodes, but using an updating rule. (Maqbool and Babri, 2007, Table 3) describe the four basic strategies for this computation:

Single Linkage

$$Sim(C_i, C_{jk}) = Max(Sim(C_i, C_j), Sim(C_i, C_k)) \tag{4.2}$$

Complete Linkage

$$Sim(C_i, C_{jk}) = Min(Sim(C_i, C_j), Sim(C_i, C_k)) \tag{4.3}$$

Weighted Average Linkage

$$Sim(C_i, C_{jk}) = \frac{1}{2}(Sim(C_i, C_j) + \frac{1}{2}(Sim(C_i, C_k)) \tag{4.4}$$

Unweighted Average Linkage

$$Sim(C_i, C_{jk}) = \frac{(Sim(C_i, C_j) * Size(C_j) + (Sim(C_i, C_k) * Size(C_k))}{(size(C_j) + (size(C_k))} \tag{4.5}$$

In the equations C_i to C_k denote the set of clusters before the current clustering step and C_{jk} the cluster created in the current clustering step by merging the clusters C_j and C_k, with $C_j \neq C_k$. $Max(X,Y)$ and $Min(X,Y)$ compute the maximum and the minimum of X and Y, where X and Y are similarities of clusters. $Size(C_x)$ returns the number of vertices in the cluster C_x.

The equations recursively base on the distance of clusters containing a single vertex. Thus, $Sim(C_i, C_j) = Sim(v_i, v_j)$ for two vertices v_i and v_j, where $C_i = \{v_i\}$ and $C_j = \{v_j\}$. The similarity of two vertices depends on the usage context of the clustering algorithm. The computation of similarity in the context of MARE is discussed in Section 8.2.4.

4.3.1.4 Arbitrary Clustering Decisions

In the single steps of a hierarchical clustering more than two cluster pairs can have the same distance. In this case an arbitrary decision is taken by the clustering implementation. This leads to non-deterministic behaviour of the clustering algorithm, since, depending on the data set and the progress of the clustering, another decision would have led to a potentially extremely different result.

Maqbool and Babri (2007) state that arbitrary decisions are the consequence of a lack of involvement of necessary information. Thus, they propose a clustering algorithm that recomputes the distance between a newly formed cluster and existing clusters based on available information instead of combining the already computed distances, which is the case in the basic four strategies introduced in the previous section.

4.3.2 Partitional Clustering

Instead of hierarchical clustering that creates clusters with a hierarchical order of its elements, partitional clustering algorithms do not consider such relations between the elements, but only provide the division of a set of objects into separate clusters. One of the most widely used partitional clustering algorithms is the k-means algorithm that will be briefly described in the following. More details about the algorithm can e.g. be found in (Tan et al., 2005, Chapter 8).

The k-means algorithm partitions a set of objects in k groups. Thereby, k is a parameter that is defined by the user and represents the number of resulting clusters. The algorithm starts with the selection of k centroids. A centroid is defined as the mean of a group of objects. Usually the centroids are not actual objects from the set of objects to be clustered, but abstract entities. The selection of the initial centroids is crucial, since it influences the quality of the clustering result. Tan et al. (2005) discuss strategies that lead to a good choice.

Clusters of the objects are formed by assigning each object to the closest centroid. Based on this assignment new centroids are computed. This is repeated until the centroids do not change anymore and a stable assignment of objects to clusters is found.

The decisive aspect of the algorithm is the definition of the proximity measure for the objects to compute their distance to the centroids. The Euclidean distance is often used, if the objects can be defined in Euclidean space, but also other notions are proximity are possible. Nonetheless, the measure should not be too complex, since the distances have to be recomputed in each iteration.

Partitional clustering is not used in MARE, since the Euclidean distance can not be used so that another definition of distance between the objects and the centroids would have to be defined. It is assumed that this computation and the definition and computation of the centroids themselves are too complex to be practically used in the context of MARE. Furthermore, it is not intended to include knowledge of the user, e.g. in terms of a fix manual mapping of single objects to clusters, which can be realised with hierarchical clustering.

4.3.3 Density-Based Clustering

Density-based clustering algorithms separate regions of high density from regions of low density. Thus, they can recognise arbitrarily shaped and sized clusters, if the underlying objects have a notion of space. One of the most prominent density-based clustering algorithms is DBSCAN that will be briefly described in the following. More details about the algorithm can e.g. be found in (Tan et al., 2005, Chapter 8).

The DBSCAN algorithm has two main parameters: Eps is a user-specified radius around each point and $MinPts$ is a number that defines the required density of a cluster. The basis of the algorithm are the definitions of core points, border points and noise points. Core points are points inside of a cluster. A point is a core point if it has at least $MinPts$ neighbouring points in Eps. A point is a border point if is has less than $MinPts$ points in Eps, but it has at least one core point in Eps. All other points are noise points.

The algorithm itself is relatively simple. All pairs of core points that are in the radius Eps of each other are assigned to the same cluster. All border points are assigned to their neighbouring core points. If a border point has more than one core point in Eps a cluster for the point has to be chosen. The original definition of DBSCAN by Ester et al. (1996) describes the algorithm from a more technical point of view and assigns the border point to the cluster of the core point for which is was found first.

Density-based clustering is not used in MARE, since the delimitation of source elements for different target components is often not clear, so that the definition of border points and noise points is difficult. Furthermore, noise points are not acceptable in the context of MARE, since a complete mapping of all source elements is required.

4.4 Applications of Graph Clustering

The most important application scenario for the context of this thesis is software clustering. However, clustering itself is used for a broad number of applications. These will be briefly described in Section 4.4.2.

4.4.1 Software Clustering

The clustering of software is one important application scenario for graph clustering. This section will show how software artefacts are mapped to a graph structure, which are the common application scenarios for software clustering, and which typical problems arise when software is clustered.

4.4.1.1 Software Graphs

A graph representation of a software system is the basis for the clustering of software systems. Graphs are frequently used to analyse and visualise software systems. Thereby, the level of detail of the graph varies depending on the rationale of the graph. E.g. Ebert et al. (2008), present a fine-grained graph of a Java program. Typically each analysis tool has its own graph representation of certain programming languages. The *Graph eXchange Language (GXL)*, presented by Holt et al. (2006), is an approach to introduce a common exchange format for graphs between software reengineering tools.

4.4.1.2 Software Clustering Applications and Problems

Common applications of software clustering are concerned with the understanding and reengineering of software systems. Typical application scenarios are the redocumentation and reconstruction of the architecture of legacy software systems (cf. Section 3.4). Furthermore, it is used in approaches for the restructuring of software systems (cf. Section 3.5). In MARE , clustering is used to support the restructuring on an architectural level.

Libraries, that provide common functionalities of software systems, often lead to problems in software clustering, since most clustering algorithms target the optimisation of coupling and cohesion. Libraries tend to break these principles, since they are used all over the system and lead to high coupling. Also, they do not necessarily exhibit high cohesion (Andritsos and Tzerpos (2003)). This can lead to the problem, that source elements are clustered together with the libraries they use instead of other elements they semantically belong to.

Bauer and Trifu (2004) therefore employ a library detection step before the actual clustering to be able to treat libraries differently than rest of the system. Andritsos and Tzerpos (2003) discover libraries by using a clustering based on information theory.

Quante (2008) on the other side uses knowledge about library usage to cluster semantically similar source elements. This works well, when the semantics of the library suits the semantics of the envisioned system decomposition. Quante

(2008) shows this by employing e.g. user interface, database and network libraries to reconstruct the layered decomposition of a Java system. Libraries that do not fit the semantics of the envisioned decomposition are excluded from the clustering to avoid the effects stated above.

4.4.2 Further Applications

In computer science graph clustering is also used in other contexts than software engineering. It is e.g. used in the context of Data Mining to classify data sets or in image analysis, e.g. for object recognition. Another application scenario is the classification of digital documents, such as text files or web pages, to sort large document pools and find documents with similar content.

Besides application in computer science, clustering is also versatilely used in other sciences for the analysis and classification of large data sets. It is further used in market research to analyse customer behaviour.

5 Model-Driven Software Development

This chapter introduces model-driven software development, which is a conceptual basis of the MARE Method. Section 5.1.1 introduces basic modelling concepts as e.g. the terms model and metamodel. Section 5.2 describes model transformations, while Section 5.3 examines the role of architecture in current model-driven software development approaches. Section 5.4 presents interoperability metamodels, which are a conceptual basis for the metamodels used in the MARE Method. Section 5.5 ends the chapter with an overview of model-driven reengineering approaches, which can be used to extend MARE towards the restructuring of the implementation of a system.

Model-driven software development (MDSD) is a software development paradigm that makes models primary artefacts of the software development process. In contrast to traditional software development processes, models are not only used for documentation purposes, but serve as a central artefact for the implementation of the system. Models are either the source for the generation of source code or they are themselves executable by an interpreter. Furthermore, models can be used for various other task, like communication between stakeholders or model-based analyses. This chapter presents the basics of MDSD and its relation to the reengineering of software systems.

To provide further background and current research directions in MDSD, France and Rumpe (2007) provide a roadmap for the model-driven development of complex software. They suggest to focus on bridging the gap between problems and requirements on one side and the implementation on the other side and also support research on executable models. In a concluding vision they encourage the development of domain-specific application development environments. These environments integrate technologies and tools that currently exist side by side. France and Rumpe (2007) state that this vision is hindered by immature technologies and the lack of understanding and experience in the application of model-driven development concepts. Selic (2003) and Uhl (2008) give more information on the application of MDSD in practice.

5.1 Modelling Concepts

5.1.1 Models

Stachowiak (1973) defines three characteristics of a model: the mapping feature, the reduction feature and the pragmatic feature. The first feature means that a system is a representation of a considered system under study. In MDSD this system is the software system to be build or the domain of the system respectively. The reduction feature implies that the model is an abstraction of the system that contains the properties of the system that are relevant for the current context. The last feature highlights the purpose as an important aspect of a model and the possibility to use the model instead of the original for this certain purpose.

The ModelWare EU project uses a definition of model in the context of MDSD, that shares the theory of these characteristics:

Definition: Model (ModelWare Glossary[1]) *A formal representation of entities and relationships in the real world (abstraction) with a certain correspondence (isomorphism) for a certain purpose (pragmatics).*

Furthermore, Favre (2004a) discusses the definition of model on the basis of different definitions from the literature and ends with properties for the definition of the term model, from which the most important is, that a model is a representation of a system under study.

5.1.2 Metamodels

To automate the processing of models (e.g. in analysis, transformation or execution) a definition of the modelling elements used in the models is needed. This definition is given by metamodels. The following definition emphasises this role of a metamodel in MDSD:

Definition: Metamodel (Seidewitz (2003)) *A metamodel is a specification model for a class of systems under study (SUS) where each SUS in the class is itself a valid model expressed in a certain modelling language. That is, a metamodel makes statements about what can be expressed in the valid models of a certain modelling language.*

---

[1] http://www.modelplex.org/index.php?option=com_content&task=view&id=199&Itemid=247

A shorter definition, which will be used in the remainder of this thesis, is given by Favre (2004b):

Definition: Metamodel (Favre (2004b)) *A metamodel is a model of a modelling language.*

He additionally introduces the term *ConformsTo* for the relation between a model and its metamodel and discusses the difference to the commonly used *InstanceOf* relation. Atkinson and Kühne (2003) distinguish ontological and linguistic metamodels. The difference between both concepts is an important aspect in MDSD, especially when domain-specific languages (DSL) are created. Languages are defined by linguistic metamodels. Ontological metamodels on the other side define a specific domain vocabulary. Ontological metamodels can turn into linguistic metamodels when they are used to define a DSL (Kühne (2006)). In the remainder of this thesis linguistic metamodels are used, that define languages to describe specific aspects of software systems.

In research and practice there are a number of metamodelling approaches. The two most influential in the practical application of metamodelling are the Meta Object Facility and the Eclipse Modeling Framework. Both are described in the following subsections.

5.1.2.1 Meta Object Facility

The Meta Object Facility (MOF) is a metamodelling standard by the Object Management Group (OMG) (2006). Currently there are two versions of MOF: Complete MOF (CMOF) and Essential MOF (EMOF). CMOF contains all modelling capabilities of the standard and is e.g. used to define the UML metamodel. EMOF is a subset of CMOF, that only supports basic metamodelling mechanisms, but defines a straightforward mapping to the implementation of these mechanisms. CMOF was e.g. used to define the metamodel of the *Unified Modeling Language (UML)*.

MOF proposes a metamodel architecture with four layers that is the basis for most practical metamodelling approaches. Figure 5.1 shows the layers M0 to M4 on the left and a typical example from the OMG model stack on the right. The relations of the OMG are replaced by the relations of Favre (2004b), because they provide more clarity. As can be seen, the M0 layer has a special role, since it represents the system to be modelled, which can be a software system or a real world entity and is as such not part of the modelling stack. M1 to M3 are necessary for the definition and processing of models and modelling languages in the context of

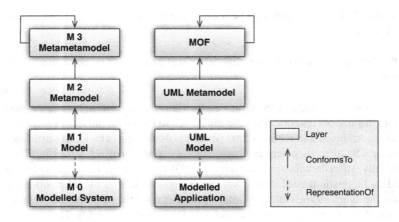

Figure 5.1: MOF Layered Metamodel Architecture

MDSD. M1 represents a model edited by a user, M2 defines the modelling language used to create the model in M1 and M3 defines a language for the definition of modelling languages. The M3 layer is usually used to defined itself for reason of simplification of the metamodelling stack.

The key concepts of MOF for the definition of metamodels are classes and their properties, associations and operations. A UML diagram showing these concepts and their relations is shown in Figure 5.2. These concepts are common in CMOF and EMOF.

5.1.2.2 Eclipse Modeling Framework

The Eclipse Modeling Framework (EMF) (Steinberg et al. (2008)) is the core subproject of the *Eclipse Modeling Project*[2]. It provides tools for the definition and implementation of metamodels. The metametamodel of EMF, called Ecore, is almost identical to EMOF. EMF is currently very popular in practice and constitutes the basis for a number of MDSD tools. It is also used as an quasi exchange standard for modelling tools (Streekmann and Kruse (2009)).

---

[2]http://www.eclipse.org/modeling/

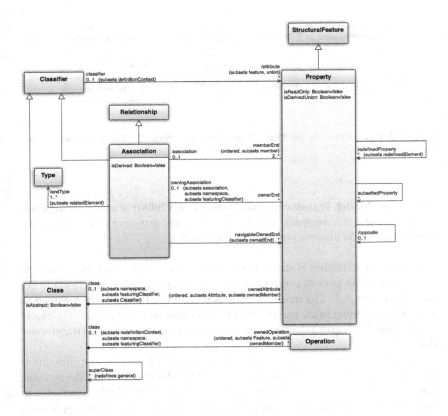

Figure 5.2: MOF Key Concepts (Source: Object Management Group (OMG) (2006))

5.2 Model Transformations

In a MDSD process, models are transformed in order to change their structure (horizontal transformation) or their level of abstraction (vertical transformation). Since the creation of a complete mapping can also be seen as model transformation from several input models to the complete mapping model, model transformations are introduced in this section. A model transformation is defined as follows:

Figure 5.3: Basic Concepts of Model Transformation (Source: Czarnecki and Helsen (2006))

Definition: Model Transformation (Baier et al. (2008)) *A model transformation is a computable mapping, that transforms model instances of a set of source models into model instances of a set of target models.*

A model transformation is defined on metamodels and executed by a transformation engine on models conforming to those metamodels. This relation is depicted in Figure 5.3. The transformation definition itself can also be regarded as a model conforming to the metamodel of the transformation language. Czarnecki and Helsen (2003) give a detailed overview on the properties of model transformations.

In practice, a difference is made between *model-to-model transformations* (M2M) and *model-to-text transformations* (M2T). Model-to-text transformations, also referred to as *code generation*, are commonly used in MDSD approaches in practice. There is also more mature tool support for several different application contexts in proprietary as well as open source tools. Model-to-model transformation languages and their tool support are still to immature for practical use and are more spread in academia. The most common model-to-model transformation languages are the ATLAS transformation language (ATL) (Jouault and Kurtev (2005)) and the QVT relations and QVT operational mappings languages as defined by the Object Management Group (OMG) (2008).

5.3 Architecture in Model-Driven Software Development

There are two main widespread approaches that introduce the notion of architecture in MDSD. Model-Driven Architecture focuses on the architecture of MDSD

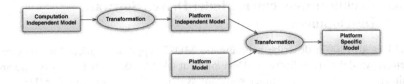

Figure 5.4: Simplified Interrelations of MDA Models

environments, while Architecture-Centric Model-Driven Software Development centres on the architecture of the system to be developed.

5.3.1 Model-Driven Architecture

The Model-Driven Architecture (MDA) is a proposal of the OMG, that provides a general architecture for MDSD environments. It focuses on the separation of concerns, especially of functional and technical architecture aspects. Since it is a standardisation effort by tool vendors, its main goals are portability, interoperability and reusability.

The MDA describes three different viewpoints on a system and according models: the computation independent model *CIM*, the platform independent model *PIM* and the platform specific model *PSM*. It further introduces the notion of a platform model (*PM*). The interrelations of these models are depicted in Figure 5.4.

The CIM covers the functional aspects of the system without relations to their implementation. The PIM defines the technical architecture of the system employing architectural styles. The PM defines a concrete technical platform on which the system is to be implemented. The PSM is build on the architectural decisions of how the architectural styles are implemented on certain concrete platforms. The PSM can be used to generate platform specific source code. The figure is simplified since the possibility of several PSM's for different platforms and further models, that support the transformations, are omitted.

In summary, the MDA is not an approach to support software architecture, but an approach for the architecture of systems for development environments for model-driven software development. Nonetheless, the separation of concerns and the differentiation of architectural models of different granularity also become important in the design of MARE.

5.3.2 Architecture-Centric Model-Driven Software Development

Stahl et al. (2007) describe a pragmatic MDSD approach called Architecture-Centric Model-Driven Software Development (AC-MDSD), that bases on the architectural aspects of the target software system. They describe AC-MDSD as a simple and low-risk approach for the introduction of MDSD. AC-MDSD focuses on technical domains. In this case the modelling languages used can be seen as configuration languages for the underlying technical libraries and frameworks. The goal of AC-MDSD is to abstract from the framework specific implementation and to generate repetitive source code. Thus, it hinders architecture erosion by the generation of architecture specific aspects. AC-MDSD is not fully automated, since only the common and repetitive parts of the source code are generate. Application domain specifics have to be added manually.

AC-MDSD is especially efficient if metamodels and generators can be reused for a number of applications. Hence, it is particularly appropriate for the development of software product lines with architectural commonalities, since it encapsulates the corresponding common architectural platform and allows modelling of varieties.

The modelling and generation of aspects from the application domain of software systems (Domain-Centric MDSD) is described as an extension of a mature AC-MDSD approach. Models are in that case more abstract and are similar to the CIM in MDA. Modelling languages in Domain-Centric MDSD are based on domain vocabulary or can be used as configuration languages for application domain specific frameworks.

5.4 Interoperability Metamodels for Reengineering

The term *Interoperability Metamodel* denotes a metamodel that is used to describe data that is exchanged between different tools. In the context of reengineering there are many tools that extract, analyse or restructure data about software systems. In most cases these tools work on proprietary data models and are not developed with the focus of an exchange of data with other tools to e.g. allow other combinations of extractor and analyser. To overcome this lack of interoperability, metamodels were developed, that constitute a common data representation for the exchange of information about software systems.

According to Lethbridge et al. (2004) an exchange format needs to offer a metamodel and a syntax. This section focuses on the metamodel aspect and will present the most common interoperability metamodels in reengineering: the Dagstuhl Middle Metamodel (Section 5.4.1) and the Knowledge Discovery Metamodel (Section 5.4.2) . Further metamodels are described by Trifu and Szulman (2005) and Koschke (2000). Additionally a short overview on existing exchange syntaxes in this context is given in Section 5.4.3.

5.4.1 Dagstuhl Middle Metamodel

The Dagstuhl Middle Metamodel (DMM) as described by Lethbridge et al. (2004) was created to represent software entities and their relationships. The abstraction level of DMM models conforms to the function level of the horseshoe model, hence it is called *middle* metamodel. A full representation of the abstract syntax of a program or information about the architecture of the system are not intended to be captured in the DMM. As such it is appropriate for the exchange of data between tools, that focus e.g. on architecture reconstruction or the analysis of the structure of a system. The DMM only describes a metamodel without elaborating on the exchange syntax. Instead GXL and TA (cf. Section 5.4.3) are suggested as appropriate exchange syntaxes.

The DMM is intended to support the most common language constructs of procedural and object-oriented programming languages such as C, C++, and Java. The metamodel is defined in UML class diagrams. Figure 5.5 shows the top level classes, of which the most important are *SourceObject*, *ModelObject* and *Relationship*.

The metamodel includes high-level syntactic entities (*SourceObject*), conceptual entities (*ModelObject*) and relationships between these entities. *SourceObjects* are e.g. files or macro definitions. *ModelElements* are subdivided in *StructuralElements* and *BehaviouralElements* which are e.g. classes or method respectively. These two kinds of elements are modelled separately since it allows for the differentiation of concepts and their programming language specific syntactical representation. This eases the analysis and restructuring of the system.

Furthermore, the specification of the DMM allows for extensions and variants of the metamodel. One example is the extension for dynamic information in Hamou-Lhadj and Lethbridge (2004).

5.4.2 Knowledge Discovery Metamodel

The Knowledge Discovery Metamodel (KDM) is a specification (Object Management Group (OMG) (2009)) of the OMG to model existing systems with the goal of modernisation of these systems. The KDM was designed to contain primary

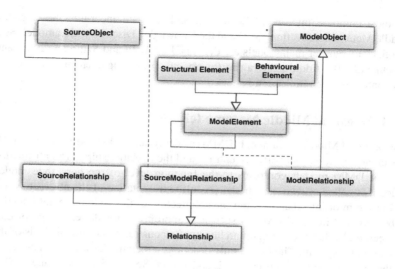

Figure 5.5: Top Level Classes of the DMM (Source: Lethbridge et al. (2004))

information (directly extracted from the source code or other artefacts) as well as aggregate information (obtained by analysis of primary information). The KDM does not only cover information about the implementation of the system, but also contains information about its intent. It consists of four layers (*Infrastructure, Program Elements, Resource,* and *Abstractions*) that can be seen in Figure 5.6. The infrastructure layer defines core elements of the KDM and the equivalent to the *SourceObjects* of the DMM.

The program elements layer defines the conceptual entities of the source code. Where the goal of the DMM is to standardise the modelling of high-level programming concepts and map all programming language specific realisations directly to these concepts, the goal of the KDM, according to Gerber et al. (2004), is to capture as much information about a system as possible. The optional method of extending the basic concepts in the DMM is the intended application of the KDM. Therefore, a stack of metamodels is proposed, starting from a general static model, suited for a large number of programming languages down to specific models for programming language versions. The metamodel is constructed to allow the straightforward definition of common transformations on the model and programming language specific extensions to these.

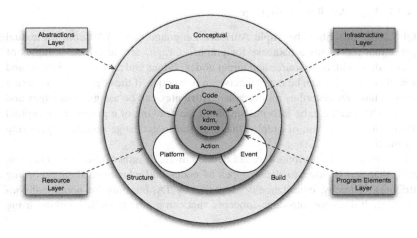

Figure 5.6: Layers and Packages of the KDM (Source: Object Management Group (OMG) (2009))

The resources layer contains elements to describe the environment of the system. The abstractions layer is intended to represent the most abstract information about the system, including architectural information about the structure of the system, its behaviour, and its build properties.

KDM and DMM represent different approaches to the modelling of existing systems. While the DMM is a consolidation of different metamodels from existing tools and research approaches and does define the elements necessary for practical analyses implemented in these tools, the KDM is a top-down approach, that covers a major part of possible systems, which makes the metamodel much more complex.

5.4.3 Exchange Syntaxes

This section describes common exchange syntaxes in current reengineering tools, which can e.g. be used to serialise DMM instances. The KDM does not use one of the exchange syntaxes described here, but defines its own serialisation using the XMI standard.

5.4.3.1 Tuple Attribute Language

Holt (2002) describes the Tuple Attribute Language (TA). TA defines a textual syntax that represents a database for graphs. Graphs are described as tuples of binary edges with their source and target nodes. Edges and nodes can be typed and more than one edge can be defined between two nodes, if the edges are of different types. Thus, TA describes multigraphs. Attributes can be assigned to edges and nodes. These can e.g. be information about the drawing of a graph or conceptual information in the case of graphs, that are used to exchange reverse-engineering information.

The semantics of attributes are not defined in TA. It rather introduces a scheme level, that can be used to define types of nodes and edges and their according attributes. Thereby, inheritance is supported by TA, but only for notational convenience. It does not introduce concepts, that can not be modelled without using inheritance.

5.4.3.2 Graph eXchange Language

The Graph eXchange Language (GXL) as described by Holt et al. (2006) is an XML based exchange format for graph-based data, that was mainly designed for the exchange of data between reengineering tools. Like TA, GXL supports graphs and their schemata. Schemata are represented in the same XML graph notation as the graphs themselves. Schemata are defined using a GXL metaschema. Metaschema, schema and graph are equivalent to the layers M1 to M3 in Figure 5.1.

Holt et al. (2006) have defined the following requirements for an exchange format in the reengineering context:

- **Universality** The format has to support multiple purposes.

- **Typing** The elements of the format have to be typed.

- **Flexibility** The format has to be adaptable to domain specific data.

- **Ease of use** Support for the format has to be easy to implement.

- **Scalability** The format has to cope with large amounts of data.

- **Modularity** The format has to support the partition of data.

- **Extensibility** The format allows the extension for additional domains.

GXL fulfils these requirements by providing the following features: It supports the standard graph elements as well as hyperedges, all of which are treated as first-class entities and may have attributes. Edges of a node are ordered. The format provides the definition of graph schemata and hierarchical graphs. It defines extension points to add new concepts.

5.5 Model-Driven Reengineering Approaches

Although MDSD technologies are mainly targeting forward engineering processes, there are a number of approaches that uses these technologies for reengineering. This section examines the current state of research.

5.5.1 Model-Driven Migration

A first group of approaches is mainly driven from industry and covers the migration of software systems. Typically the approaches deal with the migration of systems from one operating system to another or a programming language to another. A common case is the migration from COBOL to Java. Model-driven approaches to these problems (e.g. Fleurey et al. (2007), Giese (2010)) try to fully automate the migration process through the complete representation of source code concepts in abstract models, the incremental definition of transformation rules and the generation of adjusted code from the abstract models.

The methods of these approaches are quite similar. In a first phase migration tools or migration rules are defined respectively using a representative part of the system. After this phase, the remaining parts of the system are migrated using these tools. Graaf et al. (2008) employ similar methods for the automated migration between different architectures of an embedded system. They migrate the behavioural models from a style used in the source architecture to a style used in a target product-line architecture employing model-to-model transformations.

5.5.2 Model-Driven SOA-Migration

Another important topic in practice is the migration to SOA. For this goal there are also approaches that employ MDSD methods to automate the migration. These approaches (e.g. Winter and Ziemann (2006), Winter and Ziemann (2007), and Ziemann et al. (2006)) employ software models and enterprise models to model the specific aspects of the implementation and the domain-specific concepts of the services. They also use model transformations and code generation in order to automate the migration process. The MINT project (Reussner (2009)) examined how MDSD can be introduced to generate adapters for the integration of existing systems in service-oriented environments.

5.5.3 Model-Driven Integration

The aforementioned MINT project approaches integration into SOA environments as well as classic enterprise application integration (EAI) aspects. Abels et al. (2008) describe adapter generation in MINT and introduce a domain-specific case study on the integration of existing system using standardised communication. Moreno and Vallecillo (2004) also examine major issues for the integration of existing components into MDSD environments. They propose the modelling of the interfaces of existing components and process models. From these, executable processes and adapters for existing systems can be generated. Mosawi et al. (2006) give an overview on EAI approaches and propose a model-driven EAI architecture in terms of a stack of models that represent the important EAI aspects. They propose models that distinguish between inter- and intra-organisational integration and support different levels of application integration. However, they concentrate on the modelling aspect and do not elaborate on model transformations and code generation.

5.5.4 Migration to MDSD Environments

Further approaches examine the possibility to introduce MDSD in development and maintenance processes for existing software systems. Mohagheghi et al. (2003) examine how the development of a system in the telecommunication domain can be migrated to an MDSD environment. The system development already relies on models that describe certain aspects, but these models are not complete and transformations are done manually. The approach incorporates reverse engineering in order to gain more complete models. Nevertheless, for the given context it is currently not possible to create computationally complete models to generate the complete source code of the system under study. However, the introduction of model-driven techniques improved the development process.

   Reus et al. (2006) describe an approach to migrate an existing software system to an MDSD environment. They reverse-engineer the system to a generic abstract syntax tree, which they transform to UML models. These models are used for documentation and code generation purposes. The latter is currently only partially possible. As such the approach can be a first step to the migration to MDSD and is to a large extent similar to the model-driven migration approaches also discussed in this section. What is missing is the discussion which quality the reverse-engineered UML models have with regard to further development and maintenance. It has to be examined whether more abstract and domain-specific programming languages can be incorporated in order to avoid graphical programming in UML. The term graphical programming refers to the usage of UML on the same abstraction level as textual programming languages. This kind of modelling does not reduce complexity and is usually harder to understand by developers, since it does not meet their accustomed working methods.

Part II

Clustering-Based Support for
Software Architecture Restructuring

6 MARE Approach

This chapter describes the foundations of the MARE approach, which is developed in this thesis. After summarising the underlying problem description in Section 6.1, it introduces typical application scenarios in Section 6.2. Based on these, the goals (Section 6.3) and research questions (Section 6.4) of MARE are discussed. Finally, Section 6.5 defines basic terms of MARE.

6.1 Problem Description

The problems leading to an architecture restructuring are manifold. Usually, architecture restructuring is a task applied to large long-living software systems. These systems are also often called *legacy systems*, since they often suffer from architecture erosion and a lack of maintainability. But even if these problems do not arise, architecture restructuring can be a necessary task to adjust a software system to new requirements (cf. Section 6.2).

As introduced in Section 3.5.4, architecture restructuring is a reengineering task following the traditional horseshoe model (cf. Section 3.1). While the reverse engineering part of the horseshoe model is well researched in terms of architecture reconstruction and architecture conformance, and methods exist to automate the forward engineering based on architectural models (cf. Section 5.3.2), architecture transformation involves extensive manual effort by reengineers and system experts.

Current tool support for architecture transformation is limited to simulate single incremental evolutionary steps or groups thereof (cf. Section 11.1.3). During these simulations, architectural constraints can be checked and unwanted dependencies are revealed. Furthermore, a list of operations to transfer these steps to the source code can be generated as a guideline for the restructuring of the implementation. However, these methods still require a detailed understanding of the source system and do not provide support for the problem, which architectural transformation steps should be taken in order to reach a given target architecture.

6.2 Application Scenarios

There are several application scenarios in which the architecture of a system is restructured and in which the conformation of the implementation to this new architecture is needed. This section gives an overview on typical coarse-grained restructuring scenarios and sketches the application of MARE in these scenarios. However, the choice of the scenarios is not intended to be exhaustive, since restructuring projects always expose a large part of individual properties that can not be reflected by a single standard approach. MARE supports the handling of these properties by the specific selection and weighting of dependency types as well as the specific selection of source element types.

6.2.1 Evolution towards Service-Oriented Architectures

The evolution towards service-oriented architectures requires extensive restructurings of existing software systems. Today, a common strategy to integrate an existing system in a service-oriented architecture is the wrapping of the system with web services. This solution makes the functionality of the system accessible in the new environment, but does not address quality attributes such as loose coupling, high reusability and maintainability. In order to consider these, an existing system has to be restructured into functional service components with a defined set of functionality.

The latter is especially problematic for large systems with a technology-oriented decomposition and strong dependencies between different functional aspects. These dependencies are replaced by service calls in service-oriented architectures. In order to achieve the aforementioned quality attributes, functional components have to be separated and internal dependencies have to be resolved. If the functional components and their service interfaces can be defined clearly, MARE can be used to map the existing implementation to the service components and indicate which dependencies have to be resolved in order to clearly separate the components. The same problem arises, when single services are to be extracted from a system as described in Fuhr et al. (2010). When a service interface has been identified, MARE can be used to identify the implementing source code and dependencies to the implementation of other services.

In both cases, MARE can be used to transfer the architecture restructuring to the implementation of the system. The restructuring of a whole system into functional service components is the standard use case of MARE as described before. The extraction of single service components from an existing system can also be supported by MARE. In this case, the target architecture consists of two components:

the service component to be extracted and the rest of the system. The interfaces that should be considered are the services of the service component and the interface between the service component and the rest of the system. The latter is necessary, because functionality, that supports the implementation of the service, may also be needed for other purposes in the system. Thus, the explicit modelling of these interfaces and their consideration in the initial mapping supports the decision on which source elements belong to the service component and which should remain in the existing system.

6.2.2 Re-establishing Maintainability

Maintainability is defined as '*The ease with which a software system or component can be modified to correct faults, improve performance, or other attributes, or adapt to a changed environment*' (IEEE (1990)). Influence factors for good maintainability are amongst others the understandability and the changeability of the system. The former is supported by e.g. a good documentation as well as an appropriate decomposition of the system. Changeability also depends on the decomposition of the system, e.g. whether a required change was already foreseen in the decomposition of the target architecture. The maintainability can e.g. decrease, when undocumented dependencies exist and thus changes lead to unpredictable behaviour of the system. This phenomenon is called erosion (cf. 2.5). Especially for large long-living software systems the maintainability has to be re-established in order to allow for the realisability of future requirements.

In order to re-establish the maintainability and thus reduce architecture erosion, extensive architectural restructurings are necessary. These include the removal of unwanted dependencies, but also the relocation and consolidation of modules. The concrete actions depend on the concrete goals of the restructuring.

The maintainability of a software architecture depends on organisational aspects and the expected maintenance scenarios. Hence, maintainable components could be defined with certain change scenarios in mind or based on the capabilities of the developers in order to separate the work of different development teams in different components.

MARE can be used to support the re-establishment of the maintainability of existing systems. In order to rate the applicability of MARE for a concrete restructuring project different conditions of the re-establishment of maintainability have to be considered. In cases where the target components are very similar to the current architecture of the system and the maintainability problems are only caused by many unwanted dependencies, MARE will only be of little use. The

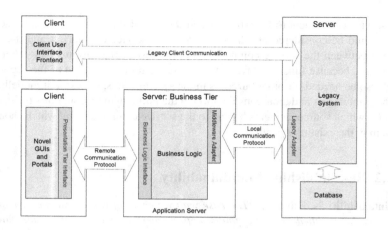

Figure 6.1: Structural View of the Dublo Pattern (Source: Teschke et al. (2004))

goal of the application of MARE would then be reduced to relocate single source elements that are assigned to the wrong modules in the implementation.

The actual potential of MARE can be used in cases of strong architecture erosion in which the intended architecture is no longer manifest in the implementation or in cases in which the target architecture is decomposed employing different maintainability criteria than the implemented architecture. MARE can then be used to relocate modules and to reveal unwanted dependencies.

6.2.3 Smooth Migration

The term smooth migration describes the stepwise migration of a software system to a new environment (also known as chicken little approach introduced by Brodie and Stonebraker (1995)). Hasselbring et al. (2004) describe a pattern called Dublo (Dual Business Logic), that supports the smooth migration of business information systems from a two-tier legacy architecture to a three-tier architecture. Hasselbring et al. (2008) discuss additional variants for the management of existing data in the context of Dublo.

Figure 6.1 shows the structural view of the Dublo pattern. The upper and the right part of the figure show the original two-tier architecture with a user client and a server that comprises the application logic as well as the data management. The database is a pure data storage in these system, where the whole data management is handled by the legacy system.

The Dublo pattern adds a new client tear as well as a pure business tier to the legacy system which is implemented in the target environment. In the example of Hasselbring et al. (2004) the legacy system is written in Informix 4GL while the business tier is implemented in J2EE. This serves future development in two ways. On the one hand new functionality can be implemented in the new business tier using already implemented functionality and data storage feature through a legacy adapter. On the other hand the existing functionality can be smoothly migrated to the new environment by replacing the interfaces of the legacy adapter with implementations in the new environment.

The details of this migration of existing functionality are not covered completely by Hasselbring et al. (2004). The selection of the interfaces provided by the legacy adapter is discussed by in detail by Teschke et al. (2004). They compare data-driven, function-driven, and object-driven approaches for this task and choose a function-driven approach for the exemplary context.

While the definition of the interfaces is thus covered, the selection of the corresponding implementing code is not discussed. Since the implementation of different functions will overlap in most cases, the migration of a certain functionality will also affect the implementation of other functionalities, that remain in the legacy system in the particular migration step. Hence, interface of which the implementation is strongly interleaved should be migrated together. Otherwise, new temporary interfaces have to be added to the legacy adapter.

The decision which parts of the implementation of the legacy system should be migrated together and the solution of the problem how to separate the implementation of the existing system to gain realisable migration increments can be supported by MARE. The target architecture for the migration can be defined based on the interfaces of the legacy adapter. Therefore, it has to be defined which source elements are needed for the implementation of an adapter interface or groups thereof. MARE can be used to identify these source elements and identify dependencies, that have to be resolved or lead to new adapter interfaces. Based on this information lowly coupled parts of the implementation that consist of one or more target components can be defined which can be migrated together in one migration step.

An initial mapping can be deduced from the mapping of the interface of the current adapters to the implementation of the existing system.

6.3 Goals of MARE

The application scenarios show that a mapping of source elements to target components is necessary in different contexts. Since this mapping is currently created

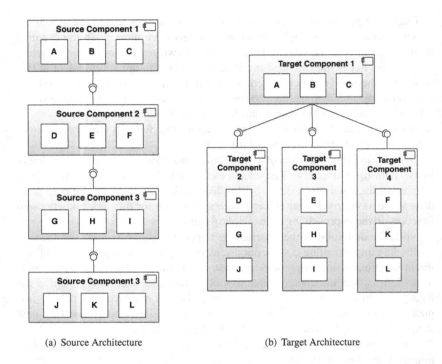

(a) Source Architecture   (b) Target Architecture

Figure 6.2: Complete Mapping Example

mostly manually and requires large effort, the main goal of MARE is to automate this task. In order to reduce the manual effort MARE creates a complete mapping of the source elements of an existing software system to the target components of a given target architecture model. In this way, the MARE approach provides support for the transformation step of the horseshoe model.

Figure 6.2(b) shows an exemplary complete mapping (This abstract example refers to the architectures of the case study presented in Section 10.1). While *Source System Component 1* is reused as whole in the target architecture, the three remaining source system components were restructured, resulting in the target components 2-4.

The creation of a complete mapping follows two concurrent goals. The first goal is to provide a mapping that maps all source elements correctly according to the semantic intentions of the target architecture components. If this goal can be obtained completely, an ideal implementation of the target architecture could be achieved based on the existing source code.

On the other hand it is usually not feasible to restructure the implementation based on such an ideal mapping, since project budgets for restructurings are limited. Furthermore, as the application scenarios have shown, restructurings of large systems have to be conducted stepwise in coordination with regular maintenance and development tasks. Thus, the second goal is to find a complete mapping that covers as much of the semantic intention as possible, while diminishing the effort for the restructuring of the implementation.

MARE does not target to provide new views on the current implementation of the system as with architecture reconstruction approaches, but rather to support the change of the implemented system. I.e. the result of MARE will be used to restructure the module structure of the implementation or to restructure the mapping of modules to runtime components, respectively. It is not used to improve the quality of the implementation with regard to the intended source architecture.

6.4 Research Questions

The problems stated in Section 6.1 lead to the main research question

> How can the architecture transformation step of an architecture restructuring task be supported in order to reduce the effort for the creation of a complete mapping of source system elements to target components?

The answer to this question is given by the MARE approach, which is described in detail in the subsequent chapters.

The development of MARE leads to a number of more detailed research questions in the different partitions of MARE. These questions are listed in Table 6.1. Each column lists a research question, the research method with which it is answered, the type of the result and the section in which the result is described.

Table 6.1: Detailed Research Questions

Research Question	Research Method	Result	Reference
How can knowledge about the target architecture be considered in the architecture restructuring process?	Method Engineering	Construction of the MARE method	Chapter 7
How can the complete mapping of source elements to target components be automated?	Method Engineering	Definition of the MARE clustering algorithm	Chapter 8
How can the MARE approach be applied in different contexts?	Argumentation	Description of application scenarios	Section 6.2
Which criteria influence the complete mapping and how can they be mapped to the clustering algorithm?	Argumentation	Source System Model Definition, Initial Mapping, Weighting of Dependencies	Sections 7.2.2 and 8.2
How can the quality of the MARE clustering algorithm be evaluated?	Construction	GQM plan	Chapter 9
Does MARE Clustering produce a complete mapping of sufficient quality?	Case Studies	Quality measures in to case studies based on reference mappings	Chapter 10
Does the MARE clustering algorithm show a stable behaviour?	Case Studies	Stability measurement in two case studies employing different input modifications	Chapter 10

6.5 Definitions

This section defines basic terms of the MARE approach.

6.5.1 Source Elements

Mitchell and Mancoridis (2006) call the structural elements of the source system, that are subject of the clustering, *modules*. They define a module as *'a source code entity that encapsulates data and functions that operate on the data'*. For the MARE approach these, entities are called *source elements* in order to avoid misunderstandings with other definitions of the term module. Since the granularity of these source elements depends on the goal of the architecture restructuring, a broader definition is used here:

Definition: Source Element *A source element is a structural element of the implementation.*

Depending on the restructuring context structural elements are e.g. files, classes, methods and functions. The factors that influence the choice of the granularity for a specific project is discussed in Section 7.1.3.

6.5.2 Detailed Design Model

The term detailed design was defined in Section 2.2.1. In MARE the detailed design model of the source system is an important input for the definition of the complete mapping. The term *Detailed Design Model* is defined as follows, using the other definitions introduced in this section.

Definition: Detailed Design Model *A detailed design model describes the structure of the implementation of a component in terms of source elements and their relationships.*

6.5.3 Target Architecture

Architecture restructuring changes the current architecture of a source system to a new architecture with desirable properties, that are not covered by the current architecture. Thus, the term target architecture is defined as follows.

Definition: Target Architecture *The desired architecture of the target system. The target architecture defines the goal of the architecture restructuring.*

More details on the assumptions about the target architecture as well as a meta-model are given in Section 7.3.3.

6.5.4 Target Components

According to Section 2.1, an architecture is defined in terms of components and their relations. Since MARE considers structure in the target architecture on different levels, the elements of this architecture, which are called *Target Components* in MARE, are also defined to represent the elements on these different levels.

Definition: Target Component *A target component is a conceptual element of the target architecture. Depending on the architecture restructuring context, a target component can refer to a module (as defined in 2.1.1) or to a component (as defined in 2.1.2).*

7 MARE Method

The MARE method is an approach to support the planning of the restructuring of the implementation of a system in an architecture restructuring process. The planning is supported by semi-automatically creating a complete mapping of all source elements to target components. MARE employs a clustering algorithm that bases on information about the source system and the target architecture. The approach includes interactions with the user in order to include the users knowledge about the source system and the decomposition criteria of the target architecture as well as to delegate key decisions to the user. An early version of MARE was published at the *Workshop on Software Quality and Maintainability (SQM 2009)* (see Streekmann and Hasselbring (2009)).

As will be discussed in Section 11, existing approaches do not provide a comparably extensive support for the transformation of an existing implementation to a target architecture in coarse-grained architecture restructuring scenarios. They concentrate mainly on the analysis of the source system or the support of an evolution of the architecture of the existing system in small steps. Furthermore, they do not include an explicit target architecture model.

MARE, in contrast, bases on explicit knowledge about the target architecture and has the goal to minimise the understanding of the implementation and architecture decomposition criteria of the existing implementation. This does reduce the manual effort in the architecture restructuring process, particularly in cases where the current architecture and the target architecture show fundamental differences. Especially in cases where the implicit architecture of the source system is not documented or shows indications of architectural erosion, the effort for architecture reconstruction can become large, with an uncertain value for the goal of the actual architecture restructuring task.

MARE is a design time approach, that supports the adjustment of the implementation to fit the target architecture. This is done by mapping source elements to the structure of the target architecture and by supporting the adjustment and refinement of the target architecture to include the constraints of the current implementation, that have to be considered to restructure the implementation with reasonable effort. In contrast to architecture reconstruction and subsequent continuous monitoring of the architecture and architectural evolution in small steps, which is supported by current tools like *Bauhaus*,[1] *Sotoarc*,[2] or *Lattix* (Sangal et al. (2005)), MARE focusses on large-scale architectural evolution, that changes the basic architectural rationale of a system and employs different decomposition criteria. This is usually not a continuous process, but will be performed in a temporally limited project.

Furthermore, the application range is not necessarily limited to software systems that suffer from architectural erosion. Even well designed and well documented software systems can be subject to fundamental architecture restructurings.

Figure 7.1 shows a complete overview of the process of the MARE method modelled as a UML activity diagram. The process includes three main activities: *Initialisation, MARE Clustering*, and *Implementation Restructuring*. The Initialisation activity includes preliminary activities that create necessary inputs for MARE Clustering. MARE Clustering creates a complete mapping on the basis of these inputs, which is implemented in the Implementation Restructuring activity.

In the following sections the parts of this process are described in detail. Section 7.1 focusses on the relation of MARE to the general reengineering process as introduced on Section 3.1 and explains the subactivities of the Initialisation and Implementation Restructuring activities. Section 7.2 describes the activities that are specific for MARE Clustering before Section 7.3 defines the data exchanged between the activities and the incorporated metamodels. The concrete sections for each activity are also annotated in Figure 7.1. Section 7.4 summarises the contributions, assumptions, and limitations of MARE.

7.1 Embedding in the Reengineering Process

MARE supports architecture restructuring and is thereby a part of a typical reengineering process. Figure 7.2 depicts the concrete activities of the Initialisation and the Implementation Restructuring in a UML activity diagram. The decision *A* indicates the architecture restructuring iteration cycle (cf. Section 7.1.1). It refers to the stepwise nature of large-scale practical reengineering projects. These are typically are not executed in a big-bang approach, but proceed in small steps to keep the restructuring effort manageable and to provide a running system at any time, which can also be adjusted to current requirements.

The vital activity of the model-based architecture restructuring process is the modelling of the target architecture. The target architecture guides the remaining process and is the reference for all decisions. It is the basis for the decision which level of detail is needed for the creation of the detailed design model of the source

---

[1] http://www.axivion.com/
[2] http://www.software-tomography.ch/

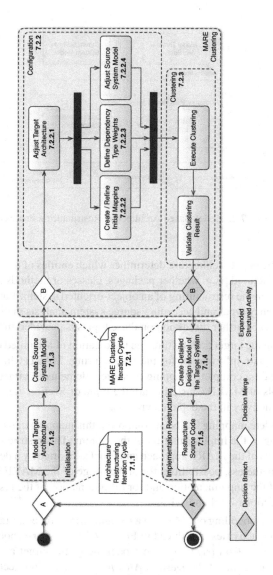

Figure 7.1: Complete MARE Method Overview

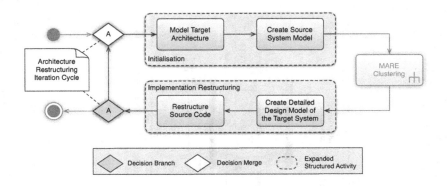

Figure 7.2: Model-Based Architecture Restructuring Process

system, since the target architecture determines which entities of the source system need to be restructured. E.g. whether packages, classes or methods are the largest indivisible units in the restructuring of an object-oriented system. Furthermore, the kind of dependency types and according source system analysis methods and tools have to be chosen. Further discussion on these topics is provided in Section 7.3.2.

After defining the target architecture and the creation of a detailed design model, containing adequate information for the restructuring, MARE Clustering can be performed to gain a complete mapping of source elements to target components. Since the details of MARE Clustering are the topic of Section 7.2, it is modelled as a structured activity in the depicted process.

After a complete mapping has been composed, this mapping can be used to plan the restructuring of the implementation of the system. This restructuring however is not in the focus of the MARE approach and is not supported by a detailed process or tooling. Nonetheless, possibilities for of the usage of the MARE results for the restructuring of the implementation and for the automation of the restructuring are discussed in Sections 7.1.4 and 7.1.5.

To clarify the embedding of MARE in a reengineering process, Figure 7.3 shows a mapping of the activities introduced in Figure 7.2 to the horseshoe model, as an overlay of Figure 3.1 on page 25. The modelling of the target architecture corresponds to the creation of the *Desired Architecture*. This architecture is not deduced directly from the architecture of the source system (*Base Architecture* in Figure 7.3), but bases on the requirements and the desired evolution properties of the target system. During the application of MARE such an ideal target architec-

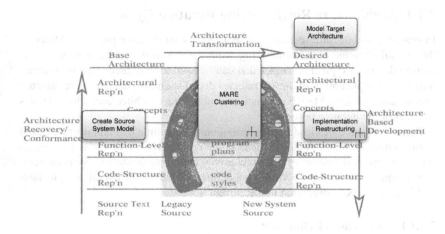

Figure 7.3: Mapping of Activities to the Horseshoe Model

ture can be refined and changed in order to regard properties of the source system
that influence the restructuring effort.

The creation of the detailed design model of the source system is part of the
reengineering or architecture reconstruction part of the horseshoe model. In contrast to the horseshoe model, which is based on architecture reconstruction and
an incremental restructuring approach, the process envisioned in MARE does not
require a detailed *Base Architecture*. It only involves reverse engineering activities
that lead to a model of the source system on the level on which structural changes
are intended. The restructuring of the implementation corresponds directly to the
Architecture Based Development in the horseshoe model.

MARE supports the *Architecture Transformation* in the horseshoe model. It
principally incorporates transformation on the layers of *Function-Level Representation* and *Architectural Representation*. Its main task is to map the functional
representation of the source system to the architectural representation of the target
system.

In the following the architecture restructuring iteration cycle in MARE and the
concrete activities in Figure 7.2 are described in more detail. The composite *MARE
Clustering* activity is the topic of Section 7.2.

7.1.1 Architecture Restructuring Iteration Cycle

In practice, architecture restructuring is typically an iterative process. Although the overall planning of a restructuring project is not in the scope of MARE, this section describes typical strategies that can be used to introduce stepwise restructuring. The applicability of these strategies depends on the goal of the architecture restructuring project. MARE assumes an overall target architecture, which defines the goal of the iterative process.

Iterations should be closed restructuring units, intending that architecture-based implementation changes made in the iteration will not have to be revised as long as the architectural decisions of the target architecture remain stable. For each iteration a target architecture is defined, that defines the part of the overall architecture, that is going to be restructured in the current iteration.

7.1.1.1 Hierarchical Refinement

In a hierarchical refinement strategy, the iteration cycle starts with the definition of coarse components that constitute the main decomposition blocks of the target system. These components are further refined into subcomponents in successive iterations. Thereby the restructuring process can be realised similar to a breadth-first or a depth-first search or a mixture of both.

Figure 7.4 shows the hierarchical refinement of the system into the subcomponents *SC 1*, *SC 2* and *SC 3*. After the iteration the components should be independent except for the defined interfaces. In a pure breadth-first approach these subcomponents can be decomposed into subsubcomponents in subsequent iterations before the next hierarchical decomposition level is restructured. In contrast, a depth-first approach restructures all relevant decomposition levels of one subcomponent before the restructuring of the next subcomponent is started. In practice, a mixture of these approaches is most probable, where the ongoing development and maintenance task of the source system is considered.

7.1.1.2 Vertical Extraction

In the vertical extraction strategy, selected components that represent functionality which is to be extracted for reuse in other contexts, are defined in detail in the target architecture. The rest of the system is modelled as one component which only provides the interface needed by the extracted components. In this way successive iterations lead to a stepwise extraction of functionality.

Ideally, extracted components should only be accessed by the rest of the system through their provided interfaces. In practice further temporal dependencies can

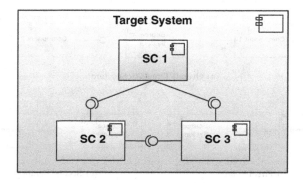

Figure 7.4: Hierarchical Refinement Example

occur, which are removed in successive iterations through the restructuring of the implementation or follow-up quality improvements. Temporal dependencies from the extracted component to the rest of the system should not occur, since that indicates, that the extracted component has to be changed, even if there is no change in the architecture. I.e. the closed character of the iteration is no longer ensured.

Figure 7.5 shows a simplified example of the vertical extraction strategy in two iterations. Each iteration extracts one component from the source system. In the first iteration (Figure 7.5(b)) *Component 1* is extracted, introducing a temporal dependency to the source system. *Component 2* is not part of the target architecture, since it is not subject of the first iteration. Figure 7.5(c) shows the target architecture of the second iteration, which extracts *Component 2* from the source system. In practice, extracted components will in many cases provide and require more than one interface. Further provided and required interfaces of the source system are not relevant for the component extraction and can therefore be omitted in the target architecture of the iteration.

7.1.1.3 Three-tier SOA

Heckel et al. (2008) describe the restructuring of a two-tier application to a three-tier architecture in the context of a SOA. They propose an iterative process, that first decomposes the system to technical layers. One of the main purposes of this step is to separate the GUI specific code in order to replace it with a service layer. The functional decomposition into services is intended for a second iteration. This

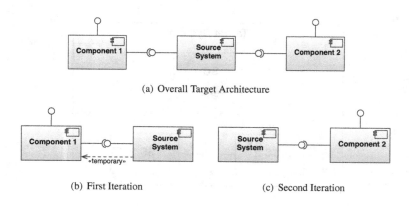

(a) Overall Target Architecture

(b) First Iteration   (c) Second Iteration

Figure 7.5: Vertical Extraction Example

strategy can be seen as a special case of hierarchical refinement in which the technical layers constitute the main decomposition of the system. The layers are then hierarchically refined into functional components.

7.1.2 Model the Target Architecture

The goal of the *Model Target Architecture* activity is to create the target architecture for the current iteration of the MARE architecture restructuring iteration cycle. This section summarises some relevant approaches for the modelling of a target architecture, but does not contain a complete guideline on how to develop this activity in a practical project. The reason is, that the modelling of a target architecture does not only depend on the goals and rationale of the future development of the system, but it is also strongly dependent on standards and processes of the developing organisation. It also bases on the functionality of the source system, since this has to be preserved during the restructuring. On the other side it should not depend on the implementation of the source system in this phase. This influence is considered later in the MARE process. Since the development and maintenance can usually not be stopped for a long-term architecture restructuring, the creation of a target architecture is also strongly interelated with these activities.

7.1.2.1 View and Decomposition

Only static views of the target architecture are considered in MARE. Requirements on the dynamics of the target system are not considered in the restructuring process. The dynamic properties of the target system result from the mapping of source elements to target components. For the computation of the complete mapping, the dynamic properties of the source system can be included by adding dependencies based on the dynamic analysis of the source system. This limitation to static views of the target architecture is adequate, since extensive in the dynamics of a system are only relevant for the restructuring of the implementation in the sense of MARE, if they also affect the structural views of the architecture.

The decomposition of the target architecture for an iteration is mainly determined by the decomposition criteria of the overall target architecture and the goals of the restructuring. The decomposition does not necessarily base on the current decomposition of the source system. Nonetheless, it may become necessary to adjust the target architecture to the current structure in later stages of the MARE process in order to reduce the effort for the restructuring of the implementation. The decomposition of the target architecture of an iteration should be chosen so that it represents a useful and realisable step for the restructuring of the implementation.

7.1.2.2 To-Be vs. Ideal Target Architecture

Engels et al. (2008) describe an approach for the evolution of application landscape architectures called Quasar Enterprise. This evolution is also described as an activity that consists of a series of projects that convert an *as-is application landscape* to an ideal application landscape. This *ideal application landscape* guides the evolution, but is not expected to be reached due to operational development and costs. Instead of the ideal, a *to-be application landscape* is taken as the goal to be reached for a series of evolutionary projects. Figure 7.6 shows the relation between *As-Is*, *To-Be* and *Ideal* application landscape and the stepwise evolution from as-is to to-be application landscape. It also depicts a *Corridor of Balance*, that should be kept in mind to not drift from the original evolution goals or the operational necessities.

As in application landscape evolution, architecture restructuring as an example of large-scale application evolution has to deal with trade-offs between an ideal target architecture and a target architecture that is feasible in a realistic project context. The ideal architecture is only influenced by current and future require-

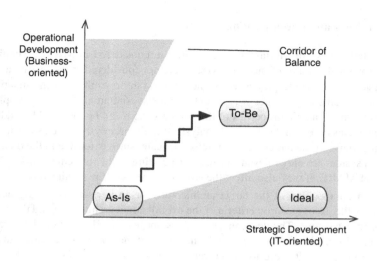

Figure 7.6: Quasar Enterprise: As-Is, To-Be and Ideal (Source: Engels et al. (2008))

ments of the target system. A realistic to-be target architecture on the other hand has to consider the source system implementation and the restructuring effort.

These considerations influence the modelling of the target architecture as well as its adjustment, which is also part of MARE (cf. Section 7.2.2). In the modelling activity, the influence of the source system concentrates on the functionality the system provides and its observable behaviour. The trade-off between the envisioned target architecture and the restructuring effort can only be made with more detailed knowledge about the source system and its dependencies, which is provided in the course of MARE. Therefore, each iteration of the architecture restructuring process should start with an ideal target architecture, which is changed to a to-be target architecture for the restructuring of the implementation using the knowledge gained during the application of MARE Clustering.

7.1.2.3 Dependencies

The designer of the target architecture can provide allowed dependencies between target components in terms of interfaces usages. These are not considered in the creation of the complete mapping, but in its visualisation and interpretation. While the detailed compliance to the interface can only be determined by a man-

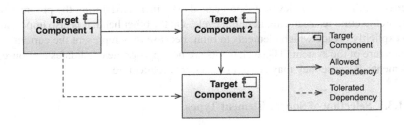

Figure 7.7: Tolerated Dependencies

ual mapping of concrete dependencies to operations of the interface, at least the coarse-grained information which component is allowed to access the interfaces of another component can be used to give initial hints on the nature of dependencies between components in the complete mapping. Unwanted dependencies, i.e. dependencies, that are not defined as allowed dependencies in the target architecture can be highlighted, since they represent the first candidates for changes in the configuration step or for the resolution of dependencies in the implementation restructuring respectively.

Furthermore, tolerated dependencies can be computed from the allowed dependencies as a further graduation of dependencies, if this fits the rationale of the target architecture. Tolerated dependencies are dependencies between two components, that do not have a direct representation in the target architecture, but can be derived from a series of allowed dependencies. This principle is depicted in Figure 7.7. It e.g. corresponds to the concept of non-strict layered architectures.

7.1.3 Create the Source System Model

The goal of the *Create Source System Model* activity is to create a model of the detailed design of the source system and to define the considered dependency types. The creation of a detailed design model of the source system is a typical reverse engineering task (cf. Section 3.3). This activity can be executed highly automated, since it is not necessary in the context of MARE to obtain an architectural representation of the system, but only a model that contains the relevant source elements and their dependencies.

The choice of source elements and dependencies that are relevant for the architecture restructuring depend on the goals of the architecture restructuring and the decomposition criteria of the target architecture as well as the level of system expertise of the user. The level of detail can also be increased during the progress of the architecture restructuring iteration cycle. On the other hand, it is also important to explicitly decide which elements to omit, because they represent the current architecture of the system. These elements are not appropriate candidates for source elements, because they may crosscut the target architecture.

7.1.3.1 Selection of Source Element Types

Source elements should be considered on the level of the system where the actual restructuring will take place. If e.g. the goal is to restructure the coarse-grained components of a large Java system, packages can be the appropriate candidates, when they are to be moved completely between components during the restructuring. On the other hand, packages often represent the module structure of a Java system. Thus, for restructurings of the module view of especially small and midsized Java systems classes and/or methods are more appropriate source elements for the detailed design model.

When smaller elements like e.g. methods are omitted, because it was decided that classes are not to be divided, it is important to lift the dependencies of these elements to their containing source elements. E.g. when methods are omitted, method calls between methods in different classes have to be lifted to the class level in order to not lose important dependency information. Method calls between methods contained in the same class can be omitted in this case.

Further criteria for the selection of source element types are the user's effort for understanding the implementation and the performance of the analysis. The effort of the user increases with the decrease of the abstraction level of source element types (e.g. from classes to methods). The reason for this is, that on lower abstraction levels more source elements have to be considered in the configuration of the clustering and the interpretation of its results. An overview of the performance of the clustering algorithm is given in the description of the case studies in Section 10.

The selection of source element types may change in the course of the architecture restructuring iteration cycle. E.g. with a hierarchical refinement strategy, more fine-grained source element types may be chosen with a more detailed target architecture in later iterations.

7.1.3.2 Selection of Dependency Types

Static Analysis The choice of dependency types, that are relevant for the architecture restructuring, depends on the architectural decisions taken in the source system. Many reverse engineering tools are able to statically extract and analyse dependencies from source code. Static dependency analysis recovers possible runtime instances of the system. E.g. a class hierarchy with several subclasses of a superclass can be defined in the source code, but it is not ensured that all classes are instantiated at runtime. The really instantiated classes can not be found using static analysis, when classes are instantiated dynamically at runtime. Another example are method calls that are defined in the source code, but never actually executed at runtime, because certain conditions are not met.

Dynamic Analysis The deficiencies of static analysis can be compensated by dynamic analysis. It employs source code instrumentation and subsequent monitoring of the system's execution or the interpretation of the code for typical use cases to reveal runtime information about the system (cf. Cornelissen et al. (2009)). This information is necessary, if e.g. the source systems architecture makes extensive use of dynamic instantiation or runtime configuration of the system. It is also useful to reveal dead code. On the other hand, dynamic analysis often has to be supplemented with static analysis to gain a complete picture of the system. The analysis itself is also costlier than static analysis since the system has to be executed for all relevant use cases to get the sought information.

Semantic Analysis A third way to gain dependencies between source elements is the analysis of their semantics. There are approaches that analyse and cluster source elements based on naming conventions, comments, participation in design patterns, etc. This semantic information can also be used in MARE in terms of dependencies, that influence the clustering. E.g. pairs of source elements with names that have exceeded a certain degree of similarity can be coupled with a respective dependency. Indicators could e.g. be a low hamming distance or the inclusion of certain domain terms or their ontological equivalents. Further semantic dependencies can also be specified by the user on the basis of his knowledge about coherence of source elements, that is not manifested in concrete relationships in the system.

Andritsos and Tzerpos (2005) show that the inclusion of directory structure and the mapping of source elements to developers lead to better results for the reconstruction of a software decomposition. For architecture restructuring, the inclusion of this information can also improve results, but this depends on the rationale of the directory structure and the developer mapping of the source system. The improvement bases on the equality of the desired decomposition result and the mapping rationale. E.g. if the target architecture complies to the technical decomposition of the system, the clustering results will not be improved by incorporating developer information, when the developers are allocated to functional tasks.

Sindhgatta and Pooloth (2007) show that the consideration data from software configuration management (SCM) systems can improve clustering results in the context of architecture reconstruction. They state that this data represents the semantics of the implementation since the joint change of files indicate that they follow a common purpose. Thus, they argument that this information better reflects the purpose of the developers of the system under study, which on the other hand can be different to the current decomposition of the system. To be useful for the restructuring of the system, it has to be assessed whether SCM data fits the decomposition criteria of the target architecture.

7.1.3.3 Handling of Libraries

The clustering of systems that incorporate library subsystems is a common problem in software clustering. Many clustering approaches employ the dependencies between source elements to compute similarity functions. Since libraries are usually used from many source elements throughout the system, this leads to clusterings that centre around library source elements. Thus, the comprehensibility and usability of the results is reduced.

In clustering for architecture reconstruction there are various approaches for the handling of the problems libraries impose. Examples are the exclusion of libraries from the clustering or the mapping of all libraries or library-like elements to a special library subsystem as e.g. proposed by Mitchell and Mancoridis (2006). Another possibility is the use of weighting schemes, that weight elements, that are used by many other elements lower than elements, that are used less. Andritsos and Tzerpos (2005) state the TF.IDF weighting scheme, which is used in information retrieval, to be applicable for this purpose.

On the other hand, libraries can also be useful to identify certain functionalities in a system. E.g. Quante (2008) introduces an approach that clusters source elements by the usage of libraries. He shows, that this can be useful to separate e.g. the implementation of the user interface, the network access and database access.

With respect to restructuring, libraries can be hindering as well as helpful for the clustering of source elements. The latter will particularly be the case for functional libraries used in the source system, that comply to the decomposition criteria of the target architecture. Common technical libraries of the programming language (e.g., java.lang) will in most cases hinder the clustering, since they are used from all over the code and do not provide a significant difference between source and target system. Functional libraries encapsulate a more special functionality, that is only used by specific source elements. It is recommended to consider uses of the library in the source system model under the following conditions: the functionality complies to a decomposition criterion of the target architecture and all source elements that use the library are supposed to be assigned to the same target component. On the other hand, if the library does not serve the decomposition of the target architecture, the consideration of uses of the library will lead to counterintuitive clustering results.

7.1.3.4 Source Code Refactoring

In some cases a manual refactoring has to be done as preparatory work for the restructuring. It becomes necessary, if the smallest source elements considered are also subject of the restructuring. An example is the mix of database accesses and user interface code in a single method, when database accesses and the user interface implementation are separated in different components of the target architecture. The goal of the refactoring in this case is to lift the level of the smallest entity considered from statement to method.

7.1.3.5 Tool Selection in Practice

In practice the decision for specific tools for the source code analysis is an important factor. Current tools are focussed on certain programming languages and types of dependencies they are able to analyse. Especially when a system is implemented in more than one language or programming paradigm (e.g. imperative or object-oriented), an appropriate tool has to be chosen carefully. Another factor is the availability of tools in an organisation. An existing tool may already be set in an organisation or the purchase of a certain tool may not be possible because of license or pricing policies.

7.1.4 Create a Detailed Design Model of the Target System

The creation of the detailed design model of the target system is the first activity of the *Implementation Restructuring*. The model is the basis for the restructuring of the source code to establish its conformity to the target architecture. The goal of the creation of the model is to provide the best quality possible in the process of restructuring and with the available effort. Thus, unwanted dependencies in the complete mapping have to be resolved. Dependencies, that can not be resolved due to high effort, should be marked as temporary in the detailed design model as well as the target architecture and resolved in subsequent projects. These projects improve the quality of the system and the conformity to the ideal target architecture.

The detailed design model of the target system bases on the detailed design model of the source system and adopts the source elements as well as the dependencies between source elements, that are allowed in relation to the target architecture. In contrast to the source system model, the target system model also contains element types, that represent the architecture of the system, e.g. packages or other high-level elements, that were omitted in the source system model.

7.1.5 Restructure the Source Code

The restructuring of the source code is the final activity to gain the intended restructured target system for the current iteration of the architecture restructuring cycle. In this activity the implementation of the system is fit to the detailed design model of the target system as defined in the preceding activity. The first steps of this activity are the identification of the affected source artefacts and the induction of the target structure. The most important and most complex part of the restructuring is the resolution of unwanted dependencies.

7.1.5.1 Identify Affected Source Artefacts

The notion of a source artefact is in this context not limited to the source code of programming languages, but also includes e.g. configuration files, such as deployment descriptors. In cases were only the mapping between components and modules of the system is affected by the restructuring, changes of deployment descriptors may be the only change of the source artefacts, while the actual programming language source code remains the same.

7.1.5.2 Induction of the Target Structure

The first task for the induction of the target structure on the level of programming language source code is the creation of new high-level structural elements, such as packages in Java or e.g. a directory structure according to modules in C. The next task is the relocation of the source elements according to the intended structure.

During the induction of the target structure all dependencies, that do not conform to the target architecture, should be resolved. The effort for the resolution of dependencies ranges from simple refactorings to complex manual restructurings. In order to introduce an engineering method for the restructuring of the implementation, a catalogue of patterns for the resolution of different dependency types in different context can be developed from existing experiences with source code restructurings. This catalogue can not be defined universally, since it depends on the languages and programming paradigms used in the source system as well as the quality criteria of the target architecture. The advantage of such a catalogue is, that the effort of the source code restructuring can be estimated on the basis of these patterns. When it is possible to rate each pattern with the effort needed to execute it, the total effort of the restructuring can be estimated from this rate and the frequency of the resolution of certain dependency types.

7.1.5.3 Automation of the Source Code Restructuring

In order to further reduce the effort of the overall restructuring process, methods can be used, that automate the restructuring of the source code. The following paragraphs sketch possible approaches for the automation.

Relocation of Source Elements   The creation of a new source code structure and the relocation of source elements in this structure can be executed based on the detailed design model of the target system, that is derived from the complete mapping created by MARE. The link to the implementation of each source element, that is contained in the complete mapping of MARE, is the only information required for this operation. Many modern development environments already provide the implementation for such relocation operations in terms of refactorings and also update all internal links to the moved elements.

Another approach, that supports patterns to change the structure of the code, is described by Hunold et al. (2008). They support the user in applying restructuring decisions as transformations to abstract source models and automate the generation of source code from these models. Hence, the approach is complementary to MARE, since MARE supports the user in taking these decisions.

Resolution of Dependencies   The automation of the resolution of dependencies based on patterns is more complex, since it requires changes to the source code, that exceed simple structural changes. Changes of control flow and data flow as well as the addition of source elements become necessary. Therefore, a more detailed model of the source system, that represents every aspect of the source code, is required in order to be able to define the pattern implementations. There are existing approaches, that provide methods to create and manipulate model representations of the source code (see e.g. Fleurey et al. (2007), Giese (2010), and Horn et al. (2009)). These approaches also allow the generation of the source code of the target system from the detailed models. Thus, the definition of a model

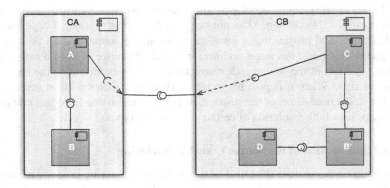

Figure 7.8: Multiple Component Instance Example

transformation on the detailed models is needed, that takes the concrete unwanted dependencies found by MARE as an input and creates a new detailed model, that only contains dependencies, that are intended in the target architecture.

Nevertheless, in practice it will not be possible to resolve all dependencies by the automatic application of patterns. Certain dependencies will be too specialised or complex to resolve to be expressible in model transformations. Furthermore, there will be several patterns to resolve certain dependencies, from which the user has to chose the appropriate solution for the specific context.

7.1.5.4 Particularities of the Component-and-Connector Viewtype

Figure 7.8 depicts an exemplary target architecture in the component-and-connector viewtype. It shows two composite components CA and CB with their subcomponents. The subcomponents are assumed to be mapped 1 : 1 to modules in a target module view. The only exception are the components B and B' which are mapped to the same module. Therefore one of them will not be mapped in the initial mapping. For the example it is assumed that B has been mapped.

Figure 7.9 depicts the dependencies from the clustering result mapped to the target architecture, whereby the source elements that were mapped to B are also considered for B' for the dependency mapping. It can be seen that most dependencies (at least in this coarse-grained view) can directly be mapped to the interfaces described in the target architecture. The only dependencies that do not fit the target architecture are the dependency from C to B and the dependency from B to

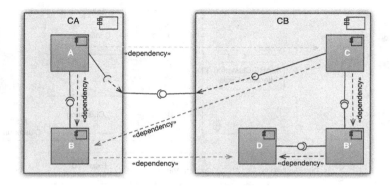

Figure 7.9: Dependencies to Multiple Component Instances

D. The dependency from C to B can be ignored, because it is just a copy of the dependency from C to B' which is part of the same composite component as C. The dependency from B to D is more problematic since there is no instance of D in CA and there is no according interface defined for CB. Possible resolutions of this unwanted dependency from B to D include the following:

- Add an instance of D to CA.

- Add an interface to CB that is delegated to the interface of D.

- Remove B and add an interface to CB that is delegated to the interface of B'.

- Add a new top-level component to the system that contains D or B and D with corresponding interfaces, which are used by CA and CB.

7.2 MARE Clustering Activities

Figure 7.10 depicts the process from Figure 7.2 with merged *Initialisation* and *Implementation Restructuring* activities and the expanded *MARE Clustering* activity. It shows that MARE Clustering contains two main activities. They represent the *Configuration* of the clustering and the *Clustering* itself. The decision *B* in the diagram represents the MARE Clustering iteration cycle. These three parts are described in the following subsections.

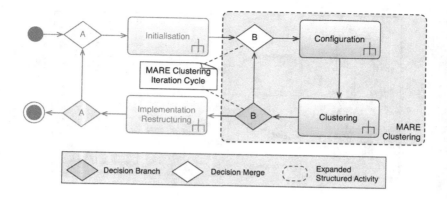

Figure 7.10: Process with Main MARE Activities

Figure 7.11: MARE Model Transformation

The clustering approach of MARE can be seen as a model transformation according to Section 5.2. Figure 7.11 shows the transformation with reference to Figure 5.3 on page 60. The clustering activity reads the defined target architecture and the source system model as well as further configurations given by the initial mapping and weights for the dependency types used in the source system model. The latter two are part of the configuration of MARE and are described in Section 7.2.2. This input is transformed to a complete mapping using clustering techniques.

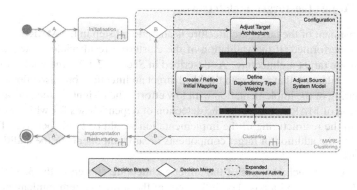

Figure 7.12: MARE Configuration Activities

7.2.1 MARE Clustering Iteration Cycle

The MARE Clustering iteration cycle, referred to by the decision *B* in Figure 7.10, is responsible for the improvement of the clustering results and represents the interactive character of the MARE process. The decision to be taken is whether the result of the *Clustering* activity is adequate to start the restructuring of the implementation. If this is the case the application of MARE Clustering in the current restructuring iteration (*A*) comes to an end and the result of the current MARE Clustering iteration is used to restructure the implementation. If the result is not adequate, the next iteration of MARE Clustering begins with the refinement of the input values of the clustering in the *Configuration* activity.

7.2.2 Configuration

The goal of the Configuration activity is to provide the information needed in the Clustering activity to create the complete mapping. It includes four optional subactivities of which *Adjust Target Architecture* is to be executed first, since it can influence the other activities. The remaining three activities, namely *Create / Refine Initial Mapping*, *Define Dependency Weights*, and *Adjust Detailed Design Model*, can be executed in parallel (see Figure 7.12). The activities create or manipulate the input values of the clustering. Thus, they provide the possibility of human interaction and the exertion of influence on the clustering result in successive MARE Clustering iterations. The following subsections describe the activities and their rationale in detail.

7.2.2.1 Adjust the Target Architecture

The adjustment of the target architecture is an optional step in the MARE process. It can be performed, if the validation of the clustering result yields new insights for the to-be target architecture. As described in Section 7.1.2.2 the goal is to find a to-be architecture that is near to the ideal target architecture, but also allows for a restructuring of the implementation with low effort. The insights gained during the application of MARE can e.g. be the detection of dependencies for which the resolution in the restructuring of the implementation would be too expensive. These can lead to the addition of target components or subcomponents or the addition of interfaces.

The need for such changes of the target architecture chosen in the *Model Target Architecture* activity based on influences of the source system implementation is mainly caused by the trade-off between restructuring effort and quality goals. Goals as e.g. cohesion of target components or the absence of certain (types of) dependencies between components may be placed back in favour of a less expensive restructuring of the implementation. However, these decisions should be recorded in the target architecture documentation. Future quality improvement projects can then be initiated to revise these decisions.

7.2.2.2 Create / Refine the Initial Mapping

An initial mapping has to be created in the first iteration of the MARE Clustering iteration cycle. The refinement of this mapping is optional for all subsequent iterations. In this activity the user has to provide a manual mapping of source elements to target components. The goal is to map a small number of source elements by hand and the rest automatically. The number of manually mapped elements should be small in order to reduce human effort for the analysis of the source system.

A necessary condition for the mapping is, that at least one source element has to be mapped to each target component that shall be included in the clustering. Reasons for not including a target component into the mapping are, that the target component is not relevant for the current iteration of the architecture restructuring iteration cycle or, in the case of a restructuring based on the component-and-connector viewpoint, that several instances of the component are used in the target architecture model. Another condition is, that a source element can only be mapped to one target component.

The choice of the source elements to be mapped underlies the user. Obvious candidates are source elements that represent the decomposition criteria of the target components and as such are central for its semantics. If the user is not a system expert, the interfaces of a component are guides to find appropriate source elements. It is assumed that a good first choice of source elements to be mapped are the equivalents of the operations and types described in the interfaces. Medvidovic and Jakobac (2006) also use this assumption in their architecture reconstruction approach to identify data components.

This assumption depends on good interface design. As a rule of thumb, interfaces should comprise types that are as general as possible, but as specialised as necessary. E.g., Strings as types in an interface can imply assumptions about their structure or numerical types be implicitly limited to a certain range of values. The mapping of operations and types can in certain cases be supported by automatic matching of similar names. Another mapping that can be made without major effort is the mapping of whole subcomponents or coarse grained modules that are known to be reused in the target architecture.

7.2.2.3 Define the Dependency Type Weights

Dependency type weights are used in the MARE clustering algorithm (cf. Section 8.2) to cluster strongly dependent source elements to the same target architecture component. The dependency types are defined during the creation of the source system model (cf. Section 7.1.3). Since the weights are needed by the clustering, this activity is required in the first iteration of MARE and optional in the subsequent iterations. The strength of the dependency between two source elements should depend on the decomposition criteria of the target architecture. This semantic information can be defined for the clustering in terms of weights of different dependency types.

When e.g. the functional decomposition is emphasised in the target architecture, a high weight for return types of methods or inheritance dependencies can lead to good results in the clustering of an object-oriented system. The impact of different dependency types on the clustering result for different types of systems and restructuring goals is discussed in Section 8.3.

Since the weighting of different dependency types is highly dependent on the usage of programming concepts in the source system and the decomposition criteria of the target architecture, it remains a manual task. During the iterations of MARE, the dependency weights can therefore be adjusted after each clustering step in order to improve the clustering result.

Experiences with dependency type weights are rarely described in the literature. Rayside et al. (2000) define weights for the reconstruction of high-level views of object-oriented systems (see Table 7.1), but they also indicate, that the weights are based on personal experiences and judgement. Furthermore, the weights are only defined informally. Christl et al. (2007) adopt the weights and map them natural numbers (low = 1, medium = 2, high = 3).

Table 7.1: Dependency Type Weights (Source: Rayside et al. (2000))

Dependency Type	Weight
Inheritance	low
Inner Class Decl.	high
Type dependence	low
Exceptions	low
Instantiation	high
Array Creation	medium
Field Read	medium
Static Field Read	low
Field Write	high
Static Field Write	high
Invocation	medium

The dependency type weights depend on the decomposition criteria of the target architecture in the context of MARE. As stated in Section 2.3.2, an important architecture decomposition criterion is the modifiability of the system. Depending on the context of the system this criterion can have different characteristics and depends on the type of modifications that are expected in the future development of the system. Therefore, e.g. the ALMA method by Bengtsson et al. (2004) bases on scenarios to assess the modifiability of a concrete architecture.

In MARE these different characteristics are modelled by different weights of dependency types, since it is assumed, that different architecture decisions lead to different types of dependencies between target components and different types of dependencies that represent the cohesion inside a target component. Experiences with dependency type weights in the context of restructuring in MARE are described in Chapter 10. The impact of dependency type weights on clustering is discussed in Section 8.3.

7.2.2.4 Adjust the Source System Model

The intention of this activity is to adjust the detailed design model of the source system due to the findings from the validation of the clustering result. Adjustments in this phase contain the following actions.

- **Removal of Source Elements.** Certain source elements like e.g. libraries or other elements, that behave like libraries, can negatively influence the automation of the complete mapping. They have strong dependencies to different parts of the system and thus lead to mappings, that do not follow the decomposition criteria of the target architecture. If this is the case for single elements, it can also be an indicator for the need of a preliminary refactoring of these elements (cf. Section 7.1.3.4).

- **Addition of Dependency Types** and corresponding dependencies. When the complete mapping reveals, that elements, that should conceptually be clustered to the same target component, are not mapped accordingly, because the conceptual relation is not represented in the source model, the inclusion of further dependency types can become necessary. A removal of dependency types is not intended, since the contained types provide useful information for the restructuring of the implementation. However, a dependency type can be excluded from the clustering by setting its weight to zero.

7.2.3 Clustering

The goal of the *Clustering* activity is the creation of the complete mapping. As depicted in Figure 7.13, it is subdivided into the activities *Execute Clustering* and *Validate Clustering Result*. The former represents the automatic clustering of source elements based on the inputs defined in the *Configuration* activity. The result is a complete mapping of source elements to target components. This mapping is the basis for the creation of a detailed design model of the target system.

MARE uses an agglomerative hierarchical clustering algorithm for the execution of the clustering. The specifics of the algorithm in relation to architecture restructuring are discussed in Section 8.2.

In the *Validate Clustering Result* activity, the resulting complete mapping is checked by the user. Based on the insights of this check the user can decide to start another iteration of the clustering with changed input values or to end the MARE Clustering activity and start the restructuring of the implementation based on the clustering result. The support for the validation of the result given by MARE and the possibilities to influence the clustering result are discussed in Section 8.5.

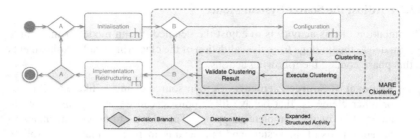

Figure 7.13: MARE Clustering Activities

7.3 MARE Metamodels

Figure 7.14 abstracts from the explicit control flow, that was shown in the activity diagrams before and depicts the data flow only. It contains all activities from the complete process model (Figure 7.1) and adds the data objects that are exchanged by the activities. Each of the data objects conforms to a metamodel. These meta-models are described in the following subsections.

Following the architecture view taxonomy of Matevska-Meyer et al. (2004) only structural views are considered in MARE. The models moreover conform to the module viewtype and the component-and-connector viewtype of Clements et al. (2003), respectively.

The source system model represents the current low-level structure of the implementation of the system. The elements of the source system model are not subject of the actual restructuring. Thus, these elements will not be changed during the restructuring process and are also the building blocks of the detailed design of the target system. The goal of MARE is to establish a mapping of these elements to the target architecture. The transfer of the actual architecture restructuring to the implementation can influence the decision which elements and dependencies are part of the source system model, such that the model is about to change in the successive iterations of MARE (cf. Section 7.1.1).

7.3.1 Applicability of Standard Interoperability Metamodels

Standard Interoperability Metamodels were introduced in Section 5.4. From the point of view of MARE such metamodels can be used to import information from other tools or to provide the complete mapping to other tools for further analysis or the automated restructuring of the implementation.

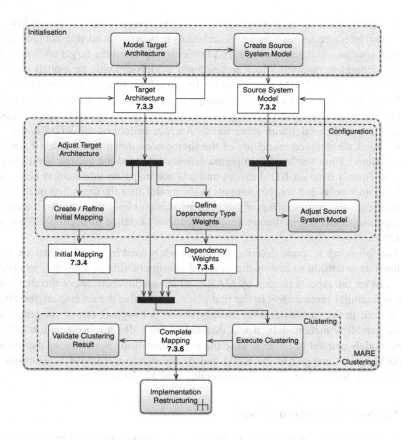

Figure 7.14: Data Flow in MARE

To serve as a metamodel for the input of MARE, a metamodel does at least have
be able to represent the source system model since this is required to be created
with an external reverse engineering tool. Thereby, it is sufficient to model elements on the function level for most use cases. A more fine-grained model that
comprises all details of the source code is not necessary. This conforms to the
limitation made in the DMM. Furthermore, the ability to model more than the syntactic dependencies of source elements should be given to be able to represent e.g.
semantic dependencies. This is possible with the KDM as well as with the DMM.

To model the complete configuration of MARE, furthermore the possibility to model architecture artefacts as well as relations between architecture artefacts and implementation artefacts is necessary in order to represent the target architecture and the complete mapping. Such architectural models can only be modelled with the KDM, since the DMM focuses on the function level of a software system.

The representation of the created complete mapping also bases on the link of the architecture level and the function level. Thus, only the KDM can be used to exchange this model with other tools. Another benefit of the KDM is that it also allows the detailed modelling of the source code down to the level of single instructions. Thus, the MARE implementation could read the needed input information from a detailed KDM model and add the mapping information between target components and source elements to the model after the execution of MARE Clustering. The restructuring of the implementation could then operate on such a complete model to put the automation scenarios sketched in Section 7.1.5 into practice.

The following sections describe the metamodels used in MARE. They are not defined as extension to one of the standard interoperability metamodels in order to focus on the aspects needed by MARE, which are independent of the standard interoperability metamodels in the first place. Since also the reverse engineering tools used in the case studies (cf. Section10) do not support one of the standard interoperability metamodels, it was decided to use a direct representation of the metamodels defined in Ecore to ease the implementation. Nonetheless, the metamodels can be mapped to the KDM and partly also to the DMM as discusssed before in order to allow for the interoperability of MARE with other tools.

7.3.2 Source System Model

The purpose of the source system model is the representation of the structural elements of the source system and their dependencies. This information is needed to semi-automatically create the complete mapping of source elements to target components.

The source system model can be seen as a detailed design view of the source system implementation leaving out information about the architectural structure of the source system such as packages, coarse-grained modules or deployment information as well as fine-grained implementation information such as single statements or control structures such as loops or conditional blocks.

Figure 7.15 shows the common metamodel of the source system model. It defines a *Source System Element* with a name and a link to the corresponding element in the implementation as attributes and a *Dependency* between source system

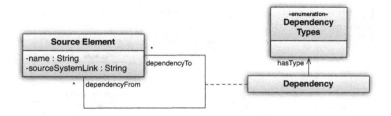

Figure 7.15: Metamodel of the Source System Model

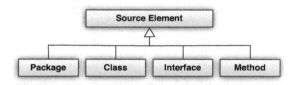

Figure 7.16: Concrete Source Elements for Java

elements as association class. Dependencies are typed. The metamodel is kept generic in order to allow to restructure source systems that follow different development paradigms as e.g. strictly imperative and object-oriented systems as well as source systems that are written in different programming languages.

The metamodel has to be extended for concrete project settings. The class *Source System Element* is then subclassed by concrete entities of the programming language of the source system. A simple example for Java is shown in Figure 7.16. The enumeration *Dependency Types* is also filled with the concrete dependency types, that are relevant for the project.

7.3.3 Target Architecture

The purpose of the target architecture model is the definition of the decomposition of the target system, which is the goal of the architectural restructuring process. The model is assumed to describe architectural elements to which source elements are to be uniquely mapped.

The target architecture metamodel as depicted in Figure 7.17 is designed to model a structural view of the target system. The core of the metamodel are target

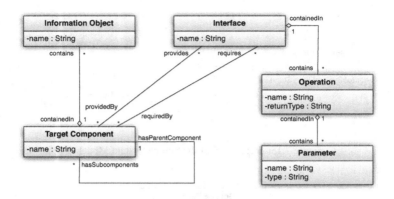

Figure 7.17: Target Architecture Metamodel

components as defined in Section 6.5. Target components can be hierarchically decomposed into subcomponents. Components can provide and require interfaces, which are defined by their operations and the parameters thereof. They can further contain information objects. Interfaces and information objects are not directly used by the MARE clustering algorithm, but support the user in the definition of the initial mapping and the interpretation of the clustering result. The metamodel is kept simple to allow for transformations from existing architecture description languages such as UML or ACME. Thus, users can model the target architecture in their preferred environment.

The architectural focus of MARE lies on the structure of software systems. This can include the implementation structure as well as the runtime structure. Thus, the module viewtype as well as the component and connector viewtype can be the basis for the description of the target architecture. The following subsections describe for which projects goals which of the viewtypes are adequate.

7.3.3.1 Viewtypes

As stated before different viewtypes can be the basis for the target architecture in MARE. For projects that aim at the development quality of the target system, the module viewpoint is adequate, since it determines the structure of the implementation entities and allows for a decomposition of source elements that supports the maintainability of the source code. In this case modules are modelled as target components.

For projects that focus on the (re-)use of elements of the source system in other contexts, e.g. by extraction of functionality as components or the migration to SOA, a structural view of the component-and-connector viewtype is more adequate. It does not focus on the source code structure, but on reusable composition units, which hold a runtime identity, since this is the way most architects think of their systems in early stages of architecture development.

Since only structural aspects are considered, both viewtypes can overlap in the definition of the target architecture. As also stated by Szyperski et al. (2002, p. 420), atomic components are modules. A change of the viewtypes from component-and-connector to module is especially probable in subsequent iterations, when the hierarchical refinement strategy is applied. This strategy leads from abstract conceptual architecture views to the concrete structure of the implementation.

Modelling of Connectors There is an ongoing discussion on whether connectors are first-class entities in component-and-connector-views (cf. Giesecke (2008, p. 42ff.)). For the task at hand connectors are modelled as second-class entities when possible, since they only have to be considered if they influence the restructuring. In most cases the connectors of the target system will not exist in the source system, so a more detailed specification is only required for the restructuring of th e implementation, but not needed for the architecture restructuring step. In cases where the connectors already exist in the source system, the respective source elements should be excluded from the clustering, because technical connectors follow different implementation rules than functional components, which might cause problems in the configuration of the clustering. When it is not possible to exclude the connector code from the source system model, since it is also subject of the restructuring, it is possible to model connectors as regular components. Since connectors usually have more than one instance, the same rules as for other multiple instance components have to be applied.

7.3.3.2 Concrete Syntax of the Target Architecture Model

To ease the use of the approach and to be able to support both viewtypes for different restructuring tasks, UML component diagrams are used to model the target architecture in the module viewtype as well as the component-and-connector viewtype. Besides differences in the semantics of modules and components regarding the runtime properties of components, an important restriction of modelling a module view with components is that (following the decomposition style defined in Clements et al. (2003, p. 53ff.)) a subcomponent is not allowed to be part of

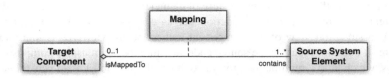

Figure 7.18: Metamodel of the Initial Mapping

more than one composite component. The MARE approach does not demand a particular target architecture view, but leaves the decision to the user, since the architectural restructuring may pursue different goals, which are reflected in the target architecture.

7.3.4 Initial Mapping

The initial mapping metamodel allows the mapping of source elements from the detailed design model of the source system to target components from the target architecture model. This generic metamodel is depicted in Figure 7.18. An arbitrary number of source elements can be mapped to each target component. On the other hand, each source element can be mapped to at most one target component. An initial mapping model contains mappings of at least one source elements for all components and subcomponents of the target architecture model of the current iteration of the architecture restructuring iteration cycle.

In reference to target architectures of the component-and-connector viewtype a further restriction is, that only one of possibly several instances of a component can be considered in the initial mapping and the clustering step, since a source element can only be mapped to one target component. The consequences for the other instances have to be analysed in the interpretation of the clustering result and the planning of the implementation restructuring.

7.3.5 Dependency Type Weights

The dependency type weights metamodel is based on the dependency types that are used in the source system model. These depend on the programming languages used in the source system and the applied analysis tools. The metamodel itself is very simple and allows the assignment of a weight to each dependency type. Figure 7.19 exemplarily shows the static dependencies of Java systems that can be

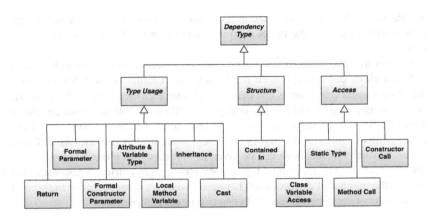

Figure 7.19: Static Dependency Types in Java

extracted with the SISSy[3] reverse engineering tool, which is based on the Recoder framework[4].

The dependency types are categorised into three abstract types. *Type Usage* refers to the usage of e.g. classes as types for return statements, parameters, variable types or inheritance relations. *Structure* covers dependencies that represent the structure of the implementation, e.g. methods and local classes that are contained in classes or classes that are contained in packages. Structural dependencies are usually not considered in MARE since they often represent the structure of the current architecture, like e.g. containment in packages. *Access* is the superclass of all dependencies that refer to accesses of variables or methods.

7.3.6 Complete Mapping

The purpose of the complete mapping model is the determination of a mapping of all source system elements to target architecture elements. The metamodel corresponds to the metamodel of the initial mapping as shown in Figure 7.18. The only difference is, that each source system element has to be mapped to exactly one target component in the complete mapping. The model resulting from the MARE Clustering activity is an instance of this metamodel. If a source system element can not be mapped to one of the target component, which can be the case if it has

---

[3]http://sissy.fzi.de/
[4]http://recoder.sourceforge.net/

no (transitive) dependencies to the initially mapped source elements, a new target component is added to the target architecture in order to illustrate this fact to the user.

In order to make the clustering result more understandable and usable for users, different views can be created on the model. One example is an UML diagram, that shows target components and their nested source elements, modelled as UML classes as depicted in Figure 6.2 on page 78. Allowed, tolerated and unwanted dependencies can be depicted as a graph (e.g. using Graphviz[5]) that shows the target components as nodes and the different types of dependencies as different edges. Further visualisations can be given as matrices with target components as rows and columns and different dependency measures as entries. These measures are e.g. the number of dependencies between two target components or the sum of the weights of the dependencies between two target components.

7.4 Summary

This chapter introduced the MARE Method. The core of the method is an iterative process model that covers the whole process of architecture restructuring. MARE is a design-time approach that employs abstract models of the source and the target system to support the planning of an architecture restructuring project. In contrast to other approaches, the target architecture is the guiding artefact of the restructuring process.

The MARE process model conforms to the horseshoe model, which is a common model for reengineering processes. A mapping of the activities of MARE to the horseshoe model was presented in Section 7.1. The architecture restructuring iteration cycle of MARE reflects the requirement of a stepwise character of restructuring projects that leads to lower risks and faster results of such projects. The decisive factor of the iterations is the stepwise adjustment of the target architecture of each iteration to an intended to-be target architecture. Possible strategies for this procedure are the hierarchical refinement of the target architecture and the vertical extraction of target components.

The second important model that is needed by MARE besides the target architecture is a detailed design model of the source system. This model comprises all source elements that are affected by the restructuring and their dependencies. The selection of source element types and dependency types is based on the decomposition criteria of the target architecture. The source element types should be chosen such that they do not reflect the decomposition criteria of the source architecture.

---

[5]http://www.graphviz.org/

The abstraction level of the source elements should also be not too low in order to allow for the traceability of the results and a good performance of the clustering algorithm. The dependency types should reflect the distinctive decomposition criteria of the target architecture as well as the structural dependencies that influence the effort of the restructuring of the implementation.

The creation of these two models as well as the restructuring of the implementation are part of the MARE process model, but are not in the focus of the contribution of MARE. They rather define the requirements from the point of view of MARE. They same applies to the actual restructuring of the implementation. This chapter described how a detailed model of the target system can be created from the complete mapping resulting from MARE and how the restructuring of the implementation can be automated using current methods from industry and research.

The focus of the MARE method lies on the creation of the complete mapping and the configuration needed for this activity. The configuration comprises the adjustment of the target architecture and the source system model as well as the definition of dependency type weights and an initial mapping. The adjustment of the target architecture is included to be able to include temporary changes that reduce the effort of the restructuring of the implementation. The adjustment of the source system model targets the ability to remove source elements that negatively influence the automatic mapping of MARE or to add further knowledge in terms of dependencies between source elements. The initial mapping is created and refined manually and serves as a seed for the automatic creation of the complete mapping. It is furthermore used to include human knowledge and decisions in the clustering. A minimal initial mapping of one source element per target component is necessary to start the automatic mapping process. The dependency type weights also reflect the user's knowledge about the system and the decomposition criteria of the target architecture.

Besides the activities of the MARE process model the chapter described the metamodels used to define the information needed to create the complete mapping. These include the target architecture and the source system model as well as the initial mapping and the dependency type weights. The metamodels are kept very generic in order to support the restructuring of systems that follow different implementation paradigms and to support a variety of target architecture views.

It was also emphasised that standard interoperability metamodels are suitable to exchange information between MARE and other reengineering tools. However, these metamodels are not used as a basis for the definition and the implementation of the MARE metamodels to keep the focus on the information that is specific for MARE and since they are not implemented in the external tools used in the MARE case studies.

The actual creation of the complete mapping and the definition of an according graph clustering algorithm are the topic of the next chapter.

8 MARE Clustering

This chapter describes the creation of the complete mapping in MARE Clustering on the basis of graph clustering. Section 8.1 describes the goals and criteria of MARE Clustering. Section 8.2 introduces the actual clustering algorithm and its underlying graph model. Section 8.3 discusses the impact of dependencies and their weights on the clustering, while Section 8.4 examines the role of arbitrary decisions taken by the clustering algorithm. Section 8.5 discusses the validation of the clustering result before Section 8.6 summarises the results of the chapter.

8.1 Goals and Criteria of the Clustering

The goal of MARE Clustering is to provide the complete mapping of source elements to target components in order to support the user with the restructuring of the implementation of a system towards a target architecture. Since the manual definition of such a mapping demands an enormous effort, the MARE approach is designed to automate as much of this effort as possible. It targets the inclusion of the available knowledge of the user and the creation of a mapping that comes close to the manual mapping the user would make.

The following subsections list the main criteria for ensuring the quality of the resulting complete mapping. They are the basis for the selection and definition of an appropriate clustering algorithm.

8.1.1 Complete Mapping

The primary goal of the clustering is the complete mapping of source elements to target components, as described in Section 6.3. In order to improve the comprehensibility of the results, the examination of intermediate results and the traceability of inputs to the resulting mapping should be possible.

The presentation of the results should clearly reflect the complete mapping, so that the user does not have to interpret the result with regard to the mapping of single source elements or groups thereof.

8.1.2 Mapping Quality

Besides the goal of a complete mapping, this mapping also has to fulfil quality requirements. The criteria for the definition of quality in this context are described in the following subsections. They influence the adoption of hierarchical agglomerative clustering as described in Section 8.2.

8.1.2.1 Similarity to a Manual Mapping

An important criterion for the creation of a complete mapping using clustering is the similarity to a manual mapping of the same source elements and target architecture. Since a purely manual mapping is to be replaced by MARE, its criteria have to be formalised as well as possible. A manual mapping is oriented towards the decomposition criteria of the target architecture and the knowledge about the existing implementation. Information about the decomposition criteria of the target architecture is captured in the components and interfaces of the target architecture model as well as the dependency type weights. The knowledge about the existing implementation and its relation to the target architecture is captured in the initial mapping and also in the dependency type weights.

This information has to be processed in the clustering algorithm in an adequate way. Furthermore, the results of the clustering have to be presented such that the user can easily interpret them and is able to derive changes in the configuration in order to improve the clustering result to suit him.

8.1.2.2 Cohesion

Another important criterion for the mapping is the cohesion of the target components according to the decomposition criteria of the target architecture. The decomposition criteria are assumed to be expressible in the dependency type weights. Hence, these have a strong influence on the execution of the clustering. Regarding a high cohesion of target components, it is assumed, that dependency types, that reflect the decomposition criteria are more likely to be found inside a target component than between target components.

8.1.2.3 Coupling and Non-Conforming Dependencies

In software engineering, high cohesion and low coupling are common quality attributes of a system architecture. While this is also true for cohesion in the case of restructuring, the situation for coupling is different. Low coupling is still a

goal for the target system, but since the restructuring is based on the source implementation, which is build with different architecture decomposition criteria, low
coupling will not always be achievable for the complete mapping. Even when
source elements are correctly assigned to a target component according to the decomposition criteria of the target architecture, there can be unwanted dependencies
to other target components through dependencies, that conform to the decomposition criteria of the source architecture. This can lead to high coupling in terms
of a high number of unwanted dependencies. However, the weights of the dependencies should still be low as compared to the dependencies of source elements
assigned to the same target component.

These unwanted dependencies lead to a conflict of interests for the semi-automatic creation of the complete mapping. While low weights for dependencies,
that represent the source architecture, lead to a good mapping of source elements
to target components, they can also lead to a high number of these dependencies
between target components. This becomes a problem in the restructuring of the
implementation. In that phase, the dependencies that do not conform to the target
architecture have to be resolved in order to gain a high-quality target implementation. Thus, the clustering algorithm needs to focus on high cohesion more than on
low coupling.

8.2 Target-Architecture-Driven Clustering

MARE employs an agglomerative hierarchical clustering algorithm to create the
complete mapping of source elements to target components. Hierarchical clustering is a well-researched method in the reconstruction of the structure of software
systems (cf. e.g. Maqbool and Babri (2007)). In contrast to the reconstruction of
an existing structure, the goal of MARE is to adapt the implementation to a new
structure given by the target architecture. Nevertheless, the fundamental idea is
similar in both contexts. The main difference is, that the criteria for the clustering of the system emphasise different aspects of the system. Where architecture
reconstruction incorporates the presumed decomposition criteria of the architects
and developers of the source system, architecture restructuring has to incorporate
the decomposition criteria of the target architecture.

Still, the influence of the existing implementation is high. On the one hand,
it contains knowledge about the implemented functionality, which should be preserved. On the other hand, the architecture decomposition criteria behind the existing implementation strongly influence the effort to change the implementation

towards the target architecture and can thus also influence the target architecture in order to keep the restructuring project budget low.

8.2.1 Adaptation of Hierarchical Graph Clustering

The target architecture and the knowledge of the reengineer about the functionality and implementation of the system are the most important inputs for the clustering. In order to be able to incorporate this information in the computation of the complete mapping, restructuring-specific adaptations to standard hierarchical clustering as described in Section 4.3.1 are necessary. This subsection describes the conceptual adaptations while the subsections 8.2.2 to 8.2.4 describe the hierarchical clustering algorithm used in MARE.

8.2.1.1 Stopping Condition

As described in Section 4.3.1 typical stopping conditions include reaching a predefined number of clusters or the dropping of the similarity between clusters below a given threshold. Since the goal in MARE is to gain one cluster of source elements for each target component, a special stopping condition is introduced. It stops the clustering, when each source element, that has a connection to one or more source elements of the initial mapping, is part of a cluster, that can be mapped to a target component.

The mere definition of the number of target components will not be sufficient to gain adequate clusters, since the resulting clusters will not be directly mappable to the target components. The definition of a similarity threshold will also not produce adequate clusters and furthermore conflicts with the goal of automating as much of the creation of the complete mapping as possible. A clustering using a similarity threshold will leave a large number of decisions to the user. The same applies to hierarchical clustering without a stopping condition, since the cut through the dendrogram that represents the clustering result has to be defined by the user and requires an intensive analysis.

8.2.1.2 Merging of Clusters

Knowledge of the reengineer about the mapping of certain source elements to target components can be expressed in the initial mapping. This is adopted in the clustering algorithm by the creation of initial clusters in a pre-clustering phase. The initial clusters contain all source elements, that were mapped to a certain component in the initial mapping. Since the initial clusters represent the target components during the clustering, they are called *component clusters*. The representation of component cluster leads to the rule, that component clusters are not allowed to be merged. A merge of two component clusters would make it impossible to directly map the resulting clusters of the algorithm to target components. Thus, this restriction to standard hierarchical clustering has to be made to gain a clustering result with the required properties.

8.2.1.3 Similarity Function

The knowledge of the reengineer on how the decomposition criteria of the target architecture can be mapped to the existing implementation is reflected in the dependency type weights. The dependency types that reflect the desired decomposition in the target architecture, should be weighted higher than other dependency types. E.g. when the target architecture is based on a domain decomposition of the system and it is known that inheritance relations in the system reflect cohesion in terms of domain-specific functionality, this dependency type should be weighted high. The reflection of decomposition criteria in dependency type weights indicates that also the definition of similarity between clusters is based on these weights. Thus, similarity of nodes and clusters in the context of MARE does not describe the similarity of these elements in terms of their properties, but similarity in terms of their mapping to the same target component.

8.2.2 Graph Model

In order to compute the complete mapping using hierarchical clustering an underlying abstract graph model is created. This model is the basis for the graph clustering algorithm and contains the information from the models created in the Configuration activity. Thus, the clustering algorithm creates a complete mapping on the basis of these models and implements the model transformation introduced in Section 7.2. This section describes the metamodel of the graph model and the creation of model instances.

8.2.2.1 Graph Metamodel

The metamodel used as the basis for the hierarchical clustering is a simple graph model. Figure 8.1 shows the classes of the graph metamodel. It basically contains nodes which are mapped to source elements and edges representing their dependencies. Nodes have a name and a link to the according source element in the source system model. Edges have a weight and allow to model more than one relationship of the same type between two nodes, indicated by the *count* attribute.

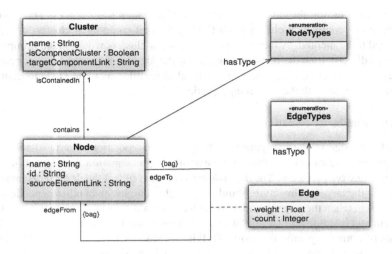

Figure 8.1: Graph Metamodel

Nodes and edges are typed. The types are represented by enumerations, which contain all possible types. Thus, the metamodel can be extended and to implemented easily. Since the types are specific to the programming language of the source system and the used reverse engineering tool, details are omitted in the figure. Nodes can be contained in a *Cluster*. A cluster is named, can be marked as component cluster and does in that case have a link to the according target component in the target architecture.

Based on the links from nodes to source elements and from clusters to target components, the clustering result can be mapped back to a complete mapping model and be visualised to the user as described in Section 7.3.6. This is necessary to enable the user to execute the validation of the clustering results as described in Section 8.5.

The edges are modelled as an association class to highlight their character as a relation between two nodes as well as their character as an object with specific properties. The association ends are bags, since there can be several edges between two nodes, even of the same type. As can be concluded from the association end names, the edges of the graph are directed. This feature is not used in the current similarity functions (cf. Section 8.2.4), but provides the possibility to define more complex similarity functions. Examples for concrete *DependencyTypes* in Java systems are shown in Figure 7.19 on page 115. To simplify an instance of the metamodel, all edges of the same type between the same nodes can be merged to one edge for which the count is set to the number of edges of this type between the same nodes. The default count for edges, that are not merged, is 1.

To simplify the definition of the similarity function between clusters, the notion of an edge between nodes can also be lifted to edges between clusters. Then, an edge exists between two clusters for each edge between two nodes which are contained in two different clusters. Thus, $(v_1, v_2) \in E_{C_1, C_2}$ with $v_1 \in C_1$ and $v_2 \in C_2$ is the set of all edges between the clusters C_1 and C_2.

Since multiple edges are allowed between two nodes, the model is a multigraph. It can be transformed into a simple graph by merging all edges between two nodes into a single edge. The edges between two nodes n_1 and n_2 can be merged by replacing them with a new single edge e_{12} with the weight $\omega_{e_{12}}$ defined as follows:

$$\omega(e_{12}) = \sum_{e \in E_{12}} \omega(e) * \chi(e) \qquad (8.1)$$

with E_{12} being the set of all edges between n_1 and n_2 and $\chi(e)$ being the count of edge e. The merging simplification and the introduction of the count attribute improves the performance the recomputation of distances during the execution of the clustering algorithm. However, it is not applicable in the whole MARE life cycle, since changes to the dependency type weights in the configuration phase of MARE are only meaningful on the multigraph representation.

8.2.2.2 Creation of the Graph Model

To create the adequate graph representation of the source system, all elements of the source system model (cf. Section 7.3.2) are mapped to graph elements. The source elements are mapped to nodes while dependencies between these elements are modelled as edges. The dependency weights defined in the Configuration activity are assigned to the edges of the respective type. The information from the target architecture and the initial mapping are included in the model in the pre-clustering phase of the clustering algorithm (cf. Section 8.2.3).

Internal attributes of source elements can also be modelled as edges between nodes in order to consider their similarity for the interrelation of the nodes. E.g. the attribute *developer* used by Andritsos and Tzerpos (2005) can be included by creating pairwise edges between all nodes that represent source elements, that were implemented by the same developer.

In order to reduce the complexity of the graph and to improve the performance of the clustering, some optimisations can be made during the creation of the graph

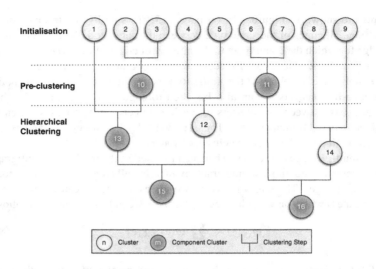

Figure 8.2: Adjusted Hierarchical Clustering Algorithm

model. One is the transformation into a simple graph as mentioned before. Furthermore, all dependencies with weight 0 can be removed from the graph model, since they do not influence the clustering result. Still, these edges should be visible to the user during the interpretation of the result, since also edges between two clusters that have a weight of 0 influence the restructuring of the implementation and can therefor lead to the decision to change the configuration for a subsequent clustering run. When the removal leads to nodes without edges, they are also removed for the clustering run.

8.2.3 Clustering Algorithm

MARE uses agglomerative hierarchical clustering to create the complete assignment. Figure 8.2 depicts an exemplary dendrogram of the adjusted hierarchical clustering algorithm. The stages of the clustering algorithm are described in the following paragraphs. Listing 8.1 explains the algorithm in pseudocode.

```
ALGORITHM MARE_Clustering (graphModel, targetArchitecture,
            initialMapping)

    // Initialisation
    FOREACH ( Node n IN graphModel )
        Cluster c = createCluster(n);
    END FOREACH

    // Pre-clustering
    FOREACH ( TargetComponent tc IN targetArchitecture )
        Merge all clusters c where c.contains(n)
        AND n is initially mapped to tc;
    END FOREACH

    // Hierarchical Clustering
    WHILE (∃ Cluster c:c.isConnected AND !c.isComponentCluster))
        Search for two clusters c1 and c2 with the
        highest similarity where
        NOT ( c1.isComponentCluster AND c2.isComponentCluster );

        Cluster c12 = merge(c1, c2);

        IF ( c1.isComponentCluster OR c2.isComponentCluster )
            c12.isComponentCluster = true;
        END IF
    END WHILE
```

Listing 8.1: Clustering Algorithm in Pseudocode

8.2.3.1 Initialisation

The algorithm starts with a simple initialisation step, that assigns each node of the graph model to a single cluster (Clusters 1-9 in Figure 8.2). The similarities of the clusters are computed using the similarity function for singular clusters as described in Section 8.2.4. The creation of clusters in the FOREACH loop in Listing 8.1 is deterministic and the order of the creation will not influence the clustering result. However, the order of the clusters in the target data structure can influence the choice of the most similar clusters in the *Hierarchical Clustering* phase depending on the implementation.

8.2.3.2 Pre-clustering

In the pre-clustering phase, initial clusters are created for each target component and are marked as component clusters (Clusters 10 and 11). The clusters representing the source elements that are mapped to the according target component in the initial mapping are merged to the new cluster. The similarities of the clusters are computed using the similarity function for composite clusters as described in Section 8.2.4. The hierarchy of target components is flattened in the pre-clustering. I.e. hierarchical relations between target components have no influence on the resulting component clusters. The order of the processing of the target components in the FOREACH loop does not influence the clustering result, since it is not allowed to map source elements to more than one target component in the initial mapping.

8.2.3.3 Hierarchical Clustering

After the pre-clustering phase, the actual hierarchical clustering begins. The similarities of the clusters are computed using the similarity function for composite clusters as described in Section 8.2.4. As described in Section 8.2.1 it is not allowed to merge two component clusters, even if they have the highest similarity value. In such a case the two clusters with the highest similarity value, that are not both component clusters, are merged.

In the case that more than one pair of clusters has the same highest similarity value, it has to be decided which pair of clusters will be merge in the current step. This decision is of prime importance for the result of the clustering, since it potentially influences the similarity values and the component clusters of the following iterations of the WHILE loop. Hence, this issue is discussed in detail in Section 8.4.

8.2.3.4 Stopping Condition

The clustering stops, when only component clusters and disconnected clusters are left. Thus, the clustering creates n_{TC} clusters (with n_{TC} = number of target components) for connected graphs. For disconnected graphs the clustering creates at most $n_{TC} + n_{DP} - 1$ (with n_{DP} = number of disconnected graph partitions), when only nodes in one graph partition are mapped in the initial mapping.

8.2.4 Similarity of Clusters

The mapping of nodes to a component cluster is based on the decomposition criteria of the target architecture. This has to be mapped to properties of the graph elements in order to be available to the similarity function and can thereby influence the clustering.

8.2.4.1 Similarity of Singular Clusters

Singular clusters are clusters, that only contain a single node. These clusters are created in the initialisation phase of the clustering algorithm. The rationale to assign two source elements to the same target component is mapped to the dependencies between the source elements in MARE. Thus, the similarity function ($Sim : C_i \times C_j \rightarrow \mathbb{R}$) for two singular clusters C_i and C_j computes the similarity value for two clusters by summing up the weights of the edges between the clusters. The direction of edges is not considered, since the similarity value represents the reasonability to assign both clusters to the same target component and for this task edges in both directions are of interest. The similarity function can be formalised as follows:

$$Sim(C_i, C_j) = \sum_{x=1}^{k} \omega(e_x) * \chi(e_x) \tag{8.2}$$

with $e_x \in E_{C_i, C_j}$, where E_{C_i, C_j} is the set of edges between the nodes in C_i and C_j, k being the number of edges in E_{C_i, C_j} and $\chi(e_x)$ being the count of edge e_x.

8.2.4.2 Similarity of Composite Clusters

Following the criterion of high cohesion for the clustering, this section introduces possible similarity functions to compute the similarity between an existing cluster C_i and a new cluster C_{jk} merged from the clusters C_j and C_k, and discusses their differences. Functions that do compute the similarity of new clusters to existing clusters from their predecessors (as e.g. the functions introduced in Section 4.3.1) are called *updating rules* by Wiggerts (1997). This term will also be used in the remainder of the thesis. A straight-forward way to define the similarity of composite clusters is to adopt the definition in Equation 8.2 for the computation of the similarity of a cluster to a newly formed cluster as follows:

$$Sim(C_i, C_{jk}) = Sim(C_i, C_j) + Sim(C_i, C_k) \tag{8.3}$$

This sums up the weights of all edges between nodes in C_i and the newly formed cluster C_{jk}, hence this updating rule is called *Sum* in the remainder of this thesis.

With respect to cohesion the definition is assumed to be not ideal, since it also leads to a high similarity for clusters that contain a few nodes, that are connected by highly weighted edges, and a large number of nodes that only have edges to these but not among each other.

Section 4.3.1 already described standard updating rules for hierarchical clustering. Since the literature indicates, that updating rules, that base on average linkage, lead to clusters with high cohesion, the functions defined in Equations 4.4 and 4.5 on page 49 are preferable here.

Furthermore, Koschke (2000, p. 190) defined a similarity function for composite clusters, that also bases on average linkage and can in this context be formalised as follows:

$$Sim(C_i, C_{jk}) = \frac{\sum_{x=1}^{n} \omega(e_x) * \chi(e_x)}{|C_i| * |C_{jk}|} \tag{8.4}$$

with $e_x \in E_{C_i,C_{jk}}$ and n being the number of edges in $E_{C_i,C_{jk}}$. This function is not an updating rule since it computes the similarity of composite clusters based on the properties of the clusters and not the existing similarity values of the predecessor of the new cluster.

Another similarity function for composite clusters that will be called *Sum Relative to Nodes* in the remainder of the thesis, can be defined. It uses previously computed similarity values, but computes a new value based on the edges between the single nodes in the clusters. To do this, the function has to extend Equation 8.2 by the notion of multiple nodes per cluster. This results in the following function:

$$Sim(C_i, C_{jk}) = (Sim(C_i, C_j) + Sim(C_i, C_k)) * \frac{|N_{Inv}|}{|N_{All}|} \tag{8.5}$$

where $|N_{Inv}|$ is the number of nodes in C_i and C_{jk} that have edges to nodes in the other cluster and $|N_{All}|$ the total number of nodes in these clusters. Thus, the weight of the edges between the clusters is rated with the connectedness of the nodes of the two clusters. If all nodes in both clusters have connections to nodes in the other cluster the latter term evaluates to 1 and the whole weight is taken as new similarity value. If only some part of the nodes has connections to nodes in the other cluster, only a fraction of the weight is taken. Figure 8.3 shows two small examples and the corresponding similarity values. Since the similarity function takes into account the number of nodes, that contribute to the edges between the two clusters, and therefore prefers highly connected clusters, it is assumed, that it leads to a higher cohesion of the resulting component clusters.

The *Unweighted Average Linkage* updating rule and the Sum updating rule defined above as well as the latter two functions, that do not only compute the simi-

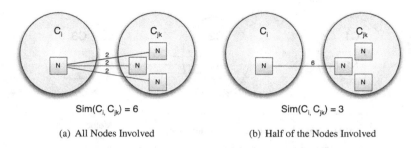

(a) All Nodes Involved   (b) Half of the Nodes Involved

Figure 8.3: Example for Equation 8.5

larity of the existing clusters to a new composite cluster from the existing similarities but also include further information, will be evaluated in the case studies in Chapter 10.

8.3 Impact of Dependencies on the Clustering

Since dependencies form the basis of the computation of the similarity of two clusters, they have a determinant impact on the clustering result. As Equation 8.2 shows, the clustering bases on the sum of the weights of all edges between two nodes. Thus, the weight and the number of dependencies are the main factor for the mapping of source elements to target components. This section shows how the weight and the number of edges interact in the clustering and how this has to be considered in the weighting of dependency types.

Figure 8.4 shows an example in which the nodes are classes. $N2$ inherits from $N1$ and calls methods in $N3$. Each of the nodes is mapped to a singular cluster. For the example it is assumed, that the decomposition criteria of the target architecture indicate to map two classes, that have an inheritance relation, to the same target component.

If all dependencies are weighted equally with e.g. a weight of 1, $C2$ will be merged with $C3$. Under the assumptions described above, this would not be the intended result of the clustering. On the other hand the number of edges of a certain type can be compensated by the weight of other edges of which less occur between two nodes. In order to gain the intended result of a merge of $C2$ and $C1$, the weight of the inheritance type has to be at least 4. This shows the interaction of the number of dependencies of a certain type and the dependency type weights. It can be argued, that the number of equally typed edges between two clusters

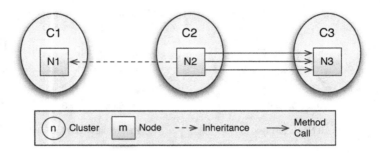

Figure 8.4: Example for the Impact of Dependencies

should not be considered in the computation of the similarity of these clusters. E.g. the mere fact, that a function calls another function more than once does not necessarily make the functions more similar. For the example described above this would mean, that a weight of 2 for the inheritance edge would lead to a clustering of *C2* to *C1*.

On the other hand, keeping in mind that for the restructuring of the implementation the similarity between two clusters also represents the effort for the resolution of dependencies between two target components, also the number of equally typed edges is an important information in relation to the clustering decision. Therefore, the default behaviour in MARE is to map all occurrences of dependencies to edges in the graph model. Nevertheless, a user can decide to map all occurrences of dependencies of the same type between two source elements to only one edge with a count of 1 in the creation of the graph model.

Mitchell (2002) also outlines the importance of dependency weights for the result of clusterings. But he also indicates that current clustering approaches do not provide knowledge on the concrete impact of dependency type weights and their change on clustering results. In the Bunch tool described in the thesis, a weight of 1 is assumed for each dependency type. This weight can be adapted by users. However, hints for a procedure of how the weights can be adapted to a certain application context are not given. They are described as topics for future research. For the context of architecture restructuring MARE examines the possible indicators for the change of dependency type weights. This topic is discussed in Section 8.5.

Andritsos and Tzerpos (2005) evaluate the influence of weighting schemes for the application of clustering based on information theory for architecture reconstruction. Similarly, the influence of dependency type weights on the presented clustering algorithm will be evaluated in Chapter 10.

8.4 Arbitrary Decisions

The presented clustering algorithm has to make arbitrary decisions when the result of the similarity value is the same for several cluster pairs. As a consequence, two clustering runs that take different decisions will result in a different complete mapping. Figure 8.5 shows a simple example for the influence of arbitrary decisions using the similarity function from Equation 8.3. Similar but more complex examples can also be found for the other similarity functions.

Figure 8.5(a) depicts the initial situation allowing the decisions to merge the clusters 1 and 2 or 3 and 4. The clusters 1 and 4 are initially mapped to different target components. 8.5(b) shows the complete clustering for the decision to merge 1 and 2 first, while 8.5(c) shows the clustering for the complete clustering for the decision to merge 3 and 4 first. The results illustrate, that cluster 3 is always merged with cluster 4, while cluster 2 is clustered depending on the decision, which clusters are merged first.

In order to cope with this situation different strategies can be applied. These strategies are described in the following subsections.

8.4.1 Allow Arbitrary Decisions

The most simple strategy is to allow arbitrary decisions by introducing a fixed rule to determine the decision. A simple to implement rule is to always take the first or the last occurrence of the similarity value. This strategy leads to a deterministic result of the clustering as long as the order of the clusters remains the same. It will however not necessarily lead to good complete mappings when a big number of arbitrary decisions occurs or the decisions occur early in the clustering process and have a major influence on the clustering result.

8.4.2 Reduce Arbitrary Decisions

Maqbool and Babri (2007) investigate the influence of arbitrary decisions for the similarity functions presented in Section 4.3.1. They argument, that arbitrary decisions do not negatively influence the clustering result, when the information reflected in the underlying model appropriately covers the characteristics of interest of the clustering. They argue that the negative influence of arbitrary decisions can

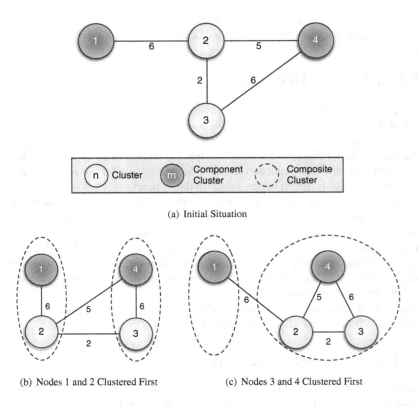

(a) Initial Situation

(b) Nodes 1 and 2 Clustered First   (c) Nodes 3 and 4 Clustered First

Figure 8.5: Example for Arbitrary Decisions

be compensated by the inclusion of more information in the similarity function. Thus, they propose the use of clustering algorithms that include more knowledge about the system and recompute the similarity value for each cluster merge instead of computing the similarity based on previous similarity values. They evaluate this using two such algorithms called LIMBO as introduced by Andritsos and Tzerpos (2005) and the Weighted Combined Algorithm defined by Maqbool and Babri (2004). They come to the conclusion, that the algorithms lead to less arbitrary decisions in later stages of the clustering process and to better results compared to the use of updating rules. On the other hand, they state that the algorithms also lead to less stable results.

In MARE the similarity functions for composite clusters as defined in Equation 8.4 and Equation 8.5 also include further information in the computation of the similarity of merged clusters. Their influence on the stability of the clustering is examined in the open source case study in Section 10.2.

8.4.3 Compute All Decisions

The optimal solution to avoid the influence of arbitrary decisions is to compute all possible decisions and compare the results of all the different clustering runs. For the small example in Figure 8.5, the two possible results are shown in 8.5(b) and 8.5(c). Based on the comparison, the optimal clustering solution can then be chosen. E.g. 8.5(c) could be chosen, because it provides better values for the sums of weights of internal and external dependencies than 8.5(b). For large systems the computation of all alternatives and the automatic decision for the best solution can become very complex and computation-intensive.

8.4.4 Consolidating Iterations

A practical strategy, that bases on the advantages of the previous strategy is to compute several clustering runs with a different order of clusters in the initialisation phase and to consolidate their results. This strategy leads to non-determinism in the clustering runs. I.e. every run on the same input data can create a different complete mapping, depending on the decision taken, when several cluster pairs have the same similarity value. Compared to the optimal solution, this strategy does not include all possible arbitrary decisions, but can be computed with less effort and is assumed to lead to more stable results than single clustering runs.

A possibility to consolidate the result and to gain a better clustering quality is to take the results of several runs and extract the nodes, that were mapped to the same component cluster in each run. These can be used to complement the initial mapping for another series of cluster runs. It is assumed that then more nodes will be clustered uniquely. The strategy is depicted in Figure 8.6 and called *Consolidating Iterations* in the remainder of the thesis.

The strategy can be further clarified using the example from Figure 8.5. A first series of clustering runs will produce the clusterings shown in 8.5(b) and 8.5(c). Since each clustering maps cluster 3 to component cluster 4, this information will be added to the initial mapping for the next series of clustering runs. In this series, component 2 will also be clustered to component cluster 4 in all clustering runs. Thus, the iterative clustering ends with 8.5(c) as the complete mapping.

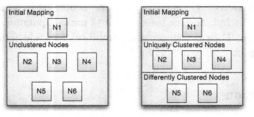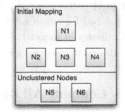

(a) Input of the First Series   (b) Result of the First Series   (c) Input of the Second Series

Figure 8.6: Example for Several Clustering Runs

In summary, the concept of consolidating iterations is to introduce an iterative clustering to resolve as many arbitrary decisions as possible by incrementally adding uniquely clustered elements to the component clusters. This does not preclude arbitrary decisions, but leads to a reduction of arbitrary decisions and their negative impact on clustering results. However, there are cases in which nodes cannot be clustered uniquely. In these cases arbitrary decisions have to be taken or the user is requested to extend the mapping for the next series of clustering runs.

Since arbitrary decisions are not processed in a schematic way, but by randomly changing the input for different clustering runs, it cannot be ensured, that all possible decisions are taken during a clustering series. Hence, an optimal complete mapping cannot be guaranteed, but the strategy provides more accurate results, than the strategy described in Section 8.4.1 and is not as computation-intensive as the strategy presented in Section 8.4.3. Therefore, this strategy has been chosen for the creation of the complete mapping in MARE. It is compared to the basic strategy presented in Section 8.4.1 in the evaluation of MARE (cf. Chapter 10).

8.5 Result Validation

The validation of the clustering result is a manual task, that is supported by simple tools in the prototypical MARE implementation. This section shows how the clustering result can be interpreted in order to find weaknesses of the complete mapping and how these weaknesses can be approached by changing the configuration of the clustering.

8.5.1 Interpretation of the Result

The criteria for the interpretation of the results are to gain a functionally meaningful mapping of source elements and target components with a high cohesion in relation to the highly weighted dependency types. Furthermore, with regard to the restructuring of the implementation unwanted dependencies should be reduced as much as possible.

8.5.1.1 Measuring Cohesion

In Section 2.4.2, existing metrics for cohesion were described. Since these are defined on the class-level, they are not suited for the measurement of cohesion of the more coarse-grained target components of MARE. There is no known metric to measure the cohesion of an arbitrary set of source elements with individually selected and weighted dependency types. However, the redefinition of LCOM by Hitz and Montazeri (1995) can easily be extended to measure the cohesion of target components in relation to the source elements mapped to it. It is defined employing the connectivity of a graph of methods with method calls and instance variable accesses as edges. Based on this definition one can derive a metric for the *Lack of Cohesion in Source Elements* (LCOSE) by extending the graph to the graph model defined in Section 8.2.2. LCOSE is then defined as the number of connected subgraphs of the graph. However, it is not clear whether all dependency types should be considered for the computation of LCOSE, which would lead to the highest possible level of cohesion, or only selected dependency types, which better reflect the intended decomposition criteria and probably give a more realistic view.

Furthermore, the criticism of Hitz and Montazeri (1995), that LCOM returns a value of 1 for all kinds of connected graphs, also holds for the the definition of LCOSE. In many cases the source elements mapped to a target component will form a connected graph and a more fine grained graduation of cohesion is necessary. Therefore, the connectivity metric of Hitz and Montazeri (1995), which is defined as $2 * \frac{|E| - (n-1)}{(n-1)*(n-2)}$ (cf. Equation 2.1 on page 21) can also be adopted here.

Since the edges in the MARE graph are weighted and the weights have a decisive meaning for the restructuring process, an extended metric called *Weighted Connectivity* can also be defined.

$$WeightedConnectivity = 2 * \frac{|D_{tc}| - (n_{tc} - 1)}{(n_{tc} - 1) * (n_{tc} - 2)} * \frac{\sum \omega(d_{tc})}{|D_{tc}| * \bigcap_{d \in D} \omega(d)} \quad (8.6)$$

with n_{tc} being the number of source elements in the target component, D_{tc} being the set of dependencies in the target component, and $d_{tc} \in D_{tc}$. $\sum \omega(d_{tc})$ denotes the sum of the weights of all dependencies between the source elements mapped to the target component and $\bigcap_{d \in D} \omega(d)$ denotes the average weight of all dependencies in the graph model.

Weighted Connectivity considers the ratio of the weights of internal dependencies of the target component to the weights of all dependencies in the graph. Thus, the connectivity value is higher if the average dependency weight inside the target component is higher than the average dependency weight of the whole graph. Thus, results of complete mappings created with different dependency type weights are more comparable.

However, the reference mappings used in the case studies in Chapter 10, which represents the optimal complete mapping, indicate that the cohesion metrics defined above are at least not appropriate in every case to characterise a high quality of the complete mapping. The reference mapping of the preliminary case studies shows acceptable cohesion values for the metrics. The LCOSE value is 1 for all target components and the values for Connectivity and Weighted Connectivity have a mean value of 0.33 and 0.43, respectively. However, the single values are widely scattered, between 0.14 and 0.66 as well as 0.17 and 0.94, respectively. The reference mapping open source case study on the other hand has an average LCOSE value of 3.12 with a maximum value of 10. The five target components with a LCOSE value of 1 also have a very low average connectivity of 0.02. This shows, that the intended cohesion is not in any case measurable with the available metrics.

Hence, it is not clear whether the presented metrics for cohesion can be used to indicate a good quality of the complete mapping. Therefore, they are not used in the evaluation of MARE. Instead, the examination whether existing metrics for cohesion are suited for the rating of the quality of the complete mapping or whether new metrics for the cohesion of coarse-grained modules are needed that better reflect the decomposition criteria of the target architecture and the intentions of the architects are needed is subject to future work.

Sindhgatta and Pooloth (2007) question the role of coupling and cohesion for the definition of the decomposition of software systems in the context of architecture reconstruction. They state that developers decompose systems rather on the basis of a similar purpose of the source elements than on the basis of low coupling and high cohesion. Thus, the modules in such decompositions often have a high coupling and a low cohesion in terms of structural dependencies between source elements. In the context of architecture restructuring it is meaningful to consider high coupling in terms of structural dependencies, because the coupling of target components influences the restructuring of the implementation in terms of the resolution of unwanted dependencies. However, cohesion in the context of

MARE should be measured in terms of the decomposition criteria of the target architecture, which includes the similarity of purpose and depends on the developers intention. Thus, coupling and cohesion can have a different measurement basis and high cohesion can not be equated with low coupling.

Furthermore, cohesion can only be an indicator for the quality of the complete mapping. Provided that the dependency weights represent a good mapping of the decomposition criteria of the target architecture, high cohesion can indicate, that a good mapping has been found. Nevertheless, high cohesion of the target components in the complete mapping alone does not guarantee a good clustering result with respect to the feasibility of the restructuring of the implementation. A high coupling caused by unwanted dependencies can still make the restructuring unfeasible or cause the necessity of an adjustment of the target architecture. On the other hand, high coupling is no indicator for a low quality of the complete mapping, because it may not be possible to produce a complete mapping with low coupling because of the dependencies in the existing implementation.

Since it is unclear whether the presented cohesion metrics are suitable, a weaker indicator for the common goals of high cohesion and low coupling in software architectures is used in the evaluation. It is assumed, that a good quality is given, when a component has more internal dependencies than external dependencies. Therefore, the ratio between internal and external dependencies is considered as an indicator for the quality of a clustering. It is assumed, that a higher value of this ratio implies a higher quality of the complete mapping.

8.5.1.2 Wrongly Mapped Source Elements

In many cases, a user with a certain knowledge about the system can find wrongly mapped elements by browsing the mappings of single target components. However, especially for complex systems, a more goal-oriented approach is necessary. There are several strategies for how a user can approach the interpretation of the result and find wrongly mapped source elements.

Examine elements first, that were mapped early in the clustering process
Source elements that are mapped wrong early in the clustering process have a high impact on the subsequent clustering process and can cause the wrong mapping of further source elements that have a high similarity to them. Hence, the examination of early clustered source elements can reveal wrongly mapped source elements with a high influence on the quality of the overall complete mapping. If the *Consolidating Iterations* strategy is used to reduce the negative influence

of arbitrary decisions, also the examination of the intermediate initial mappings produced by the strategy can be helpful to find such source elements.

Examine unwanted dependencies   Another approach to find wrongly mapped elements is to examine the unwanted dependencies between two target components. Since these dependencies have to be resolved during the restructuring of the implementation, they are good candidates to find source elements that are mapped adversely for the restructuring of the implementation.

8.5.2 Criteria for Configuration Changes

This section lists criteria for the change of the clustering configuration in order to gain a clustering result, that better suits the requirements of the restructuring of the implementation. The main influence factor for the effort of the restructuring of the implementation are the unwanted dependencies between two target components. In order to reduce the effort, these dependencies have to be reduced by changing the clustering configuration. Thereby, the adjustment of the target architecture takes a special role.

8.5.2.1 Adjustment of the Target Architecture

An important problem that arises in the creation of the complete mapping are concurrent goals, that are pursued with this complete mapping. On the one hand, the conformance between the restructured implementation and the target architecture is expected to be high, in order to ease future maintenance of the system. On the other hand, the effort of the restructuring should be as low as possible, in order to provide a usable system as soon as possible. Furthermore, the effort should be below the effort for the implementation and migration to a completely new system.

When it becomes clear during the interpretation of the clustering result, that it is unfeasible to restructure the implementation to the given target architecture, a possibility to still enable the restructuring is to adjust the target architecture. The adjustment is a crucial configuration change, since all other inputs for the clustering are possibly affected as well. Possible adjustments of the target architecture range from the extension of interfaces to allow for further dependencies to changes in the component structure and decomposition criteria.

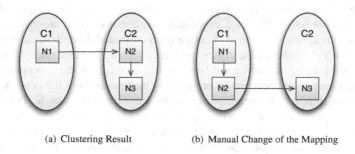

(a) Clustering Result   (b) Manual Change of the Mapping

Figure 8.7: Example for the Change of the Initial Mapping

8.5.2.2 Further Configuration Changes

Whether a dependency is unwanted or not, depends on the target architecture. This especially means, that not only dependencies, that result from maintenance tasks, that did not respect the source architecture of the system, tend to be classified as unwanted, as it is mostly the case in architecture reconstruction. On the contrary, such dependencies may even conform to the target architecture, while other dependencies, that conform to the source architecture may be unwanted in the target architecture, since the source and target source element are mapped to different target components.

Unwanted dependencies can be reduced by changing the configuration of the clustering. The main influence factors for the reduction are the initial mapping and the dependency type weights. However, some dependencies cannot be removed in this way and have to be resolved in the restructuring of the implementation.

Change of the Initial Mapping   The initial mapping allows the user to define manual mapping decisions. Thus, for the case that two elements, that are mapped to different clusters, lead to an unwanted dependency and the user is able to manually map them to a common target component, this decision can be expressed in the initial mapping. The decision should also regard further dependencies of the source elements, as they can lead to new dependencies between the affected clusters. Figure 8.7 shows a simplified example of this situation. Furthermore, the manual mapping of a single source element can induce the unforeseen automatic mapping of further source elements, which may also lead to unwanted dependencies or wrongly mapped source elements.

Change of Dependency Type Weights   By changing dependency type weights, a user does not only influence a single mapping decision, but a number of equal decisions throughout the system. Starting from unwanted dependencies, it can be analysed, which kinds of dependency types are affected more than once. If in these cases a mapping of the source and target source elements of the dependencies to the same target component can be preferred to the resolution of the dependencies in the restructuring of the implementation, the increase of the weight for this dependency type can be used to influence the clustering result. Since the weight is an attribute of the edge in the graph model and not an attribute of the edge type, it can also be changed for single dependencies. However, the manual change of single dependency weights leads to an enormous human effort in the analysis of a system, wherefore the change of weights on the level of dependency types is preferred.

8.6 Summary

This chapter introduced the clustering algorithm used by MARE to create the complete mapping of source elements to target components. The chapter discussed the quality criteria of the complete mapping. The main criteria are that all source elements are mapped and that the clusters created by the clustering algorithm can be clearly mapped to target components so that the user does not have to interpret the clustering result in order to be able to use the mapping in the further restructuring process. Based on this, the quality criteria are the similarity to an according manual mapping and measures like coupling and cohesion, whereas the latter are only partially applicable.

In Section 8.2 the MARE clustering algorithm was introduced. The section introduces the underlying analyses model and discusses differences to conventional hierarchical clustering algorithms. The MARE clustering algorithm is an adjusted graph clustering algorithm that includes a pre-clustering phase to incorporate the initial mapping and stops when only component clusters and disconnected clusters are left. The similarity of singular clusters is computed by the sum of the dependency type weights of the dependencies between two connected nodes. The similarity to newly merged composite clusters can be computed by applying different updating rules and similarity functions. The properties of these are subject of the following evaluation.

Furthermore, the chapter discussed the impact of dependencies on the clustering. It is exemplarily shown that different types of dependencies should be considered in the clustering and how weights can be used to rate the influence of the types. It was also shown, why it can be useful to consider the number of several dependencies of the same type between two source elements.

Another relevant influence factor on the clustering are arbitrary decisions. It is shown how arbitrary decisions can negatively influence the stability of a clustering algorithm. Section 8.4 discusses different strategies to cope with this influence. The strategies include the reduction of arbitrary decisions by using more detailed information in the computation of the similarity of clusters during the clustering and the introduction of consolidating iterations to find constantly clustered source elements and use this information to stabilise the final clustering result.

The validation of the clustering result is another important task in the MARE process. This chapter showed how the result can be interpreted in terms of cohesion and wrongly mapped source elements. Particularly, the measurement of cohesion is an open challenge in the MARE context. Existing cohesion metrics are not applicable since the are mostly defined for small-grained modules such as classes or files. Since the modules considered by MARE are more coarse-grained, the portability of the existing metrics is discussed and according metrics are proposed. However, the examination of the reference mapping of the evaluation shows that it is not clear whether the presented metrics for cohesion can be used to indicate a good quality of the complete mapping. Therefore, the measurement of the cohesion of coarse-grained modules will be subject of future work. Hence, a weaker indicator to measure the quality in terms of high cohesion and low coupling in the evaluation is proposed. It computes the ratio of internal to external dependencies of a target component.

Finally, the chapter introduced criteria for the change of the configuration based on the validation of the clustering result. These include the adjustment of the target architecture when it is unfeasible to restructure the implementation to the given target architecture.

Part III

Evaluation

9 Evaluation Methods

This chapter describes the goals and methods of the evaluation of MARE. Section 9.1 introduces the two main goals of the evaluation: the quality and the stability of the clustering algorithm. Section 9.2 gives an introduction to the GQM method and defines the MARE GQM plan which is the basis of the evaluation.

9.1 Goals of the Evaluation

The main goal of the evaluation is to show the applicability of MARE. The focus of the evaluation lies on the evaluation of the clustering algorithm. It is subdivided into two subgoals: the evaluation of the quality of the clustering results and a sensitivity analysis to show the stability of the results for changing inputs of the clustering.

The complete MARE process can not be evaluated in practice, since it covers the complete process of the restructuring of a system. This process can reach over a long time span and requires a suitable restructuring project, which was not feasible in the scope of this dissertation. Nonetheless, some parts of the GQM plan deal with the reaction of the MARE clustering algorithm on changing inputs and thus provide insights to the execution of the architecture restructuring iteration cycle.

9.1.1 Quality of the MARE Clustering

The quality of the MARE clustering algorithm is crucial for the use of MARE. The resulting complete mapping has to provide a high quality since it is the basis for the restructuring of the implementation. In order to provide helpful support in the restructuring of a system the automatic mapping executed by the clustering algorithm needs to have a significant impact on the creation of the complete mapping. Therefore, a high degree of the source elements have to be mapped correctly. To measure the correctness of the complete mapping, reference mappings can be employed for the evaluation of MARE. The reference mappings are created by experts or derived from the implementation of completed restructuring projects and can thus be used to assess the quality of the complete mapping created by MARE.

Another indicator for the quality of the complete mapping is the cohesion of target components, which was discussed in Section 8.5.

Another criterion for the quality of MARE is the traceability of the influence of the configuration on the complete mapping. An important aspect thereof is also, that strategies can be specified for the definition of dependency type weights and the creation of the initial mapping. Since MARE has not been applied in long-term industrial projects yet, no mature strategies can be defined in this dissertation. Nonetheless, the results of the case studies in Chapter 10 can give first hints about important influencing factors.

Furthermore, the technical clustering algorithm quality is another aspect of the evaluation. It is examined which impact the consolidating iterations for the reduction of the negative influence of arbitrary decisions has on the clustering result.

9.1.2 Stability

The stability of the clustering algorithm is an important factor for the applicability of MARE. Changes to the configuration should always result in more or less predictable changes of the resulting complete mapping. Stability of the clustering algorithm is important for the usability of a clustering method, since unpredictable changes of the result as a reaction to small changes in the input values or configuration of a clustering algorithm will reduce the users trust in the method.

Tzerpos and Holt (2000) define a clustering algorithm to be stable *if the obtained clusters are not grossly affected by slight modifications in its input*. Since they use clustering in the context of continuous architecture reconstruction, the input to be modified is different to the input in MARE. The only input modification Tzerpos and Holt (2000) consider is the modification of the source system. In MARE, however, the source system is not changed and also the source system model and the target architecture are not subject to frequent changes. On the other hand, dependency type weights and the initial mapping are more likely to change. Thus, these are the main subject of a sensitivity analysis performed in one of the case studies in Chapter 10.

The term *slight modification* also has to be refined for the MARE context. Tzerpos and Holt (2000) define it by means of the modifications to a software system during a few days of development. For MARE a slight modification can be defined as a modification typically made to the configuration in the course of one iteration of MARE Clustering. Since there is no extensive experience of the use of MARE in practice, a slight modification is assumed to be the change of a single dependency type weight value x in the interval $[\frac{x}{5}, 5x]$. For changes in the initial mapping a slight modification is assumed to be the addition of up to 3% of the number of source elements.

The *grossly affection* of the clustering result is defined by Tzerpos and Holt (2000) using the MoJo metric as defined in Tzerpos and Holt (1999). They use MoJo to compare the results of the clustering of the unchanged input and the slightly modified input with a large number of different modifications. They assume a clustering algorithm to be stable if 80% of the comparisons reveal a small MoJo value. Thereby, the definition of *small* is relative to the source system, since MoJo measures the absolute number of *Move* and *Join* operations needed to transfer one clustering result to another and this number depends on the number of source elements in the source system model.

9.2 GQM Plan

The evaluation of MARE is executed on the basis of a GQM plan. Section 9.2.1 briefly introduces the GQM approach. Section 9.2.2 describes the MoJo metrics, which are used in the evaluation of MARE. Further metrics are described directly in the MARE GQM plan, since their definition is less complex. The MARE GQM plan, which is the basis for the evaluation in the case studies that are describe in Section 10, is described in Section 9.2.3.

9.2.1 GQM Basics

The Goal Question Metric (GQM) approach was introduced by Basili et al. (1994). GQM is a procedure model for measurement. It bases on the assumptions, that measurements should follow certain goals and that the interpretation of results should base on predefined expected values. As depicted in Figure 9.1 GQM consists of three levels. The goals of the measurement are defined on the conceptual level. Each goal is described by a set of attributes. These are the *Purpose* of the measurement, a quality *Issue*, a measurement *Object* and a *Viewpoint*, that determines the emphases and expectations of the measurement.

For each goal a number of questions is defined on the operational level. The questions concretise the goal and determine the expected quality of the measurement. The quantitative level defines a set of metrics. These metrics are used to answer the questions defined on the operational level. Thereby, a metric can be associated to several questions. Basili et al. (1994) distinguish objective and subjective metrics. The latter depend on the object and the viewpoint of the goal, while

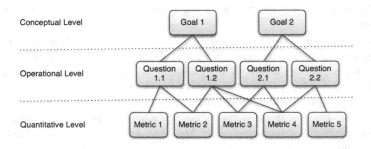

Figure 9.1: GQM Levels (Based on Basili et al. (1994))

the former only depend on the object. The MARE GQM plan employs objective metrics, which are partly supplemented by subjective expert ratings.

9.2.2 MoJo Metrics

This section gives a brief overview of the MoJo metrics, that are commonly used to measure the quality of clustering results. Further, more simple metrics, that are used in the evaluation are described in the according subsections of Section 9.2.3.

9.2.2.1 MoJo

MoJo is a common metric for the comparision of clustering results. It was originally presented by Tzerpos and Holt (1999). MoJo measures the similarity of two clustering results A and B by the minimum number of *Move* and *Join* operations $(mno(A,B))$ on nodes and clusters, that are necessary to transform one result into the other. Since it is possible that $mno(A,B) \neq mno(B,A)$, the minimum of both is taken. This case can occur, when the number of clusters is different in A and B, since the joining of cluster can be executed by a single *Join* operation, while the splitting of clusters requires several *Move* operations. The metric is formalised as

$$MoJo(A,B) = min(mno(A,B), mno(B,A)) \qquad (9.1)$$

9.2.2.2 MoJoFM

MoJoFM was introduced by Wen and Tzerpos (2004). It is a metric based on MoJo, that is used to measure the difference between a clustering result A and a reference mapping B in percent. In order to do so, the maximum distance between all possible clustering results of the clustering ($\forall A$) and the reference mapping B denoted by $max(mno(\forall A, B))$ is calculated. The metric is formalised as

$$MoJoFM(A,B) = (1 - \frac{mno(A,B)}{max(mno(\forall A,B))}) * 100\% \qquad (9.2)$$

Since the transformation from the clustering result to the reference mapping is the main interest, only $mno(A,B)$ and not $mno(B,A)$ is used. To calculate MoJo and MoJoFM the implementation by the York University was used[1] in the evaluation of MARE.

9.2.3 MARE GQM Plan

The MARE GQM plan bases on the goals defined in Section 9.1. It consists of the two goals *Quality* (cf. Section 9.1.1) and *Stability* (cf. Section 9.1.2) and according questions and metrics, that are described in the following.

9.2.3.1 Goal 1: Quality

Purpose Quantify

Issue the quality

Object of the MARE clustering algorithm

Viewpoint from the MARE user's viewpoint

Question 1.1: Which quality of the complete mapping can be reached?

This question targets the best quality of the complete mapping, that can be reached with the capabilities of MARE. This is also an indicator for the suitability of the complete mapping for the restructuring of the implementation in the last step of the MARE process.

In order to consider the iterative character of MARE, experiments with different inputs have to be conducted in the case studies. Since the dependency weights and the initial mapping are more likely to be changed than the target architecture and the source system model, these will be the emphases in the experiments. It is expected, that the quality will increase for adjusted dependency type weights and additions to the initial mapping.

---

[1] http://www.cse.yorku.ca/~bil/downloads/

Metrics for Question 1.1

Number of source elements per target component: With regard to maintainability, it can be argued, that all target components on the same hierarchical level should have the same number of source elements. In practice this will seldom be the case, because even for target components on the same hierarchical level the complexity of the implementation of a component varies. The is specially true in reengineering, since the current system will influence the target architecture. Therefore, it is at least expected, that the number of source elements per target components fits the ratio of all source elements that is expected by a system expert. Hence, concrete values for a high or low quality of the mapping depend on the concrete systems.

If a reference mapping is available, it is expected that the clustering creates target components, that fit the dimensions of the according target components in the reference mapping. Since there are more expressive metrics to compare a clustering result to a reference mapping, this metric is not computed in this case.

Ratio of internal to external dependencies: The ratio of internal to external dependencies can be seen as an indicator for the cohesion of a target component. It is expected, that the ratio is significantly higher than 1.0 for cohesive target components. However, the concrete value depends on the characteristics of the source system and the target architect as well as the chosen dependency types. A ratio under 1.0 indicates, that the target component has more external than internal dependencies which, so that the cohesion is very low for the considered dependency types. This indicates a low quality of the mapping provided that the dependency types reflect the decomposition criteria of the system.

MoJo: MoJo is used to compare the clustering result with a reference mapping. It is expected, that the MoJo value decreases for adjusted dependency weights and improved initial mappings. An absolute value can not be defined here, since it depends on the characteristics of the evaluated system.

MoJoFM: MoJoFM is used to compare the clustering result with a reference mapping. It is expected, that the MoJoFM value increases for adjusted dependency weights and improved initial mappings. A MoJoFM value of 80-90% is assumed to be useful for the subsequent implementation restructuring.

Number of correctly mapped source elements (NCMSE): To compute the number of correctly mapped source elements, all source elements, that are mapped to the same target component in the complete mapping produced by MARE and the reference mapping, are counted. It is expected that the sum of NCSME and the MoJo value of the considered complete mapping corresponds to the total number of source elements. The reason for this is, that MoJo should only measure move operations in the context of MARE , because the joining of clusters is not very likely, since the number of clusters is the same for both mappings.

Percentage of correctly mapped source elements (PCMSE): This metric computes the percentage of correctly mapped source elements in relation to the total number of source elements. Hence, the PCMSE value is 100% if all source elements are mapped correctly compared to a reference mapping. It is 0% when all source elements are mapped to other target components than in the reference mapping. Thus, the minimum PCMSE value is the percentage of initially mapped source elements of the number of all source elements in the source system model. It is expected, that the metric corresponds to MoJoFM, since both measure the difference to the reference mapping in percent.

Expert Rating: In cases where no reference mapping is available, the fact whether a complete mapping fits the decomposition criteria of the target architecture can only be rated by a system expert. This metric is the only subjective metric used in the MARE GQM plan. It is applied only if no reference mapping exists.

Question 1.2: What is a good choice for dependency type weights?

The question targets the finding of the best possible set of dependency type weights for the respective case studies. In order to find a good choice, the complete mapping resulting from several clustering runs that employ different dependency type weights, while the rest of the configuration remains stable, have to be compared.

It is assumed that a good choice of dependency type weights depends on the decomposition criteria of the target architecture and the characteristic dependency types of the system under study. Therefore, the criteria for the definition of the dependency type weights, that lead to the complete mapping with the best quality, are also of interest. They can give useful hints for the definition of common strategies to define good choices of dependency type weights for the first iteration of MARE Clustering in practical restructuring projects.

Metrics for Question 1.2
The metrics used to answer this question, are the same metrics that are defined to determine the best overall quality of the resulting complete mappings for Question 1.1. The expected values also conform to the expectation described for Question 1.1.

Question 1.3: Which characteristics should source elements in the initial mapping have?
The question targets the finding of the best possible strategy to define the initial mapping for the respective case studies. In order to find a good strategy, the complete mapping resulting from several clustering runs that employ initial mappings, that were created using different strategies, while the rest of the configuration remains stable, have to be compared. It is assumed, that such a strategy can be used for the definition of initial mappings for the first iteration of MARE Clustering in practical restructuring projects.

Metrics Question for 1.3
The metrics used to assess this question, are the same metrics that are defined to determine the best overall quality of the resulting complete mappings for Question 1.1. The expected values also conform to the expectation described for Question 1.1.

Question 1.4: How do consolidating iterations influence the quality of the clustering result?
This question does not target the MARE process model, but only the technical implementation of the MARE clustering algorithm. It examines the decision to use consolidating iterations to reduce the negative influence of arbitrary decisions.

Metrics for Question 1.4
The metrics defined for Question 1.1 can also used to approach this question. It is expected, that the quality of the complete mapping is more stable with the use of consolidating iterations and that it is averagely higher, since the number of low quality results is reduced. It is also assumed, that the number of consolidating iterations also increases the quality up to a level at which the quality of the results remains stable.

9.2.3.2 Goal 2: Stability

Purpose Quantify

Issue the stability

Object of the MARE clustering algorithm

Viewpoint from the MARE user's viewpoint

Question 2.1: How does the complete mapping change for modifications to the dependency type weights?

This question targets the stability of the MARE clustering algorithm regarding slight modifications of the dependency type weights. To measure the stability only single dependency weights are modified. The examination of the stability regarding modifications of several dependency type weights as once is more complex, since the interactions of different dependency types have to be regarded. Therefore, the extension to the change of the weights of different dependency types at once is left for future work.

Metrics for Question 2.1

Comparison with a reference mapping:

To measure the change of the complete mapping for slight modifications of the dependency weights, the same metrics as for Question 1.1 can be used, if a reference mapping is avaiable. It is expected, that the values for the metrics will also only change slightly. I.e. e.g. up to 2% for MoJoFM and PCMSE.

Comparison of complete mappings without reference mapping:

Beside the usage in the comparison of a given complete mapping to a reference mapping as mentioned for Question 1.1, the PCMSE metric can also be used for the comparison of two different complete mappings resulting from different configurations of the MARE clustering algorithm. Correctly clustered is interpreted as clustered identically in this case. PCMSE in contrast to MoJoFM is a symmetric metric. I.e. $PCMSE(A,B) = PCMSE(B,A)$ for two clustering result A and B. Therefore, it is better suited for the comparison of two clustering results than MoJoFM. It is expected, that the measurement of PCMSE results in values of more than 95% to fulfil the requirements for a high stability of the clustering algorithm. An algorithm with strongly unstable results is less appropriate in practice, since the results are less comprehensible and reliable.

Question Q 2.2: How does the complete mapping change for modifications to the initial mapping?

This question targets the stability of the MARE clustering algorithm regarding slight modifications of the initial mapping. To measure the stability complete mappings, that were created employing initial mappings which vary in the number of mapped source elements of about 3% are compared.

Metrics for Question 2.2

The metrics and expectations used to answer this question, are the same metrics and expectations, that are defined to measure the stability of the clustering algorithm for different dependency type weights for Question 2.1.

10 Case Studies

This chapter presents the results of three case studies, that were conducted to evaluate the quality and stability of the complete mappings created by MARE clustering. Section 10.1 describes a preliminary case study with a small Java reference implementation, that was used to examine and accentuate the concepts of MARE and create initial versions of the prototypical implementation.

The most extensive case study is presented in Section 10.2. In this section the already completed restructuring a middle-sized open source system is reproduced using MARE . Thus, the case study gives deeper insights to the usage of MARE in practice and enables the rating of the quality of the results.

Section 10.3 presents an industrial case study in which MARE is applied in a restructuring project of a large industrial system. Since the project is not yet finished, the results are not suited to rate the quality of the complete mapping created by MARE. On the other hand it shows, that MARE can also be applied to large software systems and gives insights in the quality and behaviour of the clustering algorithm.

The case studies are divided into experiments. To avoid misunderstandings it has to be stressed here that these are not experiments in terms of controlled experiments as e.g. introduced by Easterbrook et al. (2007), since the required level of control can not be ensured in the case studies. The experiments rather represent different tasks in the case studies that examine different configuration aspects of MARE.

10.1 Preliminary Case Study

10.1.1 Setting

The preliminary case study targets the restructuring of the iBATIS JPetStore 5. The JPetStore is a reference implementation of the iBATIS O/R mapper, which was meanwhile renamed to *myibatis*[1]. The current JPetStore consists of one component with a package structure that is decomposed following technical criteria. As shown in Figure 10.1 the package structure is subdivided into four packages, from

---

[1] http://code.google.com/p/mybatis/

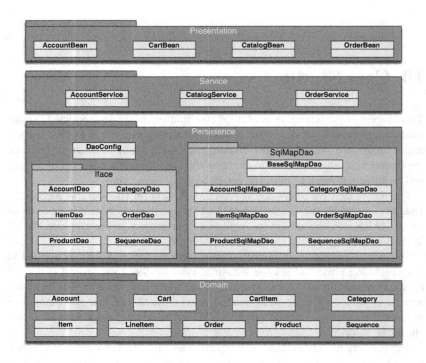

Figure 10.1: Package Structure of the JPetStore

which the *Persistence* package is further divided into an interface package and an implementation package. The figure also shows all classes and interfaces in the packages. The classes *DaoConfig* and *BaseSqlMapDao* do not contain functional code of the JPetStore, but technical code for the use of the iBATIS O/R mapper. The other classes represent the functionalities of the JPetStore and are considered in the clustering. The overall size of the considered classes and interfaces is about 1400 lines of code.

The goal of the restructuring is to divide the JPetStore into four separate components following a functional decomposition. This can be seen as an evolution towards service-oriented architectures (cf. Section 6.2.1) in the small. The target architecture of the JPetStore is depicted in Figure 10.2. The *Presentation* package is transferred unchanged into the *Presentation* component. The other target components focus on the functional aspects of the JPetStore, each implementing

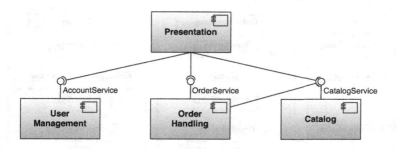

Figure 10.2: Target Architecture of the JPetStore

one of the services in the original *Service* package. The goal of the application of
MARE is to map the classes and interfaces of the packages *Service*, *Persistence*,
and *Domain* to the target components *User Management*, *Order Handling*, and
Catalog.

10.1.2 Experiment Design

To rate the results of MARE, a reference mapping was created, which is shown
in Figure 10.3. DaoConfig and BaseSqlMapDao are not included in the mapping,
since they are used in all three components. Possible solutions for this multiple
mapping problem are the duplication of the classes, the introduction of a further
target component for the classes, or the mapping to one of the existing target components. The *Presentation* component is omitted in the figure, since it remains
unchanged. The reference mapping was created by the author of this thesis based
on the functional connection of the classes with respect to the implementation of
the functionality provided by the classes in the original *Service* package.

The reference mapping includes 25 classes and interfaces. These share 170
dependencies. The reference mapping is used to compare the results of clusterings
with four different weight sets and four different initial mappings. The focus of
the experiments is Goal 1 of the MARE GQM plan, i.e. the quality of the MARE
results. The stability of the results is not target of the case study, since it is too
small to obtain meaningful results.

Table 10.1 lists the four weight sets, that are used in the experiments. The
Equal Weights set weights every dependency type with 1.0. The two *Ratio Weights*
sets are obtained from the ratio of internal and external dependencies in the reference mapping of all target components for each dependency type. Thereby, *Ratio*

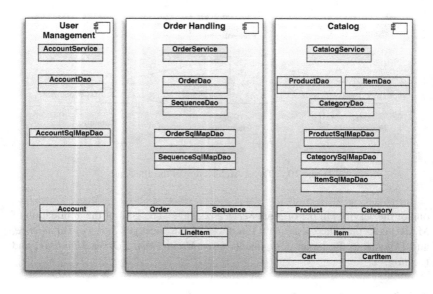

Figure 10.3: Reference Mapping of the JPetStore

Weights 1 only includes the dependencies of the functional source elements, while *Ratio Weights 2* also includes the dependencies of DaoConfig and BaseSqlMap-Dao. The *Best Weights* set is the set that led to the best complete mappings during the experiments.

The four initial mappings used in the experiments each map one source element to each target component. The source elements are taken from the same original package respectively. One mapping maps all service classes (*AccountService, OrderService,* and *CatalogService*) from the *Service* package. The remaining three initial mapping sets map the classes and interfaces that conform to the functional entities *Account, Order,* and *Product* as typical representatives of the *Domain, Persistence.Iface,* and *Persistence.SqlMapDao* packages.

The case study includes two experiments. Both experiments measure NCMSE and PCMSE for the presented weight sets and initial mappings.

Experiment 1 does only consider the source elements from the reference mapping, while Experiment 2 also considers the classes *DaoConfig* and *BaseSqlMapDao* in the clustering to see how these technical classes influence the clustering results. For this experiment the weight set (*Ratio Weights 2*) was introduced. It

Table 10.1: JPetStore Dependency Weights

DependencyType	Equal Weights	Ratio Weights 1	Ratio Weights 2	Best Weights
Return Type	1.0	21.0	21.0	17.0
Parameter Type	1.0	2.17	2.17	1.0
Constructor Parameter	1.0	3.0	3.0	1.0
Method Variable Type	1.0	7.0	7.0	1.0
Inheritance	1.0	6.0	2.0	1.0
Cast Type	1.0	6.67	6.67	1.0
Static Type	1.0	0.0	0.5	1.0
Method Call	1.0	1.29	1.24	1.0
Constructor Call	1.0	6.0	2.0	1.0

can be assumed, that this set leads to better results, since it better reflects the dependencies in the system.

There are no specific experiments regarding question 1.4, since no influence of arbitrary decisions could be detected during the work with the JPetStore. It is assumed, that the number and influence of arbitrary decision grows with the size of the system.

10.1.3 Validity

The main threats to validity lie in the external validity of the case study. The transferability of the results to other systems is limited for several reasons. The most striking reason is the size of the system. Especially in the context of an evolution to SOA, systems that have to be considered in practice are much larger and more complex. Another threat is the reference implementation character of the system. It was developed to present the capabilities of the iBATIS O/R mapper and does not show the signs of erosion, that are typical for systems with a longer maintenance history. Nonetheless, the case study allows insights to the operation of MARE and especially to the implemented clustering algorithm and gives hints to important issues that have to be regarded for the usage of MARE with larger systems.

10.1.4 Results

10.1.4.1 Experiment 1

Table 10.2 shows the NCMSE values for the clusterings without *DaoConfig* and *BaseSqlMapDao*. It can be seen, that the clustering employing the Best Weights set always maps all but one of the 25 source elements correctly (96% PCMSE). In all cases the one source element is the *LineItem* class. The reason for the wrong mapping is the strong dependency between *LineItem*, *Item*, and *CartItem*, which leads to the mapping of *LineItem* to the *Catalog* target component instead of the *Order* target component. Hence, the mapping can not be corrected by changing dependency type weights, but only by an explicit initial mapping.

Table 10.2: NCMSE Results Without DaoConfig and BaseSqlMapDao

	Service Mapping	Domain Mapping	Pers. Impl. Mapping	Pers. Iface Mapping
Best Weights	24	24	24	24
Ratio Weights 1	20	20	20	20
Equal Weights	18	21	15	18

Using the Ratio Weights 1 set, five source elements are mapped wrong in with all four initial mappings (80% PCMSE). The reason for this is similar to the reason for the Best Weights mapping. The five source elements are *Item*, *ItemSqlMapDao*, *CartItem*, *Cart* and *ItemDao*, which are clustered wrong because of their strong dependencies to *LineItem* and *Order*. The Equal Weights set provides the worst result with between 15 and 21 mapped source elements, which conforms to 60-84% PCMSE.

10.1.4.2 Experiment 2

Table 10.3 shows the NCMSE values for the clusterings with *DaoConfig* and *BaseSqlMapDao*. The two classes themselves are excepted from the calculation of NCMSE and PCMSE. The reason for this is, that both classes can be mapped correctly to all target components. Despite their exception, their dependencies influence the clustering and consequently also the mapping results as described in the following.

The weight sets Best Weights and Ratio Weights 1 lead to the same results as in Experiment 1. The Ratio Weights 2 set leads to slightly worse results, since the classes *Sequence* and *SequenceSqlMapDao* are also mapped wrong. The reason

Table 10.3: NCMSE Results With DaoConfig and BaseSqlMapDao

	Service Mapping	Domain Mapping	Pers. Impl. Mapping	Pers. Iface Mapping
Best Weights	24	24	24	24
Ratio Weights 1	20	20	20	20
Ratio Weights 2	18	18	18	18
Equal Weights	16	20	14	16

for this is supposed to be the influence of the addition of the two technical classes, which makes the ratio weights less clear, since their value is nearer to 1.0 and hence the Equal Weights set. The Equal Weights set itself again results in the worst NCMSE values.

10.1.5 Conclusions

The examination of the quality of the results show, that an almost ideal clustering with a PCMSE value of 96% can be reached. This high quality is owed to the small size and the reference implementation character of the JPetStore.

The results furthermore show that the weighting of dependency types on the basis of the ratio of the dependencies in the reference mapping leads to better results than equal weights for all dependency types. However, the best results regarding the weighting of dependency types could be obtained by weighting the *Return Type* dependency with at least 17.0 and all other dependency types with 1.0. The reason for this is assumed to be that this dependency type best reflects the decomposition criteria of the target architecture. It also has the highest ratio between internal and external dependencies of all dependency types.

Regarding the initial mappings, only minimal mappings were examined due to the low overall number of source elements. The NCMSE values for the different initial mappings only differ for the Equal Weights set. It can be seen, that the *Domain Mapping* leads to the best results, while the mapping that maps the persistence implementation classes produces the worst results. This indicates, that for the goal of a functional decomposition, the mapping of functional elements is better suited than elements with more relations to technical frameworks. However, this depends on the functionality and usage of the framework, so that in certain cases the consideration of framework usage can also lead to higher quality of the complete mapping.

In summary, the influence of the dependency weights on the result is higher than the influence of the initial mappings in this case study. However, this can not be generalised for all uses of MARE due to the small size and reference implementation character of the JPetStore.

10.2 Open Source Case Study

10.2.1 Setting

The setting of this case study is the reproduction of the integration of the opensource generator framework openArchitectureWare[2] (oAW) into the Eclipse Modeling Project[3] (EMP). During this process some parts of oAW had to be restructured to fit the projects in EMP. This kind of restructuring does not directly fit into one of the typical application scenarios described in Section 6.2, but can be seen as a kind of re-establishment or improvement of maintainability. OAW consists of four major parts: a workflow engine (called MWE in Eclipse), a facility for the extension and transformation of metamodels (Xtend), a generator (Xpand), and a framework for the creation of domain-specific languages (Xtext). The parts shared a common structure in oAW and became separate projects in EMP.

During the separation of the parts, commonly used code had to be assigned to one of the parts. Furthermore, the inner structure of the single parts was partially changed, leading to further architectural restructurings. Hence, the challenge of the integration is the decision over the target structure and the mapping of the source elements to target components. The latter can be supported by MARE. Since oAW is an open-source project and the integration is already completed, it has been chosen as a scenario for the evaluation of MARE. Furthermore, it has a size, that allows for a manual interpretation of the results. Hence, the current implementation of the oAW components in EMP can be used as a reference mapping for the validation of the results of the restructuring of the previous oAW version.

Since Xtext has been rewritten in major parts during the transition to Eclipse, it is not considered in the evaluation. Xpand is also not considered, since it is clearly separated from the other parts in both environments and remained nearly unchanged.

---

[2]http://www.openarchitectureware.org
[3]http://www.eclipse.org/modeling

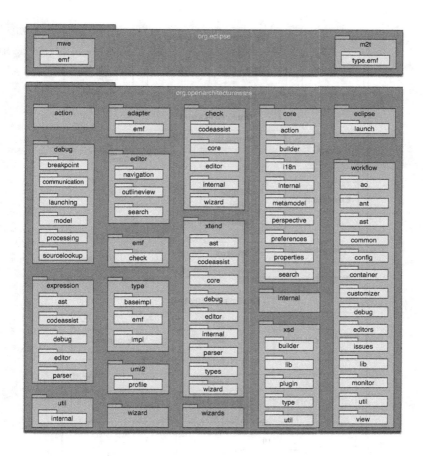

Figure 10.4: Package Structure of oAW

MWE and Xtend, however, were subject of larger restructurings and are inter-leaved in the modularisation of the source system. The considered restructurings are changes in the mapping of classes and subpackages to packages. The package structure of the considered packages is shown in Figure 10.4. MWE and Xtend contain 805 source elements (classes, interfaces and local classes), which have a total size of about 60000 lines of code. The packages were not considered as source elements, since they reflect the source architecture.

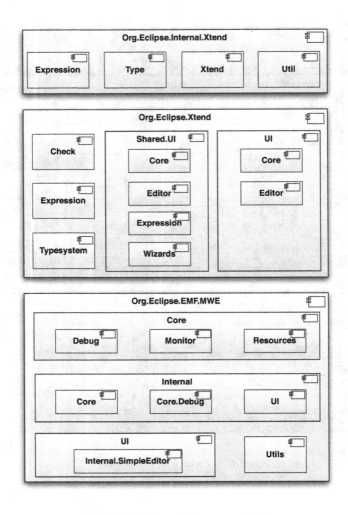

Figure 10.5: Target Architecture of oAW

The target architecture, as depicted in Figure 10.5, is derived from the pack-age structure of MWE and Xtend in EMP and consists of 25 target components to which the source elements are mapped. The figure shows 29 target compo-nents, but *Org.Eclipse.Internal.Xtend, Org.Eclipse.Xtend.UI, Org.Eclipse.EMF.-*

MWE, and *Org.Eclipse.EMF.MWE.Internal* do not contain source elements directly and are thus not considered in the mapping. Furthermore, some subpackages where not considered as target components in the target architecture, because they remained unchanged during the restructuring. Their source elements are mapped to the according parent target components. The interfaces and allowed dependencies of the target components are omitted for more clarity.

10.2.2 Experiment Design

Since the integration of oAW into EMP is already completed and thus a reference mapping exists for the target architecture, all quantitative metrics of the GQM plan can be computed and thus all questions can be processed.

For the experiments a source system model has been created using SISSy[4]. The considered dependency types are the source code dependencies of Java 5 as described in Section 7.3.5 on page 114. These dependency types can easily be extracted with the existing tooling and they represent the functional coherence of the source elements. Furthermore, they also partly reflect the semantics of the source code and the intentions of the developers, since they are used to express semantic relations between source elements.

Although structural dependencies that reflect the source architecture are usually not considered in MARE, the containment of local classes in their parent classes, is considered in this case study, since their dependencies are also important for the mapping of their parent classes. All the more, because the containment of the local classes remained unchanged during the restructuring.

For the execution of the experiments, two sets of weights have been determined. They are listed in Table 10.4. The *Equal Weights (EW)* set weights every dependency with the same weight of 1.0. The *Best Weights (BW)* set represents the best dependency weights found in the course of the case study. The basis of the set are the ratios between internal and external dependencies of the respective types for all target components (cf. Table 10.9 on page 178). The according weights were adjusted based on the knowledge about the system and the experiences made with changing weights during the experiments with oAW.

The initial mapping strategies were also varied in the experiments. The basis for the Experiments 1 and 2 are five initial mappings, that map between 5% and 25% of the source elements. They were created iteratively, beginning with one representative source element for each target component and adding wrongly mapped source elements to the initial mapping in each iteration. Thereby, source elements,

---

[4]http://sissy.fzi.de/

Table 10.4: oAW Dependency Weights

DependencyType	Equal Weights	Best Weights
Return Type	1.0	0.32
Parameter Type	1.0	0.69
Constructor Parameter	1.0	0.9
Variable Type	1.0	2.25
Method Variable Type	1.0	0.6
Inheritance	1.0	3.6
Cast Type	1.0	0.62
Contained In	1.0	10.0
Static Type	1.0	1.35
Method Call	1.0	0.42
Constructor Call	1.0	5.0

that were assumed to have a high similarity to other wrongly mapped source elements were chosen first in order to achieve the best possible mapping for the subsequent iteration. Experiment 3 evaluates further mapping strategies and does not employ these five initial mappings. In Experiment 4 another initial mapping created earlier based on knowledge about the system was used, that covers 7.7% of the source elements.

The actual settings of all four experiments are described in the following subsections. Except for Experiment 1, all experiments were executed with 10 consolidating iterations of the clustering algorithm. To enable the rating of the effect of this decision, the first experiment targets the influence of theses iterations.

10.2.2.1 Experiment 1: Influence of Consolidating Iterations and Similarity Functions

To reduce the influence of arbitrary decisions on the clustering result, the MARE clustering algorithm includes the possibility to employ consolidating iterations. To examine the effect of this configuration option, clusterings without iterations and with 10 iterations are compared in this experiment for the two aforementioned weight sets. Furthermore, the updating rules *Unweighted Average Linkage* and *Sum* as well as the two similarity functions described in Section 8.2.4 on page 130 are compared.

10.2.2.2 Experiment 2: Comparison of Different Weight Sets and Updating Rules

The focus of this experiment is the comparison of the two weight sets defined above. Clusterings are executed with both sets, the updating rules *Unweighted Average Linkage* and *Sum*, and for the aforementioned five initial mappings. The experiment targets Question 1.1 and Question 1.2 of the GQM plan. MoJo, MoJoFM, NCMSE and PCMSE are used as metrics.

10.2.2.3 Experiment 3: Comparison of Different Initial Mapping Strategies

The focus of this experiment is the examination of the application of different strategies for the creation of the initial mapping. Therefore, three different strategies are compared: the mapping of source elements, that are strongly used by other target components (incoming dependencies), the mapping of source elements, that strongly use other target components (outgoing dependencies), and the mapping of source elements, that are strongly used inside the target component. The creation of the respective initial mapping bases on the dependencies in the reference mapping.

For the creation of the five initial mappings more fine-grained steps as for the creation of the initial mappings used in the previous experiments were considered. The initial mappings include between 25 (3.1%) and 200 (24.8%) source elements with steps of 25 source elements.

10.2.2.4 Experiment 4: Sensitivity Analysis

To measure the influence of the change of dependency type weights, a sensitivity analysis was conducted. The analysis was subject of the bachelor thesis of Florian Postel (2010). It examined the influence of the change of single dependency type weights on the complete mapping. The weights were changed in 21 steps from 0.0001 to 10000.

For the sensitivity analysis the Equal Weights set and a preceding version of the Best Weights set (*Sensitivity Weights*) were used. The concrete weights of the latter are listed in Table 10.5. A comparison of this set with the Best Weight set showed that the PCMSE values were 1-4% lower for the Sensitivity Weights set, but revealed a similar behaviour.

Table 10.5: Weights for the Sensitivity Analysis

DependencyType	Best Weights	Sensitivity Weights
Return Type	0.32	0.64
Parameter Type	0.69	0.69
Constructor Parameter	0.9	0.9
Variable Type	2.25	2.25
Method Variable Type	0.6	0.6
Inheritance	3.6	1.8
Cast Type	0.62	0.62
Contained In	10.0	15.0
Static Type	1.35	1.35
Method Call	0.42	0.85
Constructor Call	5.0	1.6

Furthermore, the target architecture was varied in this experiment. Supplementing the target architecture described before, the sensitivity analysis was also executed for a simple target architecture employing only the top-level components *MWE* and *Xtend* as target components. This was done to examine the influence of a hierarchical refinement of the target architecture in the iterations of the architecture restructuring iteration cycle as described in Section 7.1.1.

10.2.3 Validity

The main threats to the validity of the results of the case study are as in the preliminary case study seen in the portability of the results to the restructuring of other systems. In contrast to the preliminary case study, this case study bases on a software system, that is actively used and developed for several years and as such better represents the systems, that are typically target of restructurings. The remaining threats are, that the results are only valid for the Java 5 language and the programming conventions used by the oAW developers. Furthermore, with regard to restructuring, this is only one type of restructuring with individual reasons and decomposition criteria of the target architecture.

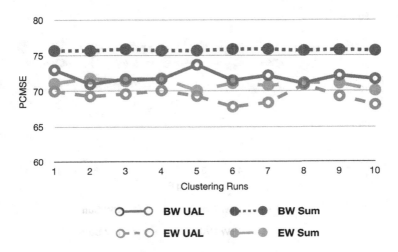

Figure 10.6: Experiment 1: Results without Consolidating Iterations for Updating Rules

10.2.4 Results

10.2.4.1 Experiment 1: Influence of Consolidating Iterations and Similarity Functions

The PCMSE results for the updating rules Sum and Unweighted Average Linkage (abbr. UAL in the figures) and the Best Weights (abbr. BW) set as well as the Equal Weights (abbr. EW) set are shown in Figure 10.6 and Figure 10.7. MoJo, MoJoFM and NCMSE lead to corresponding results. The 15% initial mapping set was chosen for all clusterings. It can be seen, that the results with 10 iterations are more stable for most configurations. Except for the Equal Weights set with the Sum updating rule, where the difference between minimum and maximum is 3.8%, the variation of the results is less than 1%.

Another exception are the results for the Best Weights set with the Sum updating rule for the clustering without iterations. It is as stable as most configurations with iterations and provides the best clustering results together with the same configuration for 10 iterations. For the other configurations without iterations the difference between maximum and minimum is between 1.7% and 3.1%.

Regarding the difference in the absolute quality for the results without and with consolidating iterations, the results are slightly different for the Best Weights set and the Equal Weights set. While for the Best Weights set the median of the results

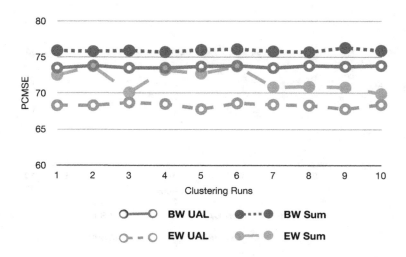

Figure 10.7: Experiment 1: Results for 10 Consolidating Iterations for Updating Rules

with iterations is 0.2% - 2% higher, it is 0.2% - 0.9% lower for the Equal Weights set. Given that also the most stable configurations vary to up to 1%, it can be said, that there is no clear difference in the absolute quality for clusterings with and without consolidating iterations.

The according PCMSE results for the similarity function defined by Koschke (2000) and the *Sum Relative to Nodes* (abbr. SumRel) function are shown in Figure 10.8 and Figure 10.9. It can be seen that the results are more stable than the result of the updating rules. The Sum Relative to Nodes function without iterations does even compute the same result for all clustering runs. Exceptions are the function defined by Kosche without iterations, which shows a variation of up to 4.1% for the Best Weights set, as well as the Sum Relative to Nodes functions with iterations, which shows a variation of up to 2.1% for the Equal Weights set. With regard to the influence of consolidating iterations no significant difference can be revealed. It is assumed, that this is a consequence of the already stable results of the clusterings without consolidating iterations. The in total higher stability conforms to the results of Maqbool and Babri (2007) who state that functions that include more information than pure updating rules lead to more stable clustering results since they reduce the number of arbitrary decisions.

Regarding the quality the result of the function by Koschke (2000) are very similar to the results of the Unweighted Average Linkage updating function. The

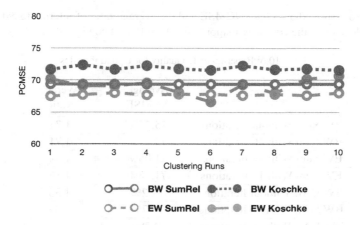

Figure 10.8: Experiment 1: Results without Consolidating Iterations for Composite Cluster Similarity Functions

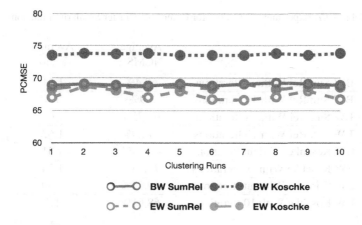

Figure 10.9: Experiment 1: Results for 10 Consolidating Iterations for Composite Cluster Similarity Functions

quality of the results of the Sum Relative to Nodes function on the other hand are the lowest of the experiment. To compare the quality in terms of similarity to the reference mapping and in terms of high cohesion and low coupling, Table 10.6 and

Table 10.7 show the average NCMSE and the average ratio of internal to external dependencies of the complete mapping for the different configurations.

Table 10.6: Experiment 1: Quality for Updating Rules

	Average NCMSE	Average Ratio
BW Sum Without Iterations	75.75%	1.71
BW Sum With 10 Iterations	75.91%	1.71
EW Sum Without Iterations	71.05%	1.84
EW Sum With 10 Iterations	71.83%	1.86
BW UAL Without Iterations	72.2%	1.33
BW UAL With 10 Iterations	73.7%	1.34
EW UAL Without Iterations	69.28%	1.5
EW UAL With 10 Iterations	68.31%	1.5

Table 10.7: Experiment 1: Quality for Composite Cluster Similarity Functions

	Average NCMSE	Average Ratio
BW SumRel Without Iterations	69,4%	1.61
BW SumRel With 10 Iterations	69%	1.6
EW SumRel Without Iterations	67.75%	1.67
EW SumRel With 10 Iterations	67.39%	1.62
BW Koschke Without Iterations	71.89%	1.31
BW Koschke With 10 Iterations	73.64%	1.34
EW Koschke Without Iterations	69.09%	1.49
EW Koschke With 10 Iterations	68.61%	1.5

It can again be seen that the results of the Unweighted Average Linkage updating rule and the similarity function defined by Koschke are almost identical. Regarding the ratio of internal to external dependencies the results indicate that the Sum updating rule and Sum Relative to Nodes function lead to more cohesive and less coupled clusters, while only the former also leads to a high quality in terms of the comparison to the reference mapping. This indicates that the two quality metrics are not equivalent.

Regarding the performance, the computation of the composite cluster similarity functions is more expensive than the computation of the updating rules. Table 10.8 shows the average computation time for the different configurations measured on a MacBook with 2GHz Intel Core Duo processor and 4GB RAM. It can be seen that especially the Sum Relative to Nodes function takes much longer to compute than the updating rules.

Table 10.8: Experiment 1: Performance for Different Configurations

	Without Iterations	With 10 Iterations
Sum	9s	12s
UAL	10s	18s
Koschke	13s	80s
SumRel	70s	700s

In summary, the results show that clustering with consolidating iterations leads to more stable results in most cases. The best results could be achieved with the Best Weights set and the Sum updating rule. However, since the Sum updating rule also created the most exceptional and therefore less predictable results and since the results of both updating rules were on a comparable level in most other experiments, the Unweighted Average Linkage updating rule is used as standard updating rule in the subsequent experiments. The composite cluster similarity functions are also not used in the subsequent experiments. The function defined by Koschke provides similar results as the Unweighted Average Linkage updating rule, but takes longer to be computed. Although the Sum Relative to Nodes function provides the most stable results, its quality and performance are the lowest of all compared functions.

10.2.4.2 Experiment 2: Comparison of Different Weight Sets and Updating Rules

Figure 10.10 shows the PCMSE values for clusterings with the two dependency type weight sets and different initial mappings. It can be seen that the Best Weights set always leads to better results than the Equal Weights set. The distance between the sets amounts to up to 5%. This can also be observed in the results of Experiment 1.

The MoJoFM values were also computed for these configurations. A result comparison of MoJoFM and PCMSE is depicted in Figure 10.11. The assumption, that both metrics lead to corresponding results could only be confirmed for a large

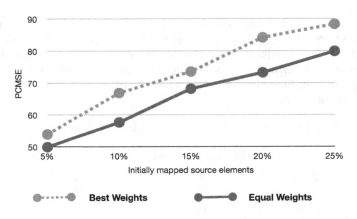

Figure 10.10: Experiment 2: Results for Best Weights and Equal Weights

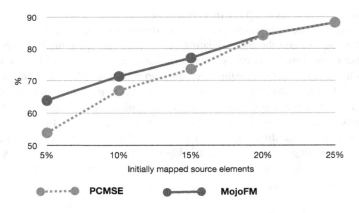

Figure 10.11: Experiment 2: Comparison of PCMSE and MoJoFM

number of initially mapped source elements or a high similarity with the reference mapping respectively. For the other initial mappings MoJoFM indicates better results than PCMSE.

The reason for these differences is, that MARE uses a fixed mapping of clusters to target components. MoJo on the other side is defined to compare clustering algorithms, that do not use such a fixed mapping. Hence, MoJoFM compares the most similar source element groups. I.e. when e.g. the assigned source elements of two clusters are exchanged completely, this will not change the MoJoFM value, but the PCMSE value will be much lower, since the groups are not correctly mapped to target compoents. This difference, however, is important for the validation of the MARE clustering results. The user examines the mapping of source elements to target components in the first place and not the possible fit of groups of the source elements to other target components. Hence, the result should reflect this in order to reduce the validation effort.

The quality of the results is not satisfactory for initial mappings including less than 20% of the source elements. The reason for this is assumed to be the low ratio of internal to external dependencies in the reference mapping. Internal dependencies are dependencies between two source elements in the same target component while external dependencies are dependencies between source elements in two different target components.

Table 10.9 lists the ratio for all dependencies in the reference mapping and for the single dependency types. It can be seen that the average ratio is only 1.15. Also the ratios for the single dependency types are mostly near to 1.0 with a maximum ratio of 2.84 for variable accesses. The ratios thus indicate no significant difference for the relation of source elements inside a target component and source elements in different target components. This is an indicator for a low cohesion of the target components in relation to the considered dependency types. In conclusion, this means that the original restructuring was not conducted with high cohesion and low coupling as a primary goal or that the chosen dependency types are not sufficient to define the cohesion of the target components.

In any case, the closeness of the ratios to 1.0 leads to a low influence of the dependency weights on the clustering result. The reason for this is, that the MARE clustering algorithm bases on the assumptions that target components have a high cohesion in relation to the decomposition criteria and that this relation can be mapped to dependency type weights. When the difference between internal an external dependencies and the difference between the ratios of different dependency types is low, the distinguishing aspect of the dependency weights declines. Thus, the initial mapping becomes the decisive factor of the clustering in this case study.

Nonetheless, the clustering results confirm that the clustering algorithm tends to create more cohesive target components. As Table 10.10 shows, the ratio is higher for clusterings with less initially mapped source elements. Hence, it can be concluded that the algorithm produces better results if the dependency type weights better reflect cohesion in relation to the decomposition criteria of the target architecture.

Table 10.9: Internal and External Dependencies

Dependency Type	Internal Dependen- cies	External Dependen- cies	Ratio
Total Number of Dependencies	4328	3748	1.15
Return Type	304	381	0.79
Parameter Type	357	452	0.79
Constructor Parameter	119	111	1.07
Variable Type	383	135	2.84
Method Variable Type	347	477	0.73
Inheritance	339	172	1.97
Cast Type	96	135	0.71
Contained In	310	0	
Static Type	261	221	1.18
Method Call	1401	1446	0.97
Constructor Call	411	218	1.89

Table 10.10: Internal and External Dependencies for Different Initial Mappings

	5%	10%	15%	20%	25%	Reference
Internal De- pendencies	4883	4955	4621	4519	4356	4328
External De- pendencies	3193	3121	3455	3557	3720	3748
Ratio	1.53	1.59	1.34	1.27	1.17	1.15

The assumption, that the sum of MoJo and NCMSE corresponds to the total number of source elements has also been examined in the experiment. Table 10.11 shows the according results. It can be seen, that the sum for the two largest initial mappings almost reaches the total number of 805 source elements. The higher difference for the other mappings is assumed to base on the same effects as the difference between MoJo and PCMSE. Thus, the assumption could be confirmed for this experiment setting.

Table 10.11: Results for MoJo and NCMSE for Best Weights and Different Initial Mappings

Metric	5%	10%	15%	20%	25%
MoJo	281	223	178	122	91
NCMSE	436	540	593	679	712
MoJo + NCMSE	717	763	771	801	803

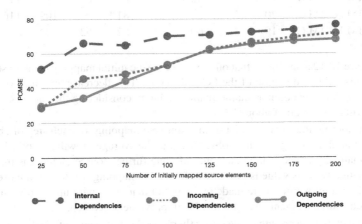

Figure 10.12: Experiment 3: Results for Different Initial Mapping Strategies

10.2.4.3 Experiment 3: Comparison of Different Initial Mapping Strategies

The results of the comparison of different initial mapping strategies are depicted in Figure 10.12. The results show, that for the oAW scenario the initial mapping of source elements with strong internal dependencies (*IM A*) provides better results than the initial mappings of source elements with strong external dependencies. Viewing only the latter shows, that the initial mapping of source elements with strong incoming dependencies (*IM B*) from other clusters induces a similar behaviour as the initial mapping of source elements with strong outgoing dependencies (*IM C*).

It was further examined whether the similarity of the results of *IM B* and *IM C* are a consequence of equal source elements in both initial mappings. Table 10.12 shows the number of different source elements in the three initial mapping sets. The pairwise comparison shows, that at least 50% of the elements are different for all pairs and sizes of the initial mapping sets. Hence, it is assumed, that the similarity results from the similarly strong binding to other target components, that is inherent to both initial mapping strategies.

Table 10.12: Number of Different Source Elements in the Different Initial Mappings

	25	50	75	100	125	150	175	200
IM A - IM B	15	30	42	59	68	85	98	110
IM A - IM C	20	39	58	70	81	97	109	116
IM B - IM C	19	39	60	73	82	93	102	111

Figure 10.12 also shows, that only in one case the initial mapping of more source elements led to a decrease of the PCMSE value. This decrease amounts to 1.2%. Hence, it does not count as major quality problem, considering the variation of the clustering algorithm of about 1%.

Considering the improvement of the complete mapping for each step of change of the initial mapping, it can be observed, that the average growth is 4-6%. I.e. for each manually added source element only one further source element is mapped automatically. This value is even lower for initial mappings of 20% and more. I.e. the major improvements are made in the initial mappings with up to 20% initially mapped source elements with up to 17% improvement per step.

The fact that the growth of the correctly mapped source elements in the complete mapping is smaller than the growth of the initial mapping and can also decrease for an initial mapping with more source elements as in IM A can have two reasons. The first is, that the creation of the initial mapping sets is not based on the clustering results with the smaller initial mapping sets. I.e. the initial mapping sets can include source elements, that were already mapped correctly by the algorithm for smaller initial mapping sets. This was since done the goal of this experiment is not to simulate the extension of the initial mapping in subsequent MARE Clustering iterations, but to find a good initial mapping strategy for the creation of an initial mapping in the first iteration.

Another reason can be, that the initial mapping of a source element SE entails the wrong automatic mapping of dependent source elements. This can be the case, when the source elements that belong to different target components are highly dependent. When all source elements were mapped to the same target component in the complete mapping created with the smaller initial mapping including a wrong mapping of SE, the initial mapping of SE can lead to the wrong mapping of the other source elements.

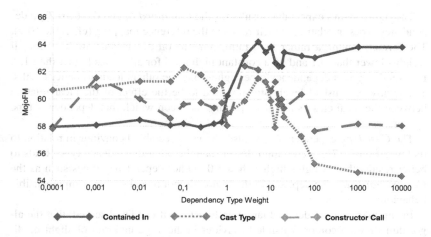

Figure 10.13: Experiment 4: Exemplary Sensitivity Analysis Results for the Detailed Target Architecture

The results indicate, that the initial mapping of core elements, that have many dependencies inside a target component, is more promising than the initial mapping of elements, that represent the interfaces of the target component. However, all three sets do not reach the quality of the results achieved with the initial mappings described in Section 10.2.2, that are based on knowledge about the system and the clustering behaviour. The results also show that the major support of the clustering algorithm can be expected for initial mappings of up to 20% of the source elements. Hence, the results indicate, that the best strategy for this case study would be to map at most 20% of the source elements that are supposed to have the many dependencies inside the target component in the first iteration of MARE Clustering, and then refine this initial mapping due to the resulting complete mapping.

10.2.4.4 Experiment 4: Sensitivity Analysis

The results of the sensitivity analysis are ambivalent. Figure 10.13 shows exemplary results for three different dependency types. All results in the figure were gained using the detailed target architecture model and the Equal Weights set for all but the analysed dependency type.

The figure shows expectable results for the *Contained In* and the *Cast Type* dependency types in relation to their ratios in the reference mapping (cf. Table 10.9). The former, having a rather high ratio, remains on a constant low level for all weights lower than 0.1 and on a constant high level for all values higher than 1.0. I.e. weighting this dependency type higher than the others leads to better results. The relatively constant levels are supposed to be the effect of the clear relation between the local classes and their parents, between which this dependency type appears.

The *Cast Type* dependency type also shows expectable behaviour in relation to its low ratio of 0.71. Weighting it lower than the other dependency types leads to better results than weights higher than 1.0. Other dependency types such as the *Constructor Call* type depicted in the figure, do not reveal such a comprehensible behaviour.

In summary for the detailed target architecture, it can be observed, that the algorithm shows a comprehensible behaviour in the large majority of slight modifications of single dependency type weights. This is valid for the Equal Weights set as well as the Sensitivity Weights set. However, in some cases inexplicable changes of more than the expected 3% for slight modifications appear. Hence, the behaviour in such cases should be further examined in future experiments.

Figure 10.14 shows exemplary results for the simplified target architecture, containing only two coarse-grained target components. The results have a much higher quality of about 90% even for the Equal Weights set and reveal less reaction of the algorithm to changing dependency weights. As can be seen in the figure, the Constructor Call dependency type represents an exception as its modification leads to unpredictable results. The reason for the higher quality and the smaller reaction to modifications is supposed to be the dependency profile of the target components. Added up, the two target components contain 7795 internal dependencies, but only 281 external dependencies. Thus, a high ratio of internal to external dependencies is also obtained for all dependency types. I.e. the separation of the two components is already high in the source system, which eases the automatic creation of the complete mapping and leads to less influence of the dependency weights and their modification.

10.2.5 Conclusions

One of the main insights this case study gives to the applicability of MARE is the role of the relation between the decomposition criteria of the target architecture and the dependency types. MARE bases on the assumption, that the target components are in a common sense cohesive and that this cohesion is reflected in

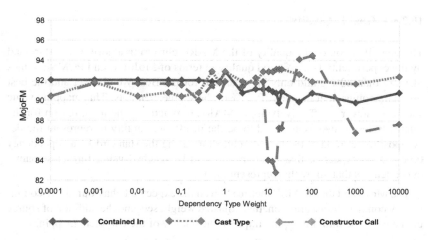

Figure 10.14: Experiment 4: Exemplary Sensitivity Analysis Results for the Coarse Target Architecture

the distribution of dependency types for internal and external dependencies of the target components.

However, the case study shows, that the cohesion of target components is not always reflected in the syntactical dependency types that are available in common programming languages. It is assumed, that the decomposition criteria applied in practice are often primarily reflected in semantic relations between source elements. To take advantage of the property of the clustering algorithm to create cohesive clusters, these semantic relations have to be mapped to according dependency types. The further examination of appropriate dependency types and a reasonable definition of cohesion on the module and component level is subject to future work.

Nonetheless, the case study also shows the promising potential of MARE in combination with conventional Java dependency types. In the following, the results of the experiments are examined according to the goals and questions in the GQM plan. The final subsection furthermore discusses further observations of the case study.

10.2.5.1 Goal 1: Quality

The quantification of the quality of the MARE clustering algorithm is addressed by the experiments 1-3. A good quality in terms of MoJoFM and PCMSE values of more than 80% could only be measured for the Best Weights set and the best initial mappings, that mapped 20-25% of the source elements. This mapping value should be lower to effectively apply MARE in practice. The main reason for the relatively low values is assumed to be the insufficient ability to represent the decomposition criteria of the target architecture using the standard Java dependency types. It is expected, that better results can be reached using further semantic dependencies that allow this representation.

The MoJo and the NCMSE metric showed the expected behaviour. They continuously confirm the assumption, that adjusted weight sets and the addition of source elements to the initial mapping improve the quality of the complete mapping.

Question 1.2, that addresses the good choice of dependency type weights, can not be answered definitely. The best values for the considered metrics could be reached with the Best Weight set. The set bases on the ratio of internal to external dependencies and knowledge about the system and the clustering behaviour. Since a large part of the this knowledge can not be gained without knowing the reference mapping no approach for a user without this knowledge can be easily derived from it. Nonetheless, it can be said, that high weights for dependency types, that reflect the decomposition criteria, and low weights for dependency types, that contradict these criteria are a good starting point. Furthermore, the examination of intermediate clustering results for dependency type weights, that cause wrong mappings of source elements is a strategy to improve the weights.

The best choice of an initial mapping also bases on knowledge about the reference mapping. Nonetheless, the results of Experiment 3 show, that source elements with high internal dependencies in the target decomposition are a better choice than source elements, that represent an interface of a target component. This again shows, that a clear definition of the decomposition criteria is necessary to gain a good complete mapping.

The influence of consolidating iterations to reduce the negative influence of arbitrary decisions could also be shown by a comparison of the clustering algorithm with and without consolidating iterations. It could be shown, that for most configurations the clustering with iterations produced more stable results and reduced the instability caused by arbitrary decisions. The expected average improvement of the results for the usage of the algorithm with consolidating iterations could only be confirmed for individual cases.

In conclusion, the quality of the complete mappings in this case study is worthy of improvement. The main point of improvement however is not MARE itself, but its use and the modelling of the decomposition criteria by dependency types. Furthermore, it was observed, that the best weight set and the best initial mapping are based on knowledge about the reference mapping. Nonetheless, strategies for the creation of both without this knowledge can be derived, that base on the precise definition of the decomposition criteria of the target architecture.

10.2.5.2 Goal 2: Stability

In Experiment 3 the complete mappings for modifications of the initial mapping in steps of 25 source elements or 3.1% were examined. Only in one case the addition of source elements to the initial mapping did not show a positive influence on the complete mapping. Nonetheless, a positive effect of the addition of source elements in terms of an improvement of the PCMSE value of significantly more than 3.1% can only be observed for initial mappings that map less than 20% of the source elements. Therefore, it can be concluded for this case study, that the addition of source elements to the initial mapping will not deteriorate the complete mapping in most cases and that the largest improvements can be made with additions up to an initial mapping size of 20% of the source elements.

Experiment 4 examined the influence of the modifications of dependency type weights on the complete mapping employing a sensitivity analysis. The result show no uniform picture. While the most modifications lead to comprehensible changes in the complete mapping, there are also a number of exceptions that can not explicable. The comparison of the results for the detailed target architecture with a simplified target architecture with two target components shows that the quality of the results strongly improve if the decomposition criteria of the target architecture is well reflected in the source system, measured by high ratios of internal to external dependencies for all dependency types. In this case, the influence of the single weights strongly decreases except for some also not explicable exceptions.

10.2.6 Further Conclusions

The course of this case study showed, that the Sum and Unweighted Average Linkage updating rules led to the best results regarding stability and quality. The similarity function defined by Koschke (2000) led to similar results as the Unweighed Average Linkage rule. The Sum Relative to Nodes function led to good results regarding stability and quality in terms of high cohesion and low coupling, but revealed low values for the quality in terms of similarity to the reference mapping. Experiment 1 furthermore indicated, that Sum leads to less stable results. Hence, Unweighted Average Linkage was preferred in the subsequent experiments.

The experiments furthermore revealed, that MoJo and MoJoFM have deficiencies in the rating of MARE results in comparison to a reference mapping. This results from the particularity of MARE, that it predefines the identity of clusters and target components, while the MoJo metrics are aimed at more general clustering techniques in the field of architecture reconstruction, where the goal is to find modules and components. NCMSE and PCMSE provide more interpretable results in the MARE context, since their measured values are lower than the values of the MoJo metrics if the grouping of source elements is correct, but the assignment to the target components does not match the user's expectation. However, this aspect is mainly significant for results with a low quality. For better complete mappings, the results of the metrics are similar.

10.3 Industrial Case Study

10.3.1 Setting

The setting of the industrial case study is a large industrial system written in C/C++. The system has been developed for about 15 years and has a size of about 3.5 million lines of code excluding comments and empty lines. The system is partially object-oriented and much of the communication and synchronisation in the system is done using global variables and shared memory objects. More details on the system can not be given here for reasons of confidentiality.

The case study was part of a project with the goal to analyse and restructure the architecture of the system. The system suffers from architectural erosion due to many years of maintenance. The goal of the project is the development of a target architecture, that allows for the planned future developments of the system, and the modernisation of the system to meet this architecture. Since the goal is the re-establishment of maintainability, the envisaged target architecture is an idealised As-Is architecture.

The case study is represents the application of parts of MARE in an industrial context. It shows the transferability of the MARE Clustering to a larger system, written in another programming language and employing other dependency types than the case studies described before. However, the quality of the results of MARE can not be assessed clearly, since no reference mapping is available, because the restructuring project is not finished and the system experts are also not yet able to create a final mapping for the system. Furthermore, the applicability of all MARE concepts can not be evaluated, since there is no fix target architecture. The restructuring of the system is still ongoing and thus only a few hints to the quality of the complete mapping of MARE are available. Parts of the results of the case study were published at the *Workshop Software-Reengineering (WSR 2010)* (see Streekmann (2010)).

10.3.2 Experiment Design

The industrial case study is divided into two experiments with different source system models and target architectures. The Experiment 2 employs the source system model of a later version of the system and a reworked target architecture. While the source system model used in Experiment 1 includes only files, the source system model used in Experiment 2 is extended by explicitly modelling global variables and shared memory objects in order to be able to map them independently from the other global variables, shared memory objects, and functions they are defined with in the same file. The number of dependencies is not influenced by this, since the dependencies to these source elements were lifted to the file level before. Apart from that, the source system models for both experiments were created using the same reverse engineering tool and involve the same dependency types.

10.3.2.1 Experiment 1

The target architecture for the experiments was designed based on Quasar categories (cf. [p. 73ff.]Siedersleben (2004)). It contains 14 target components, that represent different functionalities of the system. These reach from common functions like error handling and authentication to specific target components, that represent e.g. the data model or all customer-specific adaptations of the system. More details about the target components in particular can not be given here for reasons of confidentiality.

The source system model includes between 4821 and 5752 files. The number varies since some elements were removed during the iterations of MARE Clustering. Depending on this the number of dependencies varies from 504405 to 2.5 million. In the implementation these were reduced for performance reasons to between 87251 and 230227 dependencies by subsuming all dependencies between two nodes to one with the sum of the single weights as new weight. The initial mapping contains between 104 and 122 source elements.

The weights for the dependency types are listed in Table 10.13. The dependency types are typical structural dependencies in C/C++ systems, as e.g. reading, writing and executing accesses to global variables and functions. The weights reflect the decomposition criteria of the target architecture. E.g. inheritance is weighted high, because two classes that inherit from each other should be mapped to the same target component in the same way as functions that write the same global variable should be mapped to the same target component. On the other hand *Macro Accesses* and *Rely On* dependencies, which refer to type usages in C/C++, appear throughout the system and are appropriate for the mapping to target components. Thus, they are weighted very low.

Table 10.13: Weights for the Industrial Case Study

DependencyType	Weight
Execute	0.01
Read	0.003
Macro Access	0.000000001
Write	20
Include	0.01
Rely On	0.000000001
Contain	1.0
Inherit	200
Member Access	0.1

The experiment targets the MARE Clustering iteration cycle. In the iterations, the reaction of the clustering algorithm to the changes in the configuration are examined. Changes are the removal of source elements from the source system model, the addition of source elements to the initial mapping and changes of the dependency type weights. All clusterings in this experiment were conducted using an early version of the clustering implementation employing the Sum updating rule. In this early version, no consolidating iterations to reduce the negative influence of arbitrary decisions were employed in the clustering algorithm.

10.3.2.2 Experiment 2

The second experiment examines the influence of consolidating iterations in the clustering algorithm to avoid the negative influence of arbitrary decisions on the clustering result. To do so, 10 complete mappings, that were created with the same configuration and the same number of clustering runs are compared. The comparison is done using the PCMSE metric. The experiment is conducted without consolidating iterations and with 10 consolidating iterations. It is expected, that the complete mappings are more similar to each other for the latter algorithm. The clusterings were created using the Sum as well as the Unweighted Average Linkage updating rule.

The target architecture of Experiment 2 is a reworked version of the target architecture of Experiment 1, in which the definition of the main components was slightly changed and subcomponents were added. It contains 13 target components with 20 subcomponents. The dependency weights are the same weights as listed in Table 10.13. The source system model contains 4915 files, 361 shared memory objects and 3940 global variables. These elements share 632300 dependencies, which were subsumed as in Experiment 1 to 123330 dependencies for performance reasons. The initial mapping contains 253 files.

10.3.3 Validity

The main threat to the validity of the experiments in this case study is, that there is no reference mapping to which the complete mappings created by the clustering algorithm can be compared. Thus, the metrics can only give indications on the quality of the results. Furthermore, a detailed insight to all 5000 to 10000 source elements is not expectable of a human expert. Hence, the expert that rated the results can check the mapping on a random basis. This check is also complicated by the fact, that the target architecture of the system is not fixed.

10.3.4 Results

10.3.4.1 Experiment 1

The complete mapping gained in the MARE Clustering iterations of Experiment 1 are depicted as pie charts in Figure 10.15. For the larger target components the percent values represent the percentage of source elements mapped to the target components. The real names of the components are not used due to confidentiality reasons. The letters are used for the same target component in each subfigure.

The first iteration of the MARE Clustering iteration cycle (cf. Section 7.2.1) in Experiment 1 led to a complete mapping in which one target component contained more than 90% of the source elements. It could be seen from the sequence of the clustering, that the choice of which target component included most of the source elements depended on the clustering of a single file, that was clustered very early

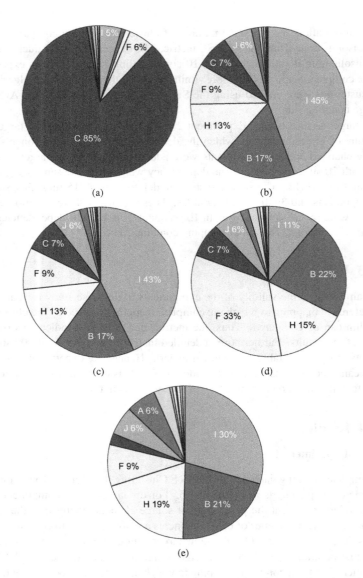

Figure 10.15: Experiment 1: Results of the MARE Clustering Iterations

in the clustering process. This single source element has 5264 incoming and 376 outgoing dependencies and was used all over the system. Hence, it facilitates the creation of large clusters.

The removal of this source element slightly improved the clustering and led to the result depicted in Figure 10.15(a). It still includes one target component containing 85% of the source elements, but also two further components containing more than 5% of the source elements.

In the next MARE Clustering iteration 769 further files, that were identified as internal libraries by domain experts, were removed from the source system model. This significantly improved the result as can be seen in Figure 10.15(b). The distribution of source elements to target components is much more homogeneous. Furthermore, the larger target components are also expected to contain more source elements by the system experts, since they represent a larger part of specific functionalities. As discussed before, the equal size of all target components is not likely in practice and also in this case study, the target components are expected to contain different amounts of source elements, which is reflected in the system experts rating of the complete mapping. Nonetheless, a certain degree homogeneity in which the size of the largest components does not diverge to much is desirable for the complete mapping in this case study.

Figure 10.15(c) shows the result after the extension of the initial mapping from 104 to 122 source elements. It can be seen, that this only resulted in small changes in the complete mapping. In the subsequent MARE Clustering iteration the number of files was further reduced to 4821, whereby further files with a library character were removed from the source system model. The consequence is a complete mapping with an again slightly more regular distribution of the size of the target components (Figure 10.15(d)), but also a strong change of the largest cluster (The share of target component I changed from 43% to 11%, while the share of target component F changed from 9% to 33%). Unfortunately, no final explanation of this phenomenon could be found during the case study. One assumption is, that both target components share the same basic files and that a large block of source elements changed the target component due to the changes caused by the removal of the source elements.

In the last MARE Clustering iteration the weights of execution accesses and reading accesses were lowered. The reason for this change is, that these kinds of accesses are allowed between different target components as well as inside target components, while e.g. writing accesses should mainly be encapsulated inside a target component. In consequence, the sizes of the target components I and F changed again. In the overall view of the complete mapping the target component sizes are again more homogeneous than in the previous results. In summary,

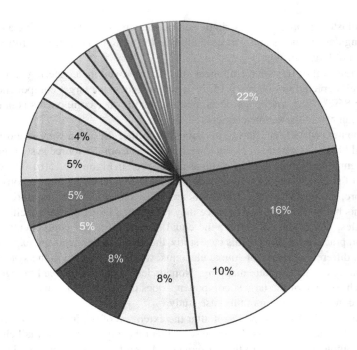

Figure 10.16: Experiment 2: Result for the Extended Target Architecture

the system expert rates this result good given the current state of the restructuring project. Reasons for this rating are that the sizes of the target components broadly match the expectations of the share of the corresponding functionalities in the system and that considered samples of the source system mappings seem to be reasonable.

10.3.4.2 Experiment 2

Figure 10.16 shows the result of a clustering with the updated configuration and the clustering implementation of Experiment 1 to give a valid comparison of the results. It can be seen, that the results are again more homogeneous, which is also owed to the larger number of target components. The largest target component subsumes a large number of specific function groups, that are not further subdivided. Thus, the difference to the size of the other target components is explicable.

Table 10.14 shows the results of the comparison of clusterings with and without consolidating iterations. For the Sum updating rule it can be seen, that the similarity of the 10 compared complete mapping is already very high without consolidating iterations with a median of 99,1%. This value also increases for the clusterings with 10 consolidating iteration with a Median of 99,4% and higher minimum and maximum values, but the difference is not significant due to the already high level of the PCMSE values.

Table 10.14: Similarity of Complete Mappings with and without Consolidating Iterations

	Minimum	Maximum	Median
Sum Without Iterations	98,5%	99,7%	99,1%
Sum 10 Iterations	98,9%	99,8%	99,4%
UAL Without Iterations	75,2%	95%	82,4%
UAL 10 Iterations	70,5%	90,5%	79,9%
UAL 20 Iterations	77,3%	91,6%	81,5%

The results for the Unweighted Average Linkage updating rule are much lower than the results obtained with the Sum updating rule. The median for clusterings without consolidating iterations is 82,4%. The values employing 10 consolidating iterations are even lower, resulting in a median of 79,9% for the comparison of 10 complete mappings. This result contradicts the expectations and can not be explained from the current experiences with the clustering. The results for 20 consolidating iterations with a median of 81.5% are nearer to the results without consolidating iterations, but still lower, so that an increase of stability by the usage of consolidating iterations can not be observed as well. Hence, further examinations of the behaviour of the clustering algorithm regarding consolidating iterations and arbitrary decisions is subject of future work.

Regarding a reason for the deterioration of the result it is assumed that the number of initially mapped source elements, which are less than 3%, may be too low. Therefore, experiments with larger initial mappings should be conducted to examine the consequent behaviour. Another aspect for future work is the increase of the number of consolidating iterations, which may be necessary to obtain the desired effect due to the larger number of possible arbitrary decisions in this case study compared to the open source case study, where the consolidating iterations led to better results. A drawback of this is the increase of computing time, that is involved by the increase of consolidating iterations.

10.3.5 Conclusions

Regarding the quality of the complete mapping, the Questions 1.1 to 1.3 of the GQM plan can not be answered to the same extent as for the preceding case studies, since no reference mapping is available for this case study. The only quantifiable metric, that is applicable, is the number of source elements per target component. The values of this metric are distributed inhomogeneously. However, in the given context this is no sign of a low quality of the complete mappings, but reflects the different natures of the target components.

It can also be concluded from Experiment 1, that the mapping quality improves with the removal of library-like source elements, the extension of the initial mapping and the change of dependency type weights. Thereby, the first shows the highest impact, while the latter led to the smallest changes.

Experiment 2 showed a high level of similarity of the complete mappings, that were obtained employing the Sum updating rule for clusterings with as well as without consolidating iterations. The Unweighted Average Linkage updating rule resulted in much less similar results and also contradicted the expectation, that the similarity increases with the usage of consolidating iterations. Hence, the experiment leaves demand of further examination of the behaviour of the MARE clustering algorithm.

Goal 2 of the GQM plan, the stability of the clustering algorithm with regard to modifications of the dependency type weights or the initial mapping, was not in the focus of the case study. The results of the experiments are also not extensive enough for meaningful statements regarding the stability.

10.4 Summary

This chapter presented the results of three case studies employing different types of restructurings for a small, a medium-sized, and a large software system. They cover the programming languages Java and C/C++ as well as open source and industrial systems with a maintenance history of up to 15 years.

The evaluation bases on the GQM plan defined in Chapter 9. Concerning the quality of the complete mappings produced by MARE, it could be shown that a high quality compared to a reference mapping can be produced. Furthermore, hints for strategies to define dependency type weights and initial mappings could be developed.

With respect to the influence of consolidating iterations to reduce the negative effects of arbitrary decisions no final answer can be read from the case studies. While the open source case study showed more stable results with a slightly higher quality for the algorithm with consolidating iterations, this could not be confirmed in the industrial case study. Further experiments with more extensive configurations are necessary here.

The stability of the approach with regard to changing initial mappings and dependency type weights could also be shown in the open source case study. A few exceptions that appeared in the sensitivity analysis of the open source case study should be further examined in future work. The choice of the best updating rule or similarity function for composite clusters used in the clustering algorithm is also subject to future work. In the preliminary and the open source case study Sum and Unweighted Average Linkage led to the best complete mappings. Regarding the stability of the results for the two updating rules, however, the results of the open source and the industrial case study are ambiguous. While Unweighted Average Linkage was slightly more stable and more or less behaviourally equivalent to Sum in the open source case study, its results were much less stable in the industrial case study.

An influence of library-like source elements on clustering results could also be observed in the preliminary and the industrial case study. In the open source case study, the source elements with the most incoming and outgoing dependencies did not lead to a deterioration of the results, but rather supported a good clustering, since the dependencies mostly connected them to other source elements in the same target architecture. Hence, libraries, frameworks, and source elements with many dependencies should be examined on for their potential role in the target system. Depending on this role they should be removed from the source system model or considered as central elements in the initial mapping.

The portability of the results in total is limited, since restructuring projects depend on a large number of influencing factors. Thus, more experience is needed to be able to make general statements. The main influencing factors are the complexity of the systems, their programming language as wells as programming conventions, and most importantly the decomposition criteria of the target architecture and the possibility to map these to dependency types.

11 Related Work

This chapter discusses related work of the MARE approach. It considers work in three categories. Section 11.1 compares MARE to other approaches that support architecture restructuring on different levels. Section 11.2 points out the differences to methodological similar approaches for architecture reconstruction and Section 11.3 examines alternative approaches for the creation of the complete mapping.

11.1 Architecture Restructuring

11.1.1 Architecture Restructuring Using Source Code Annotations and Graph Transformations

Correia et al. (2007) present an approach to architecture restructuring using graph transformation rules, which is also described in more detail in Heckel et al. (2008). They employ target architecture information for the source code transformation by semi-automatically annotating the source code with source categories. They describe the exemplary transformation of a system towards service-oriented systems employing three-tier architectures. The annotated source code is reverse engineered to a graph model, which is then transformed to a model representing the system conforming to the target architecture. From this model the source code of the target system is generated. The actual restructuring of the system is encapsulated in the graph transformation rules.

In the approach, the source code can be categorised down to the level of single statements, which principally allows for a more fine-grained restructuring than MARE. The restructuring is based on refactoring rules. The paper does, however, not state how single statements are reassembled in the target code. Furthermore, the approach is restricted to object-oriented systems.

The main differences to MARE are the code annotations and the automatic transformation of the source code. The semi-automatic annotation of source code elements can in principle be compared to the clustering of source elements based on the initial mapping in MARE. Nevertheless, it requires more detailed knowledge of the system to annotate the code manually and to define the rules for the automatic annotation. This level of detail is hard to gain for current large-scale systems and necessitates additional upfront reconstruction steps. Furthermore Correia et al. (2007) are focussed on the technological decomposition of the target architecture and leave out the challenges of the functional decomposition. Automated generation of the restructured code is subject to future work in MARE (cf. Section 13.1).

Matos (2008) extends the former work by focussing the functional decomposition. He adds a method to identify service operations in the source code and group them in order to gain coherent services. The goal for this task are loosely coupled, coarse-grained services. Several techniques are used to identify service operations in the source code, where MARE uses the target architecture as starting point for the mapping of service interfaces to source code. This kind of functional target architecture as a complement of the technological target architecture in Correia et al. (2007) is not included in the approach.

The loose coupling is obtained in the way that service operations do not depend on the use of operations of other services. However, loose coupling in the sense of loosely coupled service implementations to foster reuse in different contexts and exchangeability of services and the problems adherent to this are not discussed in detail. This is in contrast a focus of the component restructuring that is possible with MARE. Matos and Heckel (2008) summarise the whole approach, including functional and technological decomposition, targeting the migration to service-oriented architectures.

11.1.2 The SOAMIG Approach

Fuhr et al. (2010) extend the Service Oriented Modeling and Architecture (SOMA) method by IBM, as described in Arsanjani et al. (2008), in order to provide an end-to-end method for the migration of existing systems to service-oriented architectures. The method includes the identification and specification of services as well as their realisation and implementation. In the context of MARE, the identification and specification phases lead to the definition of the target architecture. MARE itself can be used in the service realisation phase, where existing implementation have to be mapped to the services. The implementation phase conforms to the *Implementation Restructuring* in MARE.

The service realisation phase in Fuhr et al. (2010) is conducted by extracting the complete but minimal code that serves as the implementation of a service interface defined in the service identification phase. This phase also identifies source elements that contain the direct equivalents to the defined service operations. The identification of the realising code is then done by querying all call, type and inheritance dependencies from a graph, which represents the complete source code. The main difference to MARE is, that this identification of the code belonging to the service implementation is based on the analysis of the dependencies of the elements already found in the service identification phase. Although this can be compared to the initial mapping in MARE, the difference is that also the interfaces of other components of the system are considered in MARE. I.e. other service implementations, that also depend on the identified code, are not considered by Fuhr et al. (2010). Furthermore, they do not discuss which required interfaces the resulting component will have. This is an important issue, because without this knowledge code maybe unnecessarily duplicated or the component may require code through its interface which could be better included in the component itself. Also, it is not discussed that components may realise more than one service. These issues can be modelled in the target architecture of MARE and are thus considered in the clustering.

11.1.3 Incremental Architecture Restructuring

Hunold et al. (2008) describe an approach for the semi-automatic transformation of a legacy system to a client-server architecture. The transformation is done on an architectural level based on refactoring patterns. These also include the extraction of functionality from a desktop application in order to execute it on a server. However, only the technical implementation of the transformation of selected parts of the code is discussed, but not how this selection can be supported. In this way the approach supports the evolution to a target architecture by incrementally applying patterns for single refactoring or restructuring operations selected by the user, who decides which steps have to be performed to reach the target architecture.

Similar methods are implemented in the tools Sotoarch[1] and Lattix (Sangal et al. (2005)), which visualise the layered architecture of object-oriented systems and dependencies between layers and single elements. On this basis, they support the planning of incremental architecture restructuring by computing the changes, that occur, when elements are moved. In all these approaches the target architecture has to be created manually in small steps from the reconstructed source architecture.

11.1.4 Automated Architecture Improvement

Approaches for automated architecture improvement in most cases use the principles of low coupling and high cohesion as criteria for the improvement. Thus, they

---

[1] http://www.software-tomography.ch/

provide useful support for the automation of refactorings to improve the maintainability of a system. In contrast to MARE they are not designed to support the coarse-grained restructuring to new architectures with significant difference to the existing architecture.

Lung (1998) presents an approach to restructure software systems using graph clustering. The goal is to improve the architecture in terms of higher cohesion and lower coupling. Therefore, a clustering algorithm is used to find a pattern that can be used to improve the architecture targeting this goal. In contrast to MARE, maintainability (addressed in terms of coupling and cohesion) is the only restructuring goal of interest. Further goals, that can e.g. be gained by the examination of a target architecture, especially restructuring based on a functional decomposition, are not considered.

Bauer and Trifu (2004) also have the goal to improve the structure of a system under study. They perform graph clustering based on architectural clues to reconstruct the intended structure of the system. By optimising the similarity function for coupling and cohesion they try to impose an improved structure, that is suited better for program understanding. In contrast to MARE, the improvement is not based on a new target decomposition, but improves the quality measures of the existing decomposition.

11.2 Architecture Reconstruction

MARE uses methods, that are similar to the methods used for architecture reconstruction, e.g. in the reflexion method and other clustering-based reconstructing approaches. The main difference to these approaches is, that the goal of MARE is not to reconstruct the implemented or intended architecture of an existing system, but creates a mapping of the implementation to a new target architecture. This changes the underlying problem and the assumptions connected to it.

11.2.1 Architecture Reconstruction Based on Source Code

The main difference of MARE to these methods is, that the results these methods provide, must be interpreted and often also reworked by the user in order to gain a consistent architectural view of the system under study. In MARE this architectural view is given by the target architecture and thus the effort for the interpretation of the result can be limited to defined aspects. These include unwanted dependencies between target components resulting from the complete mapping and the mapping of single entities or small groups of entities respectively.

11.2.2 Architecture Reconstruction Employing Architectural Information

Major methodical similarities to the MARE approach can be found in architecture reconstruction methods, that employ architectural information as a user input. The main differences to MARE is in these cases the goal of the approach, which is to obtain knowledge about the existing system, while the goal of MARE is to transfer the existing implementation to a target architecture with different decomposition criteria. In terms of the horseshoe model (cf. Section 3.1) architecture reconstruction methods focus on the reverse engineering of the base architecture, while MARE focuses on the transformation of a system towards a desired architecture.

11.2.2.1 The Extended Reflexion Method

The goal of the reflexion method is to find differences between the dependencies in a hypothesised architecture and the dependencies induced by a mapping of source elements to elements of this architecture. The extended reflexion method by Christl et al. (2007), as introduced in Section 3.4.2.1, proposes an approach for the semi-automatic creation of this mapping. To do this, a clustering approach is introduced, that iteratively creates the mapping of source elements based on the dependencies to already mapped source elements.

While the extended reflexion method and MARE both base on an architectural description as their main input, the role of these architectures differs significantly. Where the reflexion method uses a hypothesised architecture which reflects the experts expectation on the current implementation of the system, MARE uses a target architecture which reflects the experts plan of the future implementation of the system. The decompositions reflected in these architectures follow different goals and, as they can be seen as the input and output of the restructuring transformation, are assumed to show significant differences. The high-level architecture of the source system is not of interest for MARE. The addressed problem remains the same even if an extensive architectural documentation of the source system exists. Therefore it is assumed, that the hypothesised architecture is more similar to the implicit architecture of the implementation than the target architecture of MARE. This also leads to different requirements for the clustering.

Instead of a hierarchical clustering approach as described in Section 8.2.3 they use a partial clustering algorithm, that maps previously unmapped source elements to hypothesised high-level modules of the system under study. The basis for the clustering are dependencies between mapped and unmapped source elements. This causes that cohesive subclusters in the unassigned source elements are not considered. It also supports the strongly human-controlled nature of the reflexion method. In contrast to the MARE approach, the understanding of the implemented architecture of the source system is the main goal of the reflexion method. This is reflected in the partial clustering of Christl et al. (2007), while the MARE approach sets its priority on the interfaces between target components as stated in Section 8.1. The arbitrary decisions, that gain special attention in the clustering algorithm in MARE are not of interest in the extended reflexion method, since only obvious mappings are made automatically in the partial clustering.

Christl et al. (2007) also recommend to spend effort on creating a good conceptual model that resembles the implemented architecture and to provide a corresponding initial mapping. While the latter is also true for MARE, the resemblance between the target architecture and the implemented architecture cannot be assumed in the MARE approach, since restructuring may fundamentally change the implemented architecture. These differences in their objective also leads to different requirements for the approaches themselves.

MARE as well as Christl et al. (2007) make use of dependency type weights in order to indicate the impact of dependencies and the conceptual semantics they represent on the clustering result. Christl et al. (2007) use the dependency type weights proposed in Rayside et al. (2000) and leave the discussion of the role of dependency weights and the evaluation of other weights to future work. MARE on the other hand contributes a discussion on the impact of dependency type weights (cf. Section 8.3) and evaluates this impact for concrete examples (cf. Section 10).

Another difference can be found in the interpretation of the clustering result. While divergences in the reflexion model typically lead to an adjustment of the hypothesised architecture in the reflexion method, in MARE unwanted dependencies lead to changes in the implementation of the system, since they are the main targets of the restructuring of the implementation.

In summary, the extended reflexion method reveals methodical similarities to the MARE approach, but differs significantly in its objective. Table 11.1 summarises the main differences between MARE and the extended reflexion method.

11.2.2.2 Focus

In contrast to the reflexion method, Focus, as described by Medvidovic and Jakobac (2006), does not start with a hypothesised architecture of the system under study, but with an idealised logical model of the system. This model is based on the architectural style of the system, the functional user requirements and the implementation platform, e.g. the used libraries and frameworks. Unlike the reflexion

Table 11.1: Comparison Between the Extended Reflexion Method and MARE

	Extended Reflexion Method (Christl et al. (2007))	MARE
Goal	Architecture Reconstruction	Support for Architecture Restructuring
Process	Iterative adjustment of the hypothesised architecture	Iterative adjustment of the implementation to the target architecture
Assumptions	Decomposition criteria of the hypothesised architecture can be found in the source system	Support for Architecture Restructuring
Clustering Method	Partial Clustering	Complete Hierarchical Clustering
Inclusion of Architectural Knowledge	Manual Mapping, ϕ factor (allowed coupling)	Initial mapping, dependency weights
Clustering Goal	High cohesion and low coupling	High cohesion in relation to the decomposition criteria of the target architecture
Handling of Divergences	Rework of the hypothesised architecture	Change of dependency weights or adjustment of the implementation
Arbitrary Decisions	Only obvious mappings are automated	Iterative mapping, alignment of different decisions

method and MARE, Focus does only consider object-oriented systems. It follows an incremental approach to reconstruction and evolution of the system. I.e. only the part of the system that is subject to a current evolutionary requirement is reconstructed and changed.

This top-down step is complemented with a typical bottom-up architecture recovery step to reconstruct a consistent but partial architectural view of the system. During the bottom-up step, classes are clustered through the application of rules that are based on dependency types. The difference to clustering in MARE is that the groups are not assigned to target components and the set of rules is fix and is not intended to be adapted to the target decomposition.

The results of the top-down and the bottom-up step are mapped to each other in order to gain a complete architecture view. During the mapping, Focus identifies inconsistencies between the idealised and the reconstructed architecture, which is similar to the recognition of differences between hypothesised architecture and implementation in the reflexion method. Based on the reconstructed architecture, the architecture evolution is performed.

The approach incrementally starts with a high-level view of the system and hierarchically refines the parts of the system, that are relevant to the evolution task at hand, in the further iterations. This meets one of the iteration strategies described for MARE in Section 7.1.1. The reflexion method also incorporates hierarchical refinement, but describes more detailed understanding instead of the adoption of a certain evolution task as the driver of the iterations.

11.2.2.3 SARA

SARA is a semi-automatic subsystem decomposition technique defined by Girard (2005). It produces a hierarchical module view of a source system. SARA is subdivided in three phases:

1. Collapse molecular components
2. Partition and cluster
3. Integration and refinement

In each of the phases specific feedback from the user is incorporated to improve the overall result. The first phase identifies groups of source elements, that are considered as molecular components in the other phases. The techniques used in this phase focus on strong relationships of the source elements in the existing implementation, that represent the implicit architecture of the source system. As such they are not commonly usable for the restructuring of the system to a new architecture.

The second phase uses partitioning and clustering in order to create a dendrogram, that represent the hierarchical decomposition of the system. This phase is subdivided in four steps:

1. Support and driver filtering
2. Data preparation
3. Partitioning
4. Clustering

The first step removes source elements, that do not call other source elements or that call a relatively large number of other source elements. This equals the removal of libraries in MARE and leads to better results in the subsequent steps. In relation to restructuring the removal of these source elements should be further differentiated, since these elements can also be representative for the target architecture and thus should not be removed.

The second step can be compared to the creation of the source system model in MARE since it describes which relations and attributes are considered in the clustering. The structural dependencies between source elements are weighted by the number of equal dependencies to other source elements and not as in MARE by the relevance of the dependencies for the target decomposition. Further optional attributes of source elements are dominance relations, containments hierarchies, and naming conventions as well as special system-specific attributes. All these attributes can also be useful for restructuring, but should be chosen carefully for the specific project context. In MARE these attributes are modelled as further dependency types, which are weighted by their relevance for the restructuring. Such a weighting is not intended by SARA.

The third step partitions the source elements into small cohesive components. The goal is to correct the drawback of the local nature of hierarchical clustering. This can lead to the clustering of two source elements because they are highly similar, although they belong to the same component. This can e.g. happen, when two components are highly dependent. In MARE, this drawback is tackled by a higher weighting of dependencies, that indicate the intended cohesion of the component, as well as the iterative improvement of the initial mapping.

The fourth step clusters the source element or groups of source elements created in the preceding steps, respectively. SARA employs six different similarity functions to compute the similarity between clusters. The results of the clusterings are compared based on the similarity to a partial manual mapping or on coupling and cohesion measures. In the end, the clustering with the best quality is chosen as input of the third phase. MARE is also able to use different similarity functions, but does not employ the parallel execution and comparison of clustering results. In MARE, all clusterings have the same similarity to the initial mapping since component clusters are not allowed to be merged during the clustering. A comparison based on cohesion metrics would be possible, but is left to the user.

The third phase of SARA interprets the clustering result and reintegrates the source elements removed in the first step of the second phase. The interpretation of the clustering results bases on the creation of a hierarchical system decomposition based on analysis of the dendrogram created by the clustering in the second phase. Since the MARE clustering algorithm does not result in a complete dendrogram, but stops the hierarchical clustering when only component clusters are left, the mapping of source elements to target components can directly be read from the clustering result. Furthermore, the hierarchical decomposition is the same as in the target architecture. Further subcomponents are not revealed by MARE.

In summary, SARA is a sophisticated approach, that combines several techniques to execute architecture reconstruction. The main similarities to MARE are that hierarchical clustering is a central technique and that knowledge of the user is strongly integrated in the approach. The main methodological differences are that MARE does directly incorporate the initial mapping and the target architecture into the clustering algorithm while SARA mainly uses the architectural input from the user for the validation and selection of the result of specific reconstruction methods. Furthermore, MARE bases on user defined dependency weights to incorporate the decomposition criteria of the target architecture.

11.2.2.4 Further Hierarchical Clustering Approaches for Architecture Reconstruction

Maqbool and Babri (2007) review the state-of-the-art of the usage of hierarchical clustering algorithms in approaches for architecture reconstruction. Coupling and cohesion are assumed to be a good basis for architecture reconstruction approaches and often determine the metrics of their results. For architecture restructuring this only works in special cases, when the implemented principles of coupling and cohesion are similar to the principles of the target architecture. In most cases MARE will result in a complete mapping with non-optimal coupling and cohesion. Thus, further steps changing the implementation are necessary in order to ensure the quality of the implementation relating to the intended quality of the target architecture.

11.3 Alternatives to Hierarchical Clustering

In the related literature on restructuring and architecture reconstruction many methods were proposed to reveal structures in software systems and create architectural views. In the following, the most frequently used methods are described and the rationale for choosing hierarchical clustering for the creation of the complete mapping in MARE is given.

11.3.1 Formal Concept Analysis

According to Tilley et al. (2005) a typical application scenario for formal concept analysis (FCA) in software engineering is refactoring and restructuring as well as the identification of object-oriented structures. The paper also gives an overview of recent work in this area. FCA defines concepts on a set of objects and a set of attributes of these objects. A concept defines a grouping of objects with certain attributes. Thus, FCA is suitable for finding groups of source elements (objects) with certain predefined properties (attributes).

Tonella (2001) proposes the usage of FCA to restructure fine-grained modules in software systems. He defines functions as objects and the data structures they use as attributes of these objects. A module is assumed to correspond to a formal concept found with a common FCA algorithm.

A possible usage of FCA in MARE would be to map dependencies to attributes. However, this only works for dependencies that represent common attributes of source elements, but not for dependencies, that represent direct relations between source elements. Furthermore, the weighting of dependencies cannot be transferred to FCA, since a weighting of attributes, that influences the definition of concepts is not intended.

11.3.2 Data Mining Techniques

Some architecture reconstruction approaches use data mining techniques for the creation of architecture views of existing systems. Sartipi and Kontogiannis (2003) present an approach that bases on an *a priori* algorithm to determine the similarity between source elements and components. Components are defined as subsystems, that contain composite source elements (files) which again contain elementary source elements (functions, data types and variables).

The a priori algorithm computes frequent itemsets, which contain a set of elementary functions F and a set of source elements E in which every source element in E is used by every function in F. The user can thereby define the minimum number of functions in F, which is called the *minimum-support*. A k-itemset is a frequent itemset with $k = |E|$ and $k > 0$, where $|E|$ is the number of source elements in E.

The similarity of two source elements is defined as $max(|E| + \omega * |F|)$ with $0 < \omega < 1$ being a weight which is by default set to 0.5. The maximum is taken, when two source elements are contained in more than one itemset. The similarity between components is based on the sum of similarities of the source elements contained in the components.

Based on this definition of similarity a partitional clustering is executed to cluster files to components. An initial partitioning of the system is created by identifying core files with high similarities to a large number of other components. These seed files form singular clusters, while all other files are composed to a *rest-of-system* cluster. An iterative partitioning algorithm then computes in each step the similarity of each file to all other clusters and moves the file to the most similar cluster, until no file is moved anymore. The clusters are then proposed to the user as subsystems of the system. The influence of the user on the clustering is limited to the investigation of the results, including manual improvements. After the clustering, the modularity of the clusters is rated, which can lead to merging or splitting of clusters as well as a definite mapping of files to clusters, which cannot be changed in further clustering steps.

In order to be usable for the computation of the complete mapping in MARE, the a priori algorithm would have to be extended to enable the inclusion of weights for different types of dependencies between source elements. This includes the definition of another notion of frequent itemsets. The drawback would be, that the changes to dependency weights only indirectly influence the similarity measure, which leads to more effort in the interpretation of the results and the definition of changes in subsequent iterations.

11.3.3 Data Flow Analysis

An alternative approach for the extraction of components from a source system is data flow analysis. Starting from an interface of the system, the data flow through the system is analysed in order to find source elements, that are involved in the execution of the functionality defined by the interface. Horn et al. (2009) use data flow analysis to identify source elements for the extraction of a service in the course of SOA migration. While data flow analysis probably finds all source elements, that are directly needed for the service implementation, dependencies from other elements to these elements as e.g. in class hierarchies or commonly used parts of the code are not identified as such. The can lead to unwanted interfaces between the extracted components and the rest of the system. Especially, when the other interfaces and functionalities realised in the system are not considered.

11.4 Summary

This chapter discussed the related work of the MARE approach. The related work can be mainly divided into three parts: work on architecture restructuring employing different methods, work that employs similar methods for architecture reconstruction and alternatives to the graph clustering approach chosen in MARE.

Since coarse-grained architecture restructuring is not researched as well as e.g. architecture reconstruction and the most work on restructuring concentrates on restructurings on the function or class level, only two major related approaches in the of service-oriented architectures as well as several approaches for incremental restructuring and architecture improvement were identified. The latter support users in special aspects of procedures that changes architectures in small steps in contrast to the coarse-grained architecture changes targeted in MARE. The first major approach supports architecture restructuring by source code annotations and graph transformations. Thus, the abstraction layer is lower as in MARE and support for source code annotations is only existing rudimentarily. The SOAMIG approach focuses the architecture restructuring to service-oriented architectures. It provides concrete methods for the identification of service interfaces and technical support for the extraction of code, but does provide mature support for the mapping of source elements to services.

The advantage of MARE compared to the other architecture restructuring approaches is that MARE is the only approach that systematically supports the decision to which target component a source element is mapped. Furthermore, it is a generic approach that is not limited to a certain paradigm in the source system implementation or the target architecture style.

In architecture reconstruction, clustering methods are employed by a large number of research approaches. Of these, approaches that employ architectural information are the most related to MARE . Three approaches were discussed in detail. The extended reflexion method uses similar methods, but differs significantly in its objective. It supports the the manual reflexion method with partial clusterings in contrast to the complete clusterings targeted in MARE. Since it focuses on the reconstruction of the source architecture, the influence of decomposition criteria and dependency weights have another role in the approach. The Focus method employs architectural information to gain more detailed information of certain parts of a system. It employs hierarchical refinement of an idealised logical model, but focusses on more fine-grained evolution tasks, that are supported by the reconstruction. SARA is a sophisticated subsystem decomposition technique, that employs best practices from other approaches to produce a hierarchical module view of a source system. It uses hierarchical clustering as one of four reconstruction steps, but only uses architectural information to validate and classify the clustering results and not as a driving input as in MARE. It furthermore defines a number of common analyses and classifications of source system dependencies for architecture reconstruction, while MARE bases on the mapping of decomposition criteria to dependency type weights in order to define the restructuring context.

These architecture reconstruction approaches are similar to MARE, since they also employ architectural information to group source elements. The main difference is the objective and the approach to support architecture restructuring. While the aforementioned approaches support architecture restructuring by providing knowledge about the source system as a basis for human planning, MARE directly supports this planning activity by including knowledge about the target architecture and its decomposition criteria.

There are several alternative to clustering to perform the task of creating a complete mapping to support architecture restructuring. These approaches have been successfully applied in lower level restructurings or architecture reconstruction. One of these approaches is formal concept analysis (FCA) which allows the grouping of source elements with predefined properties. The problem in the application of FCA is the representation of weighted dependencies as properties. Another possibility is the use of data mining techniques. An a-priori algorithm can e.g. be used to compute frequent itemsets with highly related source elements which are then used as input for a partitional clustering algorithm. The problem in the application of this method is again the representation of dependency types and weights as well as the interpretability of the results. The last presented alternative is data flow analysis, which can be used for the extraction of components by identifying all source elements that are needed to implement a certain interface. A remaining problem is the handling of source elements that are used for the implementation of several interfaces.

The hierarchical clustering algorithm employed by MARE is that it provides a complete one-to-one mapping of source elements to target components. Furthermore, it allows a transparent inclusion of architectural knowledge and provides comprehensible and traceable mapping decision for the single source elements.

Part IV

Conclusion

12 Results

This chapter summarises the results and contributions of this thesis. The thesis introduced the MARE approach for the clustering-based support of software architecture restructuring. The chapter is organised following the main contributions of MARE: the MARE Method (Section 12.1), which represents the overall process model for architecture restructuring, MARE Clustering (Section 12.2), which introduces an adjusted clustering algorithm to create the complete mapping of source elements to target architectures, and the evaluation of MARE (Section 12.3), which examined the application of the approach in different contexts as well as the quality and stability of the clustering algorithm. The according sections base on the research questions presented in Section 6.4.

12.1 MARE Method

The research question that underlies the MARE Method is:

> How can knowledge about the target architecture be considered in the architecture restructuring process?

The MARE Method emphasises the target architecture as the basis for the architecture restructuring. All models created during the MARE process use the target architecture and its decomposition criteria as a major input.

Furthermore, the MARE process model incorporates two iteration cycles. The architecture restructuring iteration cycle structures the overall project. In the iterations the implementation is adapted to the target architecture in a number of steps. Strategies to plan the iterations are e.g. the hierarchical refinement of the target architecture or the vertical extraction of single target components. The MARE Clustering iteration cycle supports the interactive improvement of the complete mapping. The user can add knowledge about the existing system and the intended properties of the target system to the configuration of the clustering in each iteration to influence the creation of the complete mapping.

The MARE process model subdivides the overall architecture restructuring process into three phases. In the *Initialisation* phase the target architecture and the source system model are defined. Thereby, the choice of source elements and dependency types representing the source system depends on the decomposition criteria of the target architecture, since they define which source elements are reused in the target system and which dependency types have to be considered, because they characterise the cohesion of the target components or are unwanted between target components.

The *MARE Clustering* phase represents the planning of the architecture restructuring on the model level. In this phase the complete mapping is created based on the target architecture and the source system model as well as further configurations in terms of dependency type weights and an initial human mapping of source elements to target components.

In the *Implementation Restructuring* phase the complete mapping is transferred to the implementation. I.e. the source code is restructured and unwanted dependencies are resolved. This phase can be automated by using existing model-driven approaches. However, this is not in the scope of MARE, but subject of future work (cf. Section 13.1).

MARE provides metamodels for all models used for the representation of the information needed in the MARE process. These metamodels are designed as generic as possible in order to allow the application of MARE for a wide range of programming paradigms for existing systems and types of target architectures.

Another research question, that regards the applicability in different restructuring contexts is:

How can the MARE approach be applied in different contexts?

This question could not finally be answered within the scope of this thesis, because more extensive experiences in different types of restructuring projects are necessary. However, Section 6.2 described the possibility of the application of MARE in the three contexts *Evolution towards Service-Oriented Architectures, Re-establishing Maintainability*, and *Smooth Migration*.

With regard to the evolution towards service-oriented architecture MARE can be used to support for the extraction of services from a complex system. MARE can e.g. help choosing the part of the implementation that can be extracted from the system and defining the necessary interfaces between extracted services and the remaining system. The re-establishment of maintainability is a field of application in which MARE can mainly be helpful when the implemented architecture and the target architecture show major differences. In cases were the goal is the reduction architecture erosion and the re-establishment of the intended architecture and in which implemented and intended architecture are similar except for unwanted dependencies, it is assumed that other approaches are more helpful. The last use case discussed is the support of the planning of a smooth migration. In project that target the stepwise migration of an existing system to a target architecture that is given by a new development environment, MARE can be used to define the steps in which the migration will be executed. The parts of the implementation that are migrated in one step depend on the target components and their interfaces as well as the strength of the dependencies in the source system. MARE can support the planning by finding lowly coupled parts that conform to one or more target components.

12.2 MARE Clustering Algorithm

The research question that led to the development of the MARE clustering algorithm is:

> How can the creation of the complete mapping of source elements to target components be automated?

The clustering algorithm provides a solution that bases on an adjusted hierarchical clustering algorithm. The adjustments were made to incorporate knowledge about the target architecture. By representing the decomposition criteria of the target architecture in the dependency type weights that are the basis for the computation of the similarity between clusters, the algorithm adopts human mapping methods.

However, the creation of the complete mapping can not be fully automated, but is a semi-automatic task. The knowledge of the user has to be made available to the algorithm in order to create a meaningful complete mapping that can be used as a basis for the restructuring of the implementation.

An important basis for the automation of the creation of the complete mapping is the following research question:

> Which criteria influence the complete mapping and how can they be mapped to the clustering algorithm?

One of the main influences of the of the creation of the complete mapping are the decomposition criteria of the target architecture. As mentioned above, they are represented by the dependency type weights. The actual weights are depending on the project context and can be adjusted during the execution of MARE. The clustering algorithm also considers the target architecture itself. The stopping condition of the algorithm is aimed at the target components. For each of the components exactly one cluster of source elements is created. Thus, the created clusters can directly be mapped to the target components without further human interpretation.

Furthermore, MARE employs the knowledge of the user about the system and the semantics of its source elements by using a manually created initial mapping of source elements to target components. This initial mapping serves as the definition of a seed for the clusters produced by the algorithm. Further human knowledge and decisions are integrated by introducing an iterative clustering process. This process comprises the configuration of the clustering and the clustering itself. If the user observes wrongly mapped source elements or unwanted dependencies in the resulting complete mapping of an iteration, manual changes to the configuration of the clustering can be made in order to improve the result in the subsequent iteration.

Another technical influence to the complete mapping are arbitrary decisions that occur during the clustering. When several pairs of clusters have the same similarity to each other, the algorithm has to choose which of the pairs is clustered first. This decision can influence the resulting complete mapping. Thus, arbitrary decisions can reduce the stability of the clustering result, because repeated executions of the algorithm can have strongly varying results. The employed strategy of consolidating iterations of the clustering algorithm partly led to more stable results in the evaluation.

12.3 Evaluation

The basis of the implementation is formed by a GQM plan. The underlying research question for this plan is:

How can the quality of the MARE clustering algorithm be evaluated?

The evaluation of the quality of the clustering algorithm concentrates on the quality of the clustering results and the stability of the results of the clustering algorithm for changing inputs. These are also addressed in separate research questions in Section 6.4 and were chosen as goals for the GQM plan.

The question regarding the quality focusses the overall quality in terms of similarity to a reference mapping as well as expert rating. Another aspect of the quality is the influence of the consolidating iterations on repeated executions of the algorithm without changes to the input. To measure the stability regarding changing inputs, modifications of the dependency weights as well as modifications to the initial mapping are considered.

The evaluation itself comprises three case studies. A preliminary case study in which the JPetStore, a Java reference implementation of a webshop, was restructured, served a testbed to develop the concepts and the prototypical implementation of MARE. An open source case study that deals with the restructuring of the generator framework openArchitectureWare was employed to evaluate the quality and stability of the MARE clustering algorithm with a middle-sized productively used system. The final industrial case study could only be used to show the stability of the clustering algorithm and to assess the quality using expert ratings. Objective quality metrics could not be applied, since no reference mapping exists for the project that is still ongoing.

Regarding the quality of the complete mapping, the case studies showed that it depends on the choices of dependency type weights and source elements in the initial mapping. Thereby, the dependency types have to represent the decomposition criteria of the target architecture. I.e. the dependency types that represent the cohesion of the target components and that are unwanted as dependencies between different target components should be weighted high. Furthermore, libraries, frameworks, as well as library-like source elements with dependencies to many other source elements can have a strong influence on the quality of the complete mapping. They should be examined on whether they are also used in the target architecture and whether they support or contradict the intended decomposition.

With regard to the stability of the complete mapping with respect to changing dependency types and initial mappings, the open source case study showed good results with a few exceptions that have to be further examined in the future work. The evaluation also examined the stability of different updating rules. However, these results were ambiguous. While *Unweighted Average Linkage* was slightly more stable and more or less behaviourally equivalent to *Sum* in the open source case study, its results were much less stable in the industrial case study.

13 Future Work

A number of possibilities for future work on MARE were already identified throughout the thesis. This chapter supplements and discusses these possibilities. The main topics for future work are the automated restructuring of the implementation (Section 13.1), the definition of cohesion for coarse-grained modules (Section 13.2), and the further evaluation of the MARE approach (Section 13.3).

13.1 Automated Restructuring of the Implementation

The restructuring of the implementation is to some extent discussed in Section 7.1.5. A catalogue of patterns is proposed as a basis for the automation of the resolution of unwanted dependencies. It is assumed that for each dependency type one or more patterns can be described that can be used to automate the resolution of that dependency type in different contexts. It still has to be examined whether this is possible for all dependency types and all contexts or whether additional manual effort for the resolution of dependencies is necessary. Furthermore, an exemplary catalogue for the considered languages has to be composed.

Regarding the automation of the restructuring of the source code, there already is a number of model-driven approaches that are able to transform the source code on a model level. For these transformations, transformation rules are necessary that are typically created manually. Based on the aforementioned patters, model transformation rules can be defined that use a complete model of the source code and the complete mapping created by MARE as input and create a complete model of the target system. A similar approach is describe by Giese (2010).

Hence, future work on the MARE method has to examine the integration of existing approaches that allow for the transformations on complete models of the source code in order to automatically restructure the implementation. Important challenges are the definition of a pattern catalogue and according transformation rules.

A potential problem in the automation of the restructuring of the implementation occurs if the target architecture requires the use of libraries that are not used in the source system or make libraries of the source system obsolete. The replacement of a library by another library may be automatable, if both libraries use concepts that can be mapped to each other such that the dependencies to the old library can be replaced by dependencies to the new library. In other cases manual adjustments may be inevitable.

13.2 Definition of Cohesion for Coarse-Grained Modules

Section 8.5 discussed the measurement of cohesion of target components. It showed that existing cohesion metrics as e.g. LCOM are not applicable for coarse-grained modules. The problem of these metrics is that they are defined for a certain clear context. In the case of LCOM, this is the measurement of cohesion for classes in object-oriented systems based on method calls and variable uses. In these contexts the considered dependency types are obvious. For more coarse-grained modules as e.g. packages in Java systems the cohesion of the module depends on the intention of the designer of the module.

E.g. classes can be assigned to the same package when they provide a certain functionality together by calling each others methods. Another reason to assign classes the same package is that they provide a similar functionality and implement the same interfaces or inherit from the same superclass without mutually calling their methods. On the other hand frameworks provide abstract classes that are inherited from by classes in other packages. Another alternative are packages that contain classes without any structural dependencies, but common semantics. These different types of cohesion of packages should be represented by a cohesion metric in order to be able to meaningfully measure the quality of the complete mapping created by MARE.

13.3 Further Evaluation of MARE

The evaluation of MARE showed positive results for the application of MARE and the quality and stability of the clustering algorithm. However, it still leaves open questions for future work. These are discussed in the following.

- The experiments reveal exceptional results in a number of cases, e.g. some larger changes in the sensitivity analysis in the open source case study or in the measurement of the stability of the updating rules and similarity function for composite clusters in different contexts. These exceptions have to be further examined in order to gain more insight in the behaviour of the clustering algorithm and give better recommendation for the configuration of MARE in practical projects.

• Another aspect that requires further examination is the behaviour of the algorithm regarding consolidating iterations. While consolidating iterations led to more stable results in most cases, there are also cases in which consolidating iterations led to more unstable results. These have to be examined to be able to state conditions under which consolidating iterations are useful and to state a good number of iterations.

• The sensitivity analysis regarding the dependency type weights was only executed for the changes of single weights. However, the combination of changes of the weights is a remaining challenge, since in practice the combination of a higher weighting of dependency types that support the desired decomposition criteria and a lower weighting for other dependency types will lead to the best results. The interaction of dependency type weights and the relation of the dependency types to typical programming styles and conventions has to be examined to be able to define strategies for the creation of a good weight set for a concrete architecture restructuring project.

• The choice for the best updating rule or similarity function for composite clusters is another topic for the future evaluation of the clustering algorithm. The *Unweighted Average Linkage* updating rule was chosen for most experiments in the case study, because it led to relatively stable results with a high quality, but the other considered updating rules and similarity functions partly provided better results in terms of quality or stability. This has to be further examined and related to preconditions that encourage the desired behaviour.

• In order to show the applicability of MARE to industrial systems, the approach has to be evaluated employing a completed large-scale architecture restructuring project. A completed project has the advantage that a reference mapping for the evaluation can be extracted from the restructured implementation. Unfortunately, it is often not possible to obtain such conditions in a research context.

• The practical experiences will also have to show, whether initial sets of appropriate dependency type weights for certain architecture restructuring projects can be defined. While MARE provides support for the improvement of the dependency weights in the MARE Clustering iteration cycle, a process has to be described to classify the experiences from completed practical projects in a structured way. This structure should be determined by the decomposition criteria of the target architecture and the programming conventions of the source system to define the application context of MARE. This application context can then be associated to the dependency type weight sets that led to good restructuring result in similar practical projects.

- The current tools for the execution of MARE are prototypes that are constructed for the evaluation of MARE, but not for the use by users that are not involved in the development of MARE. Hence, another aspect of future work is the development of more usable tool support. This involves the integration with reverse engineering and modelling tools in order to support the *Initialisation* and *MARE Clustering* phases as well as tool support for the presentation and analysis of the complete mapping. These tools also have to be evaluated in terms of the usability. The evaluation of the applicability of a method and its supporting tools conform to a Type II validation as proposed by Eusgeld et al. (2008).

- Another precondition for the application of MARE in industrial projects is to show the reduction of effort in contrast to a manual mapping, which conforms to a Type III validation as proposed by Eusgeld et al. (2008). This could be done by performing the architecture restructuring of a system with and without MARE under realistic conditions. To show the real impact of MARE the size of the system should at least be the size of the system in the open source case study. This precondition makes it impossible to perform such a comparison in a research context as e.g. a student experiment. Also a parallel execution of a real architecture restructuring project with both approaches is too costly and not feasible. Other problems are conditions like a similar level of knowledge of the system and the target architecture of the users that perform the restructuring as well as the elimination of learning effects if the two restructurings are performed successively. Since these conditions are hard to realise in an industrial project, only positive experiences in further exemplary projects can be employed to convince users in practice.

14 Concluding Remarks

This thesis contributes to the field of architecture restructuring by introducing and evaluating the semi-automated MARE Method, which supports the transformation of the implementation of an existing system so that it conforms to a given target architecture. The second contribution of the thesis is the MARE Clustering Algorithm that creates a complete mapping of source elements to target components and thus automates an important part of the planning of the restructuring of the implementation in the course of an architecture restructuring. The third contribution is the evaluation, which mainly covers the clustering part of MARE. It shows that complete mappings with a high quality and stability can be produced and sketches strategies for the practical realisation of the configuration of the clustering.

The previous chapter discussed the remaining challenges to make MARE applicable in concrete industrial projects and open issues for future research. The main topics are the integration with other approaches to combine the restructuring of MARE on the model level with automated source code transformation, further research on the cohesion of coarse-grained modules, and the further evaluation of MARE. The execution of these topics will increase the degree of automation of architecture restructuring and improve the maturity of MARE. Even though there is much work left to make automated architecture restructuring techniques the state of the art, MARE represents a promising step towards this goal.

The iterative character of the presented process model conforms to the strategies of current reengineering projects and thus facilitates the use of MARE in practice. Furthermore, the use of generic metamodels allows for the application of MARE for the architecture restructuring of a wide range of different systems and types of target architectures. The iterative configuration of dependency type weights also allows for the fine-grained adjustment to the individual properties of concrete architecture restructuring projects.

Reengineers can benefit from MARE, because it provides a systematic process to support architecture restructuring and eases the creation of a complete mapping by the introduction of a semi-automated clustering process. In summary, MARE can be used in different architecture restructuring contexts to support the overall restructuring process and reduce human effort.

Bibliography

Sven Abels, Wilhelm Hasselbring, Niels Streekmann, and Mathias Uslar. Model-Driven Integration in Complex Information Systems: Experiences from Two Scenarios. In Jörg Rech and Christian Bunse, editors, *Model Driven Software Development: Integrating Quality Assurance*, pages 431–446. IGI Global, 2008.

Gregory D. Abowd, Robert Allen, and David Garlan. Using Style to Understand Descriptions of Software Architecture. In *Proceedings of the 1st ACM SIGSOFT symposium on Foundations of software engineering (SIGSOFT FSE 1993)*, pages 9–20. ACM, 1993. ISBN 0-89791-625-5.

Alain Abran, James W. Moore, Pierre Bourque, Robert Dupuis, and Leonard L. Tripp, editors. *Guide to the Software Engineering Body of Knowledge (SWE-BOK)*. IEEE, 2004. URL http://www.swebok.org/. ISO Technical Report ISO/IEC TR 19759.

Ellen Ackermann, Rainer Gimnich, and Andreas Winter. Ein Referenz-Prozess der Software-Migration (erweiterte Kurzfassung). *Softwaretechnik-Trends*, 25 (4):20–22, November 2005. URL http://www.uni-koblenz.de/~winter/papers/ackermann+2005.pdf.

Periklis Andritsos and Vassilios Tzerpos. Software Clustering based on Information Loss Minimization. In *10th Working Conference on Reverse Engineering (WCRE 2003)*, pages 334–344, 2003.

Periklis Andritsos and Vassilios Tzerpos. Information-Theoretic Software Clustering. *IEEE Transactions on Software Engineering*, 31(2):150–165, 2005.

Mikio Aoyama. Continuous and Discontinuous Software Evolution: Aspects of Software Evolution Across Multiple Product Lines. In *Proceedings of the 4th International Workshop on Principles of Software Evolution (IWPSE 2001)*, pages 87–90, New York, NY, USA, 2001. ACM. ISBN 1-58113-508-4. doi: http://doi.acm.org/10.1145/602461.602477.

A. Arsanjani, S. Ghosh, A. Allam, T. Abdollah, S. Gariapathy, and K. Holley. SOMA: A Method for Developing Service-oriented Solutions. *IBM Systems*

Journal, 47(3):377–396, 2008. ISSN 0018-8670. doi: 10.1147/sj.473.0377. URL http://dx.doi.org/10.1147/sj.473.0377.

Colin Atkinson and Thomas Kühne. Model-Driven Development: A Metamodeling Foundation. *IEEE Software*, 20(5):36–41, 2003. URL http://csdl.computer.org/comp/mags/so/2003/05/s5036abs.htm.

Achim Baier, Steffen Becker, Martin Jung, Klaus Krogmann, Carsten Röttgers, Niels Streekmann, Karsten Thoms, and Steffen Zschaler. Modellgetriebene Software-Entwicklung. In Ralf Reussner and Wilhelm Hasselbring, editors, *Handbuch der Software-Architektur*, pages 93–122. dPunkt.verlag Heidelberg, 2 edition, December 2008. ISBN 3898645592.

Luciano Baresi, Reiko Heckel, Sebastian Thöne, and Dániel Varró. Style-based Modeling and Refinement of Service-oriented Architectures. *Software and System Modeling*, 5(2):187–207, 2006.

Victor R. Basili, Gianluigi Caldiera, and H. Dieter Rombach. The Goal Question Metric Approach. In *Encyclopedia of Software Engineering*, pages 528–532. Wiley, 1994.

Len Bass, Paul Clements, and Rick Kazman. *Software Architecture in Practice*. Addison-Wesley, 2 edition, 2003.

Markus Bauer and Mircea Trifu. Architecture-Aware Adaptive Clustering of OO Systems. In *8th European Conference on Software Maintenance and Reengineering (CSMR 2004)*, pages 3–14, 2004.

Perolof Bengtsson. Towards Maintainability Metrics on Software Architecture: An Adaptation of Object-Oriented Metrics. In *First Nordic Workshop on Software Architecture (NOSA'98)*, 1998.

PerOlof Bengtsson, Nico H. Lassing, Jan Bosch, and Hans van Vliet. Architecture-level modifiability analysis (ALMA). *Journal of Systems and Software*, 69(1-2): 129–147, 2004.

Walter R. Bischofberger, Jan Kühl, and Silvio Löffler. Sotograph - A Pragmatic Approach to Source Code Architecture Conformance Checking. In *EWSA*, volume 3047 of *Lecture Notes in Computer Science*, pages 1–9. Springer, 2004. ISBN 3-540-22000-3. URL http://springerlink.metapress.com/openurl.asp?genre=article&issn=0302-9743&volume=3047&spage=1.

Jakob Boos, Markus Voss, Johannes Willkomm, and Andreas Zamperoni. Lösungsmuster in der Planung industrieller Migrationsprojekte. In *3. Workshop Reengineering Prozesse (RePro2006)*, number 2 in Mainzer Informatik-Berichte, 2006.

Michael L. Brodie and Michael Stonebraker. *Migrating Legacy Systems: Gateways, Interfaces & the Incremental Approach*. Morgan Kaufmann Publishers Inc., 1995. ISBN 1-55860-330-1.

William J. Brown, Raphael C. Malveau, Hays W. "Skip" McCormick, and Thomas J. Mowbray. *AntiPatterns: Refactoring Software, Architectures, and Projects in Crisis: Refactoring Software, Architecture and Projects in Crisis*. John Wiley & Sons, 1998. ISBN 978-0471197133.

Kishore Channabasavaiah, Kerrie Holley, and Edward M. Tuggle. Migrating to a Service-Oriented Architecture. Technical report, IBM, 2004.

Shyam R. Chidamber and Chris F. Kemerer. A Metrics Suite for Object Oriented Design. *IEEE Transactions on Software Engineering*, 20(6):476–493, 1994. ISSN 0098-5589. doi: http://doi.ieeecomputersociety.org/10.1109/32.295895.

Elliot J. Chikofsky and James H. Cross. Reverse Engineering and Design Recovery: A Taxonomy. *IEEE Software*, 7(1):13–18, 1990. ISSN 0740-7459.

Andreas Christl, Rainer Koschke, and Margaret-Anne Storey. Equipping the Reflexion Method with Automated Clustering. In *Proc. of 12th Working Conference on Reverse Engineering*, pages 89–98, Pittsburgh, PA, USA, November 2005. IEEE Computer Society.

Andreas Christl, Rainer Koschke, and Margaret-Anne Storey. Automated Clustering to Support the Reflexion Method. *Journal Information and Software Technology*, 49(3):255–274, March 2007.

Paul Clements, Felix Bachmann, Len Bass, David Garlan, James Ivers, Reed Little, Robert Nord, and Judith Stafford. *Documenting Software Architectures - Views and Beyond*. SEI Series in Software Engineering. Addison-Wesley, 2003.

Bas Cornelissen, Andy Zaidman, Arie van Deursen, Leon Moonen, and Rainer Koschke. A Systematic Survey of Program Comprehension through Dynamic Analysis. *IEEE Transactions on Software Engineering*, 35(5):684–702, 2009.

Rui Correia, Carlos M. P. Matos, Reiko Heckel, and Mohammad El-Ramly. Architecture Migration Driven by Code Categorization. In *Proceedings of the First European Conference on Software Architecture (ECSA 2007)*, pages 115–122, 2007.

Krzysztof Czarnecki and Simon Helsen. Classification of Model Transformation Approaches. In *Proceedings of the 2nd OOPSLA Workshop on Generative Technique in the Context of the Model Driven Architecture*, Anaheim, October 2003.

Krzysztof Czarnecki and Simon Helsen. Feature-Based Survey of Model Transformation Approaches. *IBM Systems Journal*, 45(3):621–646, 2006.

Desmond Francis D'Souza and Alan Cameron Wills. *Objects, Components, and Frameworks with UML: The Catalysis Approach*. Addison-Wesley, 1999.

Stéphane Ducasse and Damien Pollet. Software Architecture Reconstruction: A Process-Oriented Taxonomy. *IEEE Trans. Software Eng.*, 35(4):573–591, 2009.

Steve Easterbrook, Janice Singer, Margaret-Anne Storey, and Daniela Damian. Selecting Empirical Methods for Software Engineering Research. In Forrest Shull, Janice Singer, and Dag I. K. Sjøberg, editors, *Guide to Advanced Empirical Software Engineering*, pages 285–311. Springer, 2007.

Jürgen Ebert, Volker Riediger, and Andreas Winter. Graph Technology in Reverse Engineering: The TGraph Approach. In *10th Workshop Software Reengineering (WSR2008)*, pages 67–81, 2008.

Thomas J. Emerson. A Discriminant Metric for Module Cohesion. In *Proceedings of the 7th international conference on Software engineering (ICSE 1984)*, pages 294–303, 1984.

Gregor Engels, Andreas Hess, Bernhard Humm, Oliver Juwig, Marc Lohmann, Jan-Peter Richter, Markus Voß, and Johannes Willkomm. *Quasar Enterprise: Anwendungslandschaften serviceorientiert gestalten*. Dpunkt Verlag, 2008.

Thomas Erl. *Service-Oriented Architecture - Concepts, Technology, and Design*. Prentice Hall, 2005.

Martin Ester, Hans-Peter Kriegel, Jörg Sander, and Xiaowei Xu. A Density-Based Algorithm for Discovering Clusters in Large Spatial Databases with Noise. In *Proceedings of 2nd International Conference on Knowledge Discovery and Data Mining (KDD 1996)*, pages 226–231, 1996.

Irene Eusgeld, Felix C. Freiling, and Ralf Reussner, editors. *Dependability Metrics*, volume 4909 of *Lecture Notes in Computer Science*, 2008. Springer. ISBN 978-3-540-68946-1.

Eric Evans. *Domain-Driven Design - Tackling Design In The Heart Of Software*. Addison-Wesley, 2004.

Hoda Fahmy and Richard C. Holt. Software Architecture Transformations. In *Proceedings of the International Conference on Software Maintenance (ICSM 2000)*, pages 88–96, 2000.

Jean-Marie Favre. Foundations of Model (Driven) (Reverse) Engineering : Models - Episode I: Stories of The Fidus Papyrus and of The Solarus. In *Language Engineering for Model-Driven Software Development*, 2004a.

Jean-Marie Favre. Foundations of Meta-Pyramids: Languages vs. Metamodels - Episode II: Story of Thotus the Baboon1. In *Language Engineering for Model-Driven Software Development*, 2004b.

Franck Fleurey, Erwan Breton, Benoit Baudry, Alain Nicolas, and Jean-Marc Jézéquel. Model-Driven Engineering for Software Migration in a Large Industrial Context. In Gregor Engels, Bill Opdyke, Douglas C. Schmidt, and Frank Weil, editors, *Model Driven Engineering Languages and Systems, 10th International Conference, MoDELS 2007*, volume 4735 of *Lecture Notes in Computer Science*, pages 482–497. Springer Verlag, 2007.

Martin Fowler. *Refactoring: Improving the Design of Existing Code*. Addison-Wesley, 1999.

Robert France and Bernhard Rumpe. Model-driven Development of Complex Software: A Research Roadmap. In *FOSE '07: 2007 Future of Software Engineering*, pages 37–54, Washington, DC, USA, 2007. IEEE Computer Society. doi: http://dx.doi.org/10.1109/FOSE.2007.14. Lesegruppe 02.08.2007.

Andreas Fuhr, Tassilo Horn, and Andreas Winter. Model-Driven Software Migration. In *Software Engineering 2010 - Fachtagung des GI-Fachbereichs Softwaretechnik, 22.-26.2.2010 in Paderborn*, pages 69–80, 2010.

Joshua Garcia, Daniel Popescu, George Edwards, and Nenad Medvidovic. Identifying Architectural Bad Smells. In *Proceedings of the 13th European Conference on Software Maintenance and Reengineering (CSMR 2009)*, pages 255–258, 2009.

David Garlan. Software Architecture: a Roadmap. In *ICSE '00: Proceedings of the Conference on The Future of Software Engineering*, pages 91–101, 2000.

David Garlan, Jeffrey M. Barnes, Bradley R. Schmerl, and Orieta Celiku. Evolution Styles: Foundations and Tool Support for Software Architecture Evolution. In *Joint Working IEEE/IFIP Conference on Software Architecture 2009 and European Conference on Software Architecture 2009 (WICSA/ECSA 2009)*, pages 131–140, 2009.

Anna Gerber, Erica Glynn, Anthony MacDonald, Michael Lawley, and Kerry Raymond. Modelling for Knowledge Discovery. In *Proceedings of the Workshop on Model-driven Evolution of Legacy Systems (MELS)*, pages 1–6. IEEE Computer Society Press, October 2004.

Cord Giese. AMELIO Modernization Platform - Architektur, Beispielszenario, Evaluierung. Technical report, Delta Software Technology GmbH, 2010.

Simon Giesecke. *Architectural Styles for Early Goal-driven Middleware Platform Selection*. PhD thesis, University of Oldenburg, 2008.

Rainer Gimnich. SOA-Migration - Vorgehen und Projekterfahrungen. *HMD - Praxis der Wirtschaftsinformatik*, 257, 2007.

Rainer Gimnich and Andreas Winter. Workflows der Software-Migration. *Softwaretechnik-Trends*, 25(2):22–24, 2005. URL http://www.uni-koblenz.de/~winter/papers/gimnichwinter2005.pdf.

Jean-François Girard. *ADORE-AR: Software Architecture Reconstruction with Partitioning and Clustering*. PhD thesis, University of Kaiserslautern, 2005.

Bas Graaf, Sven Weber, and Arie van Deursen. Model-Driven Migration of Supervisory Machine Control Architectures. *Journal of Systems and Software*, 81 (4):517–535, 2008.

Abdelwahab Hamou-Lhadj and Timothy Lethbridge. A Metamodel for Dynamic Information Generated from Object-Oriented Systems. *Electronic Notes in Theoretical Computer Science*, 94:59–69, 2004.

R. Harrison, S. Counsell, and R. Nithi. An Overview of Object-Oriented Design Metrics. In *Proceedings of the 8th International Workshop on Software Technology and Engineering Practice (STEP 1997)*, page 230, Washington, DC, USA, 1997. IEEE Computer Society. ISBN 0-8186-7840-2.

Wilhelm Hasselbring, editor. *Betriebliche Informationssysteme: Grid-basierte Integration und Orchestrierung*. GITO Verlag, 2010.

Wilhelm Hasselbring, Ralf Reussner, Holger Jaekel, Jürgen Schlegelmilch, Thorsten Teschke, and Stefan Krieghoff. The Dublo Architecture Pattern for Smooth Migration of Business Information Systems: An Experience Report. In *Proceedings of the 26th International Conference on Software Engeneering (ICSE 2004)*, pages 117–126. IEEE Computer Society Press, May 2004.

Wilhelm Hasselbring, Achim Büdenbender, Stefan Grasmann, Stefan Krieghoff, and Joachim Marz. Muster zur Migration betrieblicher Informationssysteme. In *Tagungsband Software Engineering 2008*, Lecture Notes in Informatics, München, February 2008. Bonner Köllen Verlag.

Reiko Heckel, Rui Correia, Carlos M. P. Matos, Mohammad El-Ramly, Georgios Koutsoukos, and Luis Filipe Andrade. Architectural Transformations: From Legacy to Three-Tier and Services. In *Software Evolution*, pages 139–170. Springer, 2008.

Martin Hitz and Behzad Montazeri. Measuring Coupling and Cohesion In Object-Oriented Systems. In *Proceedings of the 3rd International Symposium on Applied Corporate Computing (ISACC1995)*, October 1995.

Christine Hofmeister, Robert Nord, and Dilip Soni. *Applied Software Architecture*. Addison-Wesley, 2000.

Richard C. Holt. TA: The Tuple Attribute Language. Technical report, University of Waterloo, 2002.

Richard C. Holt, Andy Schürr, Susan Elliott Sim, and Andreas Winter. GXL: A Graph-Based Standard Exchange Format for Reengineering. *Science of Computer Programming*, 60(2):149–170, 2006.

Tassilo Horn, Andreas Fuhr, and Andreas Winter. Towards Applying Model-Transformations and -Queries for SOA-Migration. In *MDD, SOA and IT-Management (MSI 2009)*, 2009.

Sascha Hunold, Matthias Korch, Björn Krellner, Thomas Rauber, Thomas Reichel, and Gudula Rünger. Transformation of Legacy Software into Client/Server Applications through Pattern-Based Rearchitecturing. In *Proceedings of the 32nd Annual IEEE International Computer Software and Applications Conference (COMPSAC 2008)*, pages 303–310, 2008.

IEEE. IEEE 610.12:1990: Standard Glossary of Software Engineering Terminology. IEEE, 1990.

IEEE Architecture Working Group. IEEE Recommended Practice for Architectural Description of Software-Intensive Systems-Description. IEEE Standards Description: 1471-2000. ANSI/IEEE, 2000.

ISO/IEC. International Standard - ISO/IEC 14764 IEEE Std 14764-2006 Software Engineering - Software Life Cycle Processes - Maintenance. *ISO/IEC 14764:2006 (E) IEEE Std 14764-2006 Revision of IEEE Std 1219-1998)*, pages 1–46, 2006. doi: 10.1109/IEEESTD.2006.235774.

Igor Ivkovic and Kostas Kontogiannis. A Framework for Software Architecture Refactoring using Model Transformations and Semantic Annotations. In *10th European Conference on Software Maintenance and Reengineering (CSMR 2006)*, pages 135–144, 2006.

Jens H. Jahnke. Reverse-Engineering von Software-Architekturbeschreibungen. In *Handbuch der Software-Architektur*, volume 2, pages 199–211. dpunkt.verlag, 2008.

Nicolai M. Josuttis. *SOA in Practice: The Art of Distributed System Design*. O'Reilly, 2007.

Frédéric Jouault and Ivan Kurtev. Transforming Models with ATL. In *MoDELS Satellite Events*, pages 128–138, 2005.

Rick Kazman, Steven S. Woods, and S. Jeromy Carrière. Requirements for Integrating Software Architecture and Reengineering Models: CORUM II. In *5th Working Conference on Reverse Engineering (WCRE 1998)*, pages 154–163, 1998.

Jens Knodel and Daniel Popescu. A Comparison of Static Architecture Compliance Checking Approaches. In *Proceedings of the 6th Working IEEE / IFIP Conference on Software Architecture (WICSA 2007)*, page 12, 2007.

Rainer Koschke. *Atomic Architectural Component Recovery for Program Understanding and Evolution - Evaluation of Automatic Re-Modularization Techniques and Their Integration in a Semi-Automatic Method*. PhD thesis, Universität Stuttgart, 2000.

Rainer Koschke. Rekonstruktion von Software-Architekturen - Ein Literatur- und Methoden-Überblick zum Stand der Wissenschaft. *Informatik Forschung und Entwicklung*, 19(3), 2005.

Rainer Koschke and Daniel Simon. Hierarchical Reflexion Models. In *10th Working Conference on Reverse Engineering (WCRE 2003)*, pages 36–45, 2003.

Dirk Krafzig, Karl Banke, and Dirk Slama. *Enterprise SOA: Service-Oriented Architecture Best Practices (The Coad Series)*. Prentice Hall PTR, Upper Saddle River, NJ, USA, 2004.

Holger Krahn and Bernhard Rumpe. Enabling Architectural Refactorings through Source Code Annotations. In *Modellierung 2006*, pages 203–212, 2006.

Stefan Krieghoff, Wilhelm Hasselbring, Ralf Reussner, and Niels Streekmann. Migration eines Altsystems zu einer Java Enterprise Architektur. In Ralf Reussner and Wilhelm Hasselbring, editors, *Handbuch der Software-Architektur*, pages 487–497. dpunkt.verlag, 2 edition, December 2008. ISBN 3898645592.

Philippe Kruchten. The 4+1 View Model of Architecture. *IEEE Software*, 12 (6):42–50, 1995. ISSN 0740-7459. doi: http://doi.ieeecomputersociety.org/10. 1109/52.469759.

Thomas Kühne. Matters of (Meta-)Modeling. *Software and System Modeling*, 5 (4):369–385, 2006.

Matthias Kühnemann and Gudula Rünger. Modellgetriebene Transformation von Legacy Business-Software. In *3. Workshop Reengineering Prozesse (RePro2006)*, number 2 in Mainzer Informatik-Berichte, pages 20–21, 2006.

Timothy Lethbridge, Sander Tichelaar, and Erhard Plödereder. The Dagstuhl Middle Metamodel: A Schema For Reverse Engineering. *Electronic Notes in Theoretical Computer Science*, 94:7–18, 2004.

Carola Lilienthal. Architectural Complexity of Large-Scale Software Systems. In *Proceedings of the 13th European Conference on Software Maintenance and Reengineering (CSMR 2009)*, pages 17–26, 2009.

Chung-Horng Lung. Software Architecture Recovery and Restructuring through Clustering Techniques. In *Proceedings of the third international workshop on Software architecture (ISAW)*, pages 101–104, New York, NY, USA, 1998. ACM. ISBN 1-58113-081-3. doi: http://doi.acm.org/10.1145/288408.288434.

Chung-Horng Lung and Marzia Zaman. Using Clustering Technique to Restructure Programs. In *Proceedings of the International Conference on Software Engineering Research and Practice (SERP 2004)*, pages 853–860, 2004.

Dennis Mancl. Refactoring for Software Migration. *Communications Magazine, IEEE*, 39(10):88–93, 2001.

Onaiza Maqbool and Haroon A. Babri. The Weighted Combined Algorithm: A Linkage Algorithm for Software Clustering. In *Proceedings of the 8th European Conference on Software Maintenance and Reengineering (CSMR 2004)*, pages 15–24, 2004.

Onaiza Maqbool and Haroon A. Babri. Hierarchical Clustering for Software Architecture Recovery. *IEEE Transactions on Software Engineering*, 33(11):759–780, 2007.

Robert Martin. OO Design Quality Metrics - An Analysis of Dependencies. Position Paper, Workshop on Pragmatic and Theoretical Directions in Object-Oriented Software Metrics, OOPSLA 1994, 1994.

Jasminka Matevska-Meyer, Wilhelm Hasselbring, and Ralf H. Reussner. Software Architecture Description Supporting Component Deployment and System Runtime Reconfiguration. In *Proceedings of the 9th International Workshop on Component-oriented Programming*, 2004.

Carlos Matos. Service Extraction from Legacy Systems. In *Proceedings of the 4th International Conference on Graph Transformations (ICGT 2008)*, pages 505–507, 2008.

Carlos M. P. Matos and Reiko Heckel. Migrating Legacy Systems to Service-Oriented Architectures. *Electronic Communications of the EASST*, 16, 2008.

Nenad Medvidovic and Vladimir Jakobac. Using Software Evolution to Focus Architectural Recovery. *Automated Software Engineering*, 13(2):225–256, 2006.

Tom Mens and Serge Demeyer, editors. *Software Evolution*. Springer, 2008.

Tom Mens, Serge Demeyer, Bart Du Bois, Hans Stenten, and Pieter Van Gorp. Refactoring: Current Research and Future Trends. *Electronic Notes in Theoretical Computer Science*, 82(3):483–499, 2003.

Brian S. Mitchell. *A Heuristic Search Approach to Solving the Software Clustering Problem*. PhD thesis, Drexel University, 2002.

Brian S. Mitchell and Spiros Mancoridis. On the Automatic Modularization of Software Systems Using the Bunch Tool. *IEEE Transactions on Software Engineering*, 32(3):193–208, 2006.

Parastoo Mohagheghi, Jan Pettersen Nytun, Selo, and Warsun Najib. MDA and Integration of Legacy Systems: An Industrial Case Study. In Arend Rensink, editor, *Workshop on Model Driven Architecture: Foundations and Applications, MDAFA'03*, pages 85–90, University of Twente, Enschede, The Netherlands, 2003. CTIT Technical Report TR-CT I T-03-27.

Nathalie Moreno and Antonio Vallecillo. What Do We Do With Re-use in MDA? In *Position paper at the Second European Workshop on Model Driven Architecture with an emphasis on Methodologies and Transformations (EWMDA-2)*, 2004.

Adra Al Mosawi, Liping Zhao, and Linda A. Macaulay. A Model Driven Architecture for Enterprise Application Integration. In *HICSS*, 2006. URL http://doi.ieeecomputersociety.org/10.1109/HICSS.2006.18.

Hausi A. Müller, Jens H. Jahnke, Dennis B. Smith, Margaret-Anne D. Storey, Scott R. Tilley, and Kenny Wong. Reverse Engineering: a Roadmap. In *ICSE - Future of SE Track*, pages 47–60, 2000.

Gail C. Murphy, David Notkin, and Kevin J. Sullivan. Software Reflexion Models: Bridging the Gap between Source and High-Level Models. In *Proceedings of the Third ACM SIGSOFT Symposium on the Foundations of Software Engineering*, pages 18–28. ACM Press, 1995.

Gail C. Murphy, David Notkin, and Kevin J. Sullivan. Software Reflexion Models: Bridging the Gap between Design and Implementation. *IEEE Transactions on Software Engineering*, 27(4):364–380, 2001.

Object Management Group (OMG). Meta Object Facility (MOF) Core Specification Version 2.0, January 2006.

Object Management Group (OMG). Unified Modeling Language: Superstructure Version 2.1.1 (formal/2007-02-05), 2007.

Object Management Group (OMG). Meta Object Facility (MOF) 2.0 Query/View/ Transformation Specification Version 1.0, April 2008.

Object Management Group (OMG). Architecture-Driven Modernization (ADM): Knowledge Discovery Meta-Model (KDM) Version 1.1 (formal/2009-01-02), 2009.

William F. Opdyke. *Refactoring: A Program Restructuring Aid in Designing Object-Oriented Application Frameworks*. PhD thesis, University of Illinois at Urbana-Champaign, 1992.

Organization for the Advancement of Structured Information Standards (OASIS). Reference Model for Service Oriented Architecture 1.0, October 2006.

David L. Parnas. On the Criteria To Be Used in Decomposing Systems into Modules. *Communications of the ACM*, 15(12):1053–1058, December 1972.

David Lorge Parnas. Software Aging. In *Proceedings of the 16th International Conference on Software Engineering (ICSE 1994)*, pages 279–287. IEEE Computer Society Press, 1994. ISBN 0-8186-5855-X.

Ilian Pashov. *Feature-Based Methodology for Supporting Architecture Refactoring and Maintenance of Long-Life Software Systems*. PhD thesis, Technische Universit"at Ilmenau, 2004.

Ilian Pashov, Matthias Riebisch, and Ilka Philippow. Supporting Architectural Restructuring by Analyzing Feature Models. In *Proceedings of the 8th European Conference on Software Maintenance and Reengineering (CSMR 2004)*, pages 25–36, 2004.

Dewayne E. Perry and Alexander L. Wolf. Foundations for the Study of Software Architecture. *ACM SIGSOFT Software Engineering Notes*, 17(4):40–52, October 1992. ISSN 0163-5948.

Florian Postel. Evaluation des halbautomatischen Verfahrens zur modellbasierten Architekturrestrukturierung (MARE). Bachelor's thesis, University of Oldenburg, 2010.

Jochen Quante. Using Library Dependencies for Clustering. In *Workshop Software Reengineering*, pages 171–175, 2008.

Derek Rayside, Steve Reuss, Erik Hedges, and Kostas Kontogiannis. The Effect of Call Graph Construction Algorithms for Object-Oriented Programs on Automatic Clustering. In *8th International Workshop on Program Comprehension (IWPC 2000)*, pages 191–200. IEEE Computer Society, 2000.

Maryam Razavian and Patricia Lago. A Frame of Reference for SOA Migration. In *ServiceWave 2010*, volume 6481 of *LNCS*, pages 150–162, 2010.

Thijs Reus, Hans Geers, and Arie van Deursen. Harvesting Software Systems for MDA-Based Reengineering. In Arend Rensink and Jos Warmer, editors, *2nd European Conference on Model Driven Architecture-Foundations and Applications*, volume 4066 of *LNCS*, pages 213–225. Springer Verlag, 2006.

Ralf Reussner, editor. *MINT - Modellgetriebene Integration von Informationssystemen*. Universitätsverlag Karlsruhe, 2009.

Ralf Reussner and Wilhelm Hasselbring, editors. *Handbuch der Software-Architektur*. dpunkt.verlag, 2 edition, 2008.

Matthias Riebisch and Stephan Bode. Software-Evolvability. *Informatik Spektrum*, 32(4):339–343, 2009.

James Rumbaugh, Ivar Jacobson, and Grady Booch. *The Unified Modeling Language Reference Manual*. Addison-Wesley, Boston, MA, 2. edition, 2005. ISBN 978-0-321-24562-5.

Neeraj Sangal, Ev Jordan, Vineet Sinha, and Daniel Jackson. Using Dependency Models to Manage Complex Software Architecture. In *Proceedings of the 20th Annual ACM SIGPLAN Conference on Object-Oriented Programming, Systems, Languages, and Applications (OOPSLA 2005)*, pages 167–176, 2005.

Kamran Sartipi and Kostas Kontogiannis. A User-Assisted Approach to Component Clustering. *Journal of Software Maintenance*, 15(4):265–295, 2003.

Satu Elisa Schaeffer. Graph Clustering. *Computer Science Review*, 1(1):27–64, 2007.

Ed Seidewitz. What Models Mean. *IEEE Software*, 20(5):26–32, 2003. ISSN 0740-7459. doi: http://doi.ieeecomputersociety.org/10.1109/MS.2003.1231147.

Bran Selic. The Pragmatics of Model-Driven Development. *IEEE Software*, 20: 19–25, 2003. URL http://csdl.computer.org/comp/mags/so/2003/05/s5019abs.htm.

Gabriela Serban and István Gergely Czibula. Object-Oriented Software Systems Restructuring through Clustering. In *9th International Conference on Artificial Intelligence and Soft Computing (ICAISC 2008)*, pages 693–704, 2008.

Johannes Siedersleben. *Moderne Softwarearchitektur*. dpunkt Verlag, 2004.

Renuka Sindhgatta and Krishnakumar Pooloth. Identifying Software Decompositions by Applying Transaction Clustering on Source Code. In *Proceedings of
the 31st Annual International Computer Software and Applications Conference
(COMPSAC 2007)*, pages 317–326, 2007.

Harry Sneed. Migrating to Web Services: A Research Framework. In *Proceedings of the International Workshop on SOA Maintenance Evolution (SOAM
2007), 11th European Conference on Software Maintenance and Reengineering
(CSMR 2007)*, 2007.

Herbert Stachowiak. *Allgemeine Modelltheorie*. Springer, 1973.

Thomas Stahl, Markus Völter, Sven Efftinge, and Arno Haase. *Modellgetriebene Softwareentwicklung - Techniken, Engineering, Management*, volume 2. dpunkt.verlag, 2007.

Dave Steinberg, Frank Budinsky, Marcelo Paternostro, and Ed Merks. *EMF -
Eclipse Modeling Framework*. Addison-Wesley, 2 edition, 2008.

Wayne P. Stevens, Glenford J. Myers, and Larry L. Constantine. Structured Design. *IBM Systems Journal*, 13(2):115–139, 1974.

Niels Streekmann. Model-Based Architecture Restructuring of a Large Industrial
System. *Softwaretechnik-Trends*, 30(2), May 2010. ISSN 0720-8928.

Niels Streekmann and Wilhelm Hasselbring. Model-Based Architecture Restructuring Using Graph Clustering. In Massimiliano di Penta and Jens Knodel,
editors, *Workshop Proceedings of the 13th European Conference on Software
Maintenance and Reengineering*, pages 75–82, 2009.

Niels Streekmann and Steffen Kruse. MDSD Umfrage 2009 - Ergebnisse und
Trends. Technical report, OFFIS, 2009.

Clemens Szyperski, Dominik Gruntz, and Stephan Murer. *Component Software:
Beyond Object-Oriented Programming*. Addison-Wesley, 2 edition, 2002.

Pang-Ning Tan, Michael Steinbach, and Vipin Kumar. *Introduction to Data Mining*. Addison-Wesley, 2005. ISBN 0-321-32136-7.

Thorsten Teschke, Holger Jaekel, Stefan Krieghoff, Marc Langnickel, Wilhelm
Hasselbring, and Ralf Reussner. Funktionsgetriebene Integration von Legacy-
Systemen mit Web Services. In Manfred Reichert Wilhelm Hasselbring, editor,

Tagungsband zum Workshop "EAI 2004 - Enterprise Architecture Integration", pages 19–28. GITO Verlag, 2004.

Thomas Tilley, Richard Cole, Peter Becker, and Peter W. Eklund. A Survey of Formal Concept Analysis Support for Software Engineering Activities. In *Formal Concept Analysis, Foundations and Applications*, pages 250–271, 2005.

Juha-Pekka Tolvanen and Matti Rossi. MetaEdit+: Defining and Using Domain-Specific Modeling Languages and Code Generators. In *OOPSLA '03: Companion of the 18th annual ACM SIGPLAN conference on Object-oriented programming, systems, languages, and applications*, pages 92–93, New York, NY, USA, 2003. ACM. ISBN 1-58113-751-6. doi: http://doi.acm.org/10.1145/949344. 949365.

Paolo Tonella. Concept Analysis for Module Restructuring. *IEEE Transactions on Software Engineering*, 27(4):351–363, 2001.

Mircea Trifu and Peter Szulman. Language Independent Abstract Metamodel for Quality Analysis and Improvement of OO Systems. In *Proceedings of the 7th German Workshop on Software-Reengineering (WSR 2005)*, Bad Honnef, Germany, 2005.

Vassilios Tzerpos and Richard C. Holt. MoJo: A Distance Metric for Software Clusterings. In *Proceedings of the Sixth Working Conference on Reverse Engineering (WCRE 1999)*, pages 187–193, 1999.

Vassilios Tzerpos and Richard C. Holt. On the Stability of Software Clustering Algorithms. In *Proceedings of the 8th International Workshop on Program Comprehension (IWPC 2000)*, pages 211–218, 2000.

Axel Uhl. Model-Driven Development in the Enterprise. *IEEE Software*, 25(1): 46–49, 2008.

William Ulrich. A Status on OMG Architecture-Driven Modernization Task Force. In *Proceedings of the Workshop on Model-driven Evolution of Legacy Systems (MELS)*. IEEE Computer Society Press, October 2004.

Willem-Jan van den Heuvel. *Aligning Modern Business Processes and Legacy Systems - A Component-Based Perspective*. Cooperative Information Systems. MIT Press, 2007.

Arie van Deursen, Christine Hofmeister, Rainer Koschke, Leon Moonen, and Claudio Riva. Symphony: View-Driven Software Architecture Reconstruction. In *Proceedings Working IEEE/IFIP Conference on Software Architecture (WICSA'04)*, pages 122–134. IEEE Computer Society Press, 2004.

Jilles van Gurp and Jan Bosch. Design Erosion: Problems and Causes. *Journal of Systems and Software*, 61(2):105–119, March 2002.

André van Hoorn, Matthias Rohr, Wilhelm Hasselbring, Jan Waller, Jens Ehlers, Sören Frey, and Dennis Kieselhorst. Continuous Monitoring of Software Services: Design and Application of the Kieker Framework. Technical Report TR-0921, Department of Computer Science, University of Kiel, Germany, November 2009. URL http://www.informatik.uni-kiel.de/uploads/tx_ publication/vanhoorn_tr0921.pdf.

Zhihua Wen and Vassilios Tzerpos. An Effectiveness Measure for Software Clustering Algorithms. In *12th International Workshop on Program Comprehension (IWPC 2004)*, pages 194–203, 2004.

Theo A. Wiggerts. Using Clustering Algorithms in Legacy Systems Remodularization. In *Proceedings of the Fourth Working Conference on Reverse Engineering (WCRE 1997)*, pages 33–43, 1997.

Andreas Winter and Jörg Ziemann. Model-based Migration to Service-Oriented Architectures. In Andreas Winter Uwe Kaiser, Petr Kroha, editor, *3. Workshop Reengineering Prozesse (RePro 2006) Software Migration*, number 2 in Mainzer Informatik-Berichte, pages 16–17, Mainz, Germany, November 2006. Johannes Gutenberg University Mainz.

Andreas Winter and Jörg Ziemann. Model-based Migration to Service-oriented Architectures - A Project Outline. In Harry Sneed, editor, *CSMR 2007, 11th European Conference on Software Maintenance and Reengineering, Workshops*, pages 107–110. Vrije Universiteit Amsterdam, March 2007.

Tao Xie and David Notkin. An Empirical Study of Java Dynamic Call Graph Extractors. Technical report, Dept. of Computer Science and Engineering, University of Washington, 2002.

Xia Xu, Chung-Horng Lung, Marzia Zaman, and Anand Srinivasan. Program Restructuring Through Clustering Techniques. In *Proceedings of the 4th IEEE International Workshop on Source Code Analysis and Manipulation (SCAM 2004)*, pages 75–84, 2004.

Jörg Ziemann, Katrina Leyking, Timo Kahl, and Dirk Werth. Enterprise Model driven Migration from Legacy to SOA. In Rainer Gimnich and Andreas Winter, editors, *Workshop Software-Reengineering und Services*, Fachberichte Informatik, pages 18–27, Koblenz, Germany, 2006. University of Koblenz-Landau.